THE NEOCATECHUMENAL WAY
ACCORDING TO
PAUL VI AND JOHN PAUL II

The Neocatechumenal Way
according to
Paul VI and John Paul II

Edited by Ezekiel Pasotti

Introduction by Kiko Argüello and Carmen Hernández

ST PAULS

Original title: *il Cammino Neocatecumenale secondo Paolo VI e Giovanni Paolo II*
© Edizioni San Paolo, s.r.l., Cinisello Balsamo (Milano)
Translated by the Neocatechumenal Centre, London

ST PAULS
Middlegreen, Slough SL3 6BT, United Kingdom
Moyglare Road, Maynooth, Co. Kildare, Ireland

English translation © Neocatechumenal Centre, London, 1996

ISBN 085439 520 2

Set by TuKan, High Wycombe

Printed by Biddles Ltd, Guildford

ST PAULS is an activity of the priests and brothers of the Society of St Paul
who proclaim the Gospel through the media of social communication

Contents

PREFACE *by Monsignor Paul Josef Cordes*   7

INTRODUCTION
by Kiko Argüello and Carmen Hernández   9

LETTER OF JOHN PAUL II APPROVING
THE NEOCATECHUMENAL WAY   *insert*

TRANSLATION OF THE LETTER OF JOHN PAUL II
AND A BRIEF COMMENT ON IT FOR THE
VATICAN PRESS OFFICE BY KIKO ARGÜELLO   19

Chapter I
BAPTISM AND NEOCATECHUMENATE:
"YOU ARE SO NECESSARY IN THE CHURCH
OF TODAY"   23

Chapter II
CHURCH AND SECULARISATION:
"IN THIS AGE WE NEED TO REDISCOVER
A RADICAL FAITH"   38

Chapter III
"REBUILDING THE PARISH, BASING IT ON
THE NEOCATECHUMENAL EXPERIENCE"   53

Chapter IV
THE NECESSITY OF SIGNS OF FAITH:
"GIVE YOUR LIFE. I SEE THAT IN YOUR
COMMUNITIES THESE WORDS ARE MADE FLESH"   72

Chapter V
ITINERANT CATECHISTS:
"JESUS CHRIST IS ITINERANT WITH YOU"   82

Chapter VI
"THE FAMILY IN MISSION IS THE IMAGE OF
THE TRINITY IN MISSION"   93

Chapter VII
THE 'REDEMPTORIS MATER' SEMINARIES:
"IT DOES NOT SURPRISE ME THAT IN YOUR WAY
THERE ARE VOCATIONS"   108

Appendices

I. THE NEOCATECHUMENAL WAY:
A BRIEF SYNTHESIS
by Kiko Argüello and Carmen Hernández   127

II. TEXTS OF THE CONGREGATION FOR DIVINE
WORSHIP ON THE NEOCATECHUMENAL WAY   136
A Comment by the Congregation for Divine Worship   136
Note by the Congregation for Divine Worship on the
      celebration in groups of the Neocatechumenal Way   138

III. THE 'REDEMPTORIS MATER' SEMINARIES   139
What are the 'Redemptoris Mater' Seminaries?   139
Decree of erection of the 'Redemptoris Mater'
      Seminary, Rome   140

IV. LETTER OF THE HOLY FATHER JOHN PAUL II
TO THE EUROPEAN BISHOPS MEETING IN
VIENNA   142

V. SOME FRUITS OF THE NEOCATECHUMENAL
WAY   145
Some statistics on the Neocatechumenal Way in the
      diocese of Rome   145
The Parish and The Neocatechumenal Way as they
      appear in a statistical survey of the Spanish
      Episcopal Conference   156

VI. COMPLETE TEXTS OF THE SPEECHES OF
PAUL VI AND JOHN PAUL II   173

Bibliography   205

Preface

In the 1960s Werner Stark, the sociologist of Fordham University in New York, published an epoch-making five volume work entitled "The Sociology of Religion: A Study of Christendom". This historical-religious analysis proved from evidence the importance of the Papacy in the renewal of the Church. Thanks to the Bishop of Rome, charisms raised up by the Holy Spirit to deepen the faith of the people of God have been given a place for their mission, and so have remained within the ecclesial structure, which is not the case with the impulses of renewal in other Christian confessions. In this way the successor of Peter has fulfilled his ministry of communion. As early as 390 the Regional Council of Milan affirmed this and wrote to Pope Siricius that "in the Church of Rome... a heresy has never arisen". Today the voice of the Popes still provides a unique guideline with regard to the purity of doctrine and the unity of the Church.

The present publication gathers together words and teachings about the Neocatechumenal Way by two Bishops of Rome of the last thirty years, Pope Paul VI and Pope John Paul II. Delivered on various occasions, they emphasise the need, today more than ever, of a radical faith, of renewal in the parish, of total dedication to the apostolate, of the mission of the family and of the formation of future presbyters.

Without doubt the most important document is the Letter *with which John Paul II, on the 30th August 1990, solemnly recognised the Neocatechumenal Way as "an itinerary of Catholic formation, valid for the society and times of today".*

This Letter *represents an extraordinary step by the Universal Pastor with regard to lay associations and the new ecclesial realities which appeared at the time of the Second Vatican Council. It was the Pope himself who wanted it and on the 25th July*

1990, in the course of a private audience which he granted me, he decided on its publication and to whom it should be addressed. The documentation gathered here shows that it fits into the context of many other papal speeches. On the other hand, as he confirms in the Letter, *the Pontiff had been able to verify "in the many meetings he had held as Bishop of Rome, in the Roman parishes, with the Neocatechumenal Communities and their pastors and in his apostolic journeys in many nations... abundant fruits of personal conversion and fruitful missionary impulse".*

How can we not thank the Lord for this work of his! After having received from the Holy Father, on the 21st October 1986, the charge ad personam *to watch over the Neocatechumenal Way, today – together with many other Pastors of the Church – I bless God, Father of our Lord Jesus Christ, that he chose to open this itinerary of salvation for the benefit of many who live "in darkness and in the shadow of death" (Lk 1:29). The brief collection of data about the Neocatechumenal Communities in the parishes of Spain and in the Diocese of Rome, published in the appendix, represent merely a pallid statistical reflection of the story, at times dramatic, of the many who have found the Lord "Way, Truth and Life" (Jn 14:6) in the Church, thanks to this Way.*

The present collection of documents will constitute, for the members of the communities, yet another motive for communion with the successor of Peter, and for all the members of the Church, a new demonstration of the exceptional mission that the Bishops of Rome have in the renewal of the Church.

Mons. PAUL JOSEF CORDES
(Vice President of the
Pontifical Council for the Laity)

Introduction

I am moved, re-reading these texts, by the tenderness and the mercy of the Lord. How can we not thank him for all the good that he has done for us!

It was the year 1968, in the middle of June, when a priest from Seville, Carmen and myself arrived in Rome, invited by Monsignor Torregiani, founder of the Servants of the Church. He had heard us give catechesis in Avila and had insisted that we come to Rome. We went with him to the Archbishop of Madrid, Monsignor Casimiro Morcillo, who gave us a letter of recommendation for the Vicar of the Pope, Cardinal Angelo Dell'Acqua.

In Rome, poor Don Gino, already old and very saintly, went with us from parish priest to parish priest, acting as our interpreter, in the attempt to convince some of them of the necessity of opening a post-baptismal way of evangelisation in the parishes for the many people who had drifted away from the Church.

We soon became aware of the uselessness of our attempt, so we decided to go and live amongst the poor, waiting for the Lord to show us His will by opening a door for us.

Thanks to a sister who worked with the poor and who helped us, we found a chicken shed in which we could live, in Rome's Borgetto Latino, an area full of shacks. Carmen found a place with a woman who put her up in a shack nearby. Together with some seminarians from Avila, who had joined us in the meantime, we began our life among the poor.

I was invited to a meeting, held in Nemi, of young people from the parishes of Rome who were working with the slum-dwellers, to share my experience with them; and there I got to know a group from the parish of the Canadian Martyrs which was conducting an experience of a liturgical nature, with the presbyter of the Sacramentine Order, Don Guglielmo Amadei.

After having explained to the priest and these young people the need to open a way of evangelisation, forming small communities within the parish, they agreed that we should begin, and invited some older couples to participate.

As is our practice, before beginning the catecheses, we presented ourselves to Cardinal Dell'Acqua to ask his permission to preach in his Diocese. Don Francesco Cuppini, a priest from Bologna who had joined our team with the permission of his bishop, went with us. The Cardinal Vicar listened to us attentively and gave us permission to begin the catecheses – always with the agreement of the parish priest – and invited us to speak with Monsignor Ugo Poletti, who was soon to become the Cardinal Vicar and who for many years has helped and defended us in a way that is providential. After that, as if by a miracle, the first Neocatechumenal Community was born, with fifty brothers. The following year we did catecheses in the parishes of Santa Francesca Cabrini, the Natività and San Luigi Gonzaga in Parioli.

In the midst of the many miracles and fruits of conversion which we saw there were also many sufferings, but here we had the great surprise of feeling and seeing the Lord working in our favour with signs and wonders. An example was when we were called to the Congregation for the Sacraments and Divine Worship because of the doubts an Auxiliary Bishop of Rome had about the exorcisms that we were doing during the first scrutiny. We found ourselves before a Commission presided over by the Secretary of the Congregation, accompanied by experts who had worked on the *Ordo Initiationis Christianae Adultorum* (RCIA). In front of him each one had the *Ordo*, which had only just been printed but was not yet in the bookshops. Full of fear, we introduced ourselves, after having prayed a lot to the Virgin and to the Lord to stay close to us.

When we explained that we were doing nothing other than confronting people with the first part of the Baptism that they had received, of which the exorcisms constituted an important part, and having explained how the Way was born, of what it consisted, and so forth, they were dumbfounded, looking at each other. It was the practical fulfilment in the parishes of what they had elaborated over the years in the *Ordo* for the initiation of adults.

Here the Holy Spirit had already provided people and means for its realisation! This is what they told us, full of admiration and surprise.

After a period of study of the stages and rites of the Neocatechumenal Way, during which they sent observers to our celebrations, and given that Chapter IV of the RCIA extended the use of the *Ordo* to baptised persons who had not received an adequate catechesis, the Congregation issued a document entitled *Reflections on Chapter IV of the RCIA*, in which it established which rites of the Catechumenate repeated in order to relive Baptism and which then summoned again, they read the docu expressed their joy and satisfaction with th doing in the Church, and they told us th publish a laudatory Note in Latin, for u. *Notitiae*, the official magazine of the Congregation, . help us. The note begins like this: "*Omnes reformationes u Ecclesia novos gignerunt inceptus novasque promoverunt instituta, quae optata reformationis ad rem deduxerunt. Ita evenit post Concilium Tridentinum; nec aliter fieri poterat. Instauratio liturgica profunde incidit in vitam Ecclesiae. Spiritualitas liturgica novos germinare flores sanctitatis et gratiae necesse est, nec non instensioris apostolatus catholici et actionis pastoralis. Praeclarum exemplar huius renovationis invenitur in 'Communitatibus neocatechumenalibus', quae ortum habuerunt Matriti....*"[1]

Thanks to this, a very fruitful dialogue was established with the Congregation for Divine Worship, which later was to prove very important for the relationship of Paul VI with the Neocatechumenal Way. Because of certain difficulties, Cardinal Poletti (who had already put us in contact with the Director of the Catechetical Office of the Diocese of Rome, Monsignor Giulio Salimei who, impressed by the conversions and by the action of the Lord in the parishes, was a great help to us) invited us to speak with the Secretary of the Congregation for the Clergy, which was the Congregation responsible for catechesis in the Church. Again, on that occasion we were full of fear, but there, to our surprise, we found Monsignor Massimino Romero, whom we had already known when he was Bishop of Avila and who had supported and helped us.

The first thing that he did was to ask us for the schemes that we used for the catechesis, to have them examined by catechetical experts. We explained to him that they were only duplicated pages that had not even been corrected, in order not to give them too much importance: they were guidelines, given that we wanted to form the catechists, during years of a way which leads to Christian life and witness, and not merely to repeat texts written by others. Secondly, we prepared the catechists in an oral tradition of announcing the *Kerygma* and, finally, at the time of giving the catechesis, the team, which always includes a priest,

---

1. All the reforms in the Church have given rise to new principles, and have promoted new norms to enable the purposes of the reform to be put into practice. This was so after the Council of Trent; and it could not be otherwise in our own day. The liturgical renewal has a deep impact on the life of the Church. Liturgical spirituality must, of necessity, germinate new flowers of holiness and grace and also a more intense Christian apostolate and spiritual action. An excellent example of this renewal is to be found in the 'Neocatechumenal Communities' which arose in Madrid. (*Notitiae* nn. 95-96, July-August 1974, page 229, cf. the full text in Appendix II.)

made use of those guidelines. We did not have official writings as such. The duplicated copies were only indications, guidelines, the transcript of an oral preaching adapted to the people who were listening, to help them to rediscover the praxis and the liturgy of the Church within a way of conversion.

Despite all this, he asked us for them. This, too, was providential: years later, in fact, in Canada, some priests who were against the renewal of the Council and who came into possession of these photostat copies, saw heresies everywhere in them and maintained that they contained secret directives, etc... without knowing that the Congregation had had them studied, and had then let us know the opinion of the consultors which, thank God, was very positive from the doctrinal point of view. For our consolation they showed us the report of a consultor of that very Congregation which concluded: "I now intend to highlight another aspect of these catecheses, or rather, of this Neocatechumenal Way. As a scholar of the history of ancient catechesis, I must say that the attempt of Kiko and Carmen to make actual the Catechumenate is successful. Personal experience has given them an insight into the profoundly valid content of this institution of the Church of the first three centuries and it has permitted them to translate it into a structure which, whilst not retracing the ancient one, takes up its most important elements and inserts them into a new context: that of the conversion of those who, though having been baptised, have never made a personal option of faith. In this process, which takes time, these baptised members of the Neocatechumenal Communities are helped to make their global option of faith in a community climate, to open themselves to the action of the Holy Spirit who introduces them to understanding and, in an experiential way, gradually initiates them to the Word of God, to the sacraments of Christian conversion (Penance) and to the Eucharist. I find all of this very positive. Therefore I conclude my judgement by inviting those responsible in the Sacred Congregation of the Clergy to encourage this movement, helping it with understanding and paternal indulgence to remain always in the direction it has undertaken of service to the parochial communities for their authentic renewal."

We can say that the words of St Paul are true: "Everything contributes to the good of those who love God". Each time that we have been accused or slandered to the Holy See, everything, in the end, was transformed into our good.

Later we found ourselves faced with other difficulties: some said that these communities had no social commitment (it was shortly after 1968 and there were politicised basic communities all over the place), and that we wanted to repeat Baptism. The holy Virgin Mary, the mother of Jesus, came to our help.

Earlier, when we had just arrived, Don Gino had brought us to the sanctuary of Our Lady of Pompeii in order to place our mission at the feet of the Virgin. And the first words spoken by Paul VI on the Neocatechumenal Way were on the 8th of May 1974, feast of Our Lady of Pompeii, or Our Lady of the Rosary.

"How great is the joy, how great is the hope, which you give us with your presence and with your activity! ... Whilst for you, this purpose is a conscious, authentic way of living your Christian vocation, it becomes an efficacious witness for others: you do the apostolate just because you are what you are!... To live and foster this re-awakening is what you call a kind of *post baptism*, which can renew in our contemporary Christian communities the effects of maturity and depth which were achieved in the early church during the period of preparation before Baptism. You do this afterwards. **Whether *Before* or *After* is secondary**, I would say. The fact is that you aim at the authenticity, fullness, coherence and sincerity of Christian life. And this is a very great merit, I repeat, which consoles us enormously..."

Here was the Pope answering the accusations without even being aware that he was doing so: "You are doing an apostolate simply because you are what you are!" and "Before or after Baptism, I would say, is secondary". The date of the 8th of May was for us a sign that the Virgin was encouraging us and making us understand that she was helping us in our problems. In fact from then on, no one has accused us again of repeating Baptism.

We could recount innumerable facts like these in which the Lord constantly came to our help. But there was one fact which was decisive for us. At the very beginning, amongst the poor in Madrid, when the police had arrived to demolish the shacks in the area where Carmen was staying with a friend, we called the Archbishop to come to our help. When Monsignor Casimiro Morcillo came to the shanty town it was truly a miracle: he met the small community of gypsies, tramps and poor people; he heard us pray and was deeply moved by the work that the Holy Spirit was doing in that front line of the Church. After we had explained to him the need to complete the catechesis of the people there with concrete signs in a renewed liturgy, as the Council was already proposing, to our astonishment he told the parish priest of the nearest parish, who was present, to let us have the church – a wooden hut in the middle of a square – so that the community of the shanty town could celebrate the Eucharist once a week, allowing us to celebrate with both species, using unleavened bread instead of hosts, as we had asked him.

Likewise, some years later in Madrid, the celebration of the Paschal Vigil (which we were celebrating throughout the night, in the rediscovery of the power of that night in which Christ defeated death) created problems in some parishes. We discussed these problems with the parish priests in the presence of the Archbishop and the auxiliary bishops, and while we were thinking that the Archbishop might perhaps forbid us everything, he exclaimed, "How I wish that the Paschal Vigil would become the fulcrum of the life of my Diocese, while I see with sadness that in the majority of parishes it is reduced to an evening mass with only three readings and that it has already finished before the sun has set. If, thanks to you, the Paschal Vigil recovers the splendour and the strength which God intended and the liturgical reform recommends, then you are welcome. I give you all the empty churches of Madrid so that you may be able to celebrate all night until dawn, giving in this way an example and witness."

These lines of introduction are fundamentally an occasion for blessing God, for thanking Him for the gift of the Spirit who willed to found the Church upon Peter and the Apostles. Without the Bishops, and above all without Peter, the Neocatechumenal Way would not exist today.

On the 3rd of September 1979 John Paul II invited Carmen, Father Mario (a Verona Father missionary who had been in the team with us for a few years) and myself to Mass in Castel Gandolfo.

This was the first time that we had met him. We knew that he had welcomed the Way in his Diocese when he was Cardinal in Cracow and had defended the Saturday evening Eucharist in the communities in front of certain parish priests. When the Mass was finished, he came to greet us and I asked him if I could speak with him alone. He asked me "Right now, or another day?" I answered "Right now". He invited me to follow him across a corridor and he brought me into a library which, I remember, was filled with bright sunlight. He sat down behind the desk and invited me to sit in front of him and speak. With great trouble I told him how I had heard from the Virgin Mary that I should form small communities like the Holy Family of Nazareth, who were to live in humility, simplicity and praise, and where the other is Christ. My greatest difficulty came from the fact that I thought that he might imagine that he had before him a visionary, a fanatic or something of that kind. After having listened to me, and after some minutes of silence, he told me that during the Mass, whilst thinking of us, he had seen before him: ATHEISM-BAPTISM-CATECHUMENATE. I sensed that he was referring to the countries of the East and it impressed me that he had inverted the order, putting the word "catechumenate" after "baptism". The truth is that I would have liked to have got down on my knees to thank the Lord!

Later, when the Pope began to visit the parishes of Rome, where there was always a special meeting with the Neocatechumenal Communities, we had many opportunities, Carmen especially, to speak to him about the Way.

His words, as can be seen in these pages, have always been surprising, generous, always going beyond what one would have expected; like the time we asked for an audience for the Seminarians from the communities of the Way and he wanted the meeting to take place in the Sistine Chapel. We did not fit in, we were more than one thousand two hundred people, but he wanted it to be there; he wanted to speak of his election as Pope in that very place, in order to impress such a powerful experience of the Holy Spirit upon those young aspirants to the priesthood.

What can we say about the time he came to Porto San Giorgio on the 30th of December 1988, to celebrate the Eucharist with us. A few days beforehand we had received the authorisation from the Congregation for Divine Worship to move the sign of the peace to before the anaphora and to celebrate with both species every Sunday and, full of courage, he was the first to celebrate it with those changes. Furthermore, it was he himself who sent out the one hundred families, with many children, to the poorest and most dechristianised areas of Latin America and of Europe, something else that was giving rise to much criticism.

When we asked for five, he gave us a hundred. It is his style. He seems as if he recognises the real enemy, the devil, before we do, and he defends us as a father defends his children, as a shepherd defends his sheep, without fear, taking risks on his own behalf; giving an example as Bishop of Rome.

We have always been the first to be surprised by his affirmations about the Way, by his praise, by his indicating new aspects for us.

When he came to the parish of the Holy Canadian Martyrs, in November 1980 – the first parish in Rome in which we had begun the Neocatechumenal Way – there, before the eleven communities which already existed, he spoke spontaneously for more than half an hour. Bearing in mind the constant criticisms, in which we were accused of creating an elite Christianity, separate from the other realities of the parish, as if we thought we were the only ones, the Pope went still further, speaking of the terrible reality of today, of the radical confrontation: "faith and anti-faith, Church and anti-church, God and anti-God", inviting us strongly to a radical Christianity and to go ahead, giving us courage.

Things have gone like this not just with John Paul II. The same had happened also with Paul VI, who in the general audience of Wednesday 12th January 1977, at which more than five hundred parish priests who have the Way in their parishes were present, together with sixty-seven Bishops who were accompanying them, he surprised us by saying that he was dedicating that allocution to the Neocatechumenal Way, and he entitled it "After Baptism". He concluded saying, "Many people feel attracted by these Neocatechumenal communities, because they see that there is a sincerity, a truth in them, something alive and authentic, Christ living in the world." This allocution is a brief treatise on the necessity of rediscovering the riches of Baptism as the basis of evangelisation. He said "That is why the term 'catechumenate' has reappeared. This certainly does not intend to invalidate or to diminish the importance of the baptismal discipline as currently practised, but seeks to apply it with a gradual and intensive method which recalls and renews in a certain way the Catechumenate of earlier times." There was never a word of criticism. It was as if someone was pushing him to encourage us. He himself, the first time that he used the word "Neocatechumenate", added, raising his eyes from the written text, "Behold the fruits of the Council!"

But we cannot fail to remember John Paul I, whom we met personally in 1972, when he was Patriarch of Venice, and who gave us permission to open the Way in his diocese. In the following years he encouraged it and followed it, personally presiding over all the stages and scrutinies. Furthermore he erected a Diocesan Neocatechumenal Centre, putting the church of San Toma at the disposition of the Way but, above all, he allowed the Paschal Vigil to be celebrated all night, confirming our praxis in everything in front of some parish priests who had raised some difficulties. The joy of his words in the homily that he gave two months before being elected Pope still rings in our ears, when he handed over the breviary to the brothers of the first Neocatechumenal Community in the parish of Santa Maria Formosa, who had arrived at the Initiation to Prayer, and he encouraged them citing the Fathers: "I go to pray, I go to fight!"

The statistics in the appendix show that more than 50% of those who are in the Communities were outside the Church; that is, they were people who in general had prejudices against the hierarchy, against the Vatican, against the Pope. Today the love that the brothers in the Neocatechumenal Way have for the liturgy, for the Pope, for the bishops is recognised by all. These brothers have experienced the lies that the devil constantly sows in society, and it is only through the experience of gestation that they have had in the Way, within the Church, that these lies have been erased from their souls, giving birth to a deep love for the Church and for the Virgin Mary.

Years later, on the 9th May 1986, we were called before the Congregation of the Faith, which subjected us to a questionnaire on hermeneutics, on pastoral work and on doctrine. After having studied our answers, we were called by Cardinal Ratzinger to a meeting at which, he informed us, we could be accompanied by a theologian. At that meeting they told us that they had studied everything, and that they had also been kept informed and they wanted to help us. They proposed joining us to a Congregation, because it was necessary to establish a juridical settlement. We said that a real help would be a 'brief' from the Holy Father, whilst the juridical aspect was being studied more deeply. As a result, the Pope nominated Monsignor Paul J. Cordes, vice-president of the *Consilium pro Laicis*, as having the charge *ad personam* to help us and to act as our link with the Congregations. Since 'briefs' were no longer used, they agreed that the

Al Venerato Fratello
Monsignor PAUL JOSEF CORDES
Vice Presidente del Pontificio Consiglio per i Laici
Incaricato "ad personam"
per l'Apostolato delle Comunità Neocatecumenali

Ogniqualvolta lo Spirito Santo fa germinare nella Chiesa impulsi di una maggiore fedeltà al Vangelo, fioriscono nuovi carismi che manifestano tali realtà e nuove istituzioni che le mettono in pratica. E' stato così dopo il Concilio di Trento e dopo il Concilio Vaticano II.

Tra le realtà generate dallo Spirito ai nostri giorni figurano le Comunità Neocatecumenali, iniziate dal Signor K. Argüello e dalla Signora C. Hernandez (Madrid, Spagna), la cui efficacia per il rinnovamento della vita cristiana veniva salutata dal mio predecessore Paolo VI come frutto del Concilio: "Quanta gioia e quanta speranza ci date con la vostra presenza e con la vostra attività... Vivere e promuovere questo risveglio è quanto voi chiamate una forma di "dopo il Battesimo" che potrà rinnovare nelle odierne comunità cristiane quegli effetti di maturità e di approfondimento che nella Chiesa primitiva erano realizzati dal periodo di preparazione al Battesimo" (Paolo VI alle Comunità Neocatecumenali, Udienza

Generale, 8 maggio 1974, in <u>Notitiae</u> 96-96, 1974, 230).

Anch'io, nei tanti incontri avuti come Vescovo di Roma, nelle parrocchie romane, con le Comunità Neocatecumenali e con i loro Pastori e nei miei viaggi apostolici in molte nazioni, ho potuto constatare copiosi frutti di conversione personale e fecondo impulso missionario.

Tali Comunità rendono visibile, nelle parrocchie, il segno della Chiesa missionaria e "si sforzano di aprire la strada all'evangelizzazione di coloro che hanno quasi abbandonato la vita cristiana, offrendo loro un itinerario di tipo catecumenale, che percorre tutte quelle fasi che nella Chiesa primitiva i catecumeni percorrevano prima di ricevere il sacramento del Battesimo; li riavvicina alla Chiesa ed a Cristo" (cfr. Catecumenato postbattesimale in <u>Notitiae</u> 96-96, 1974, 229). Sono l'annuncio del Vangelo, la testimonianza in piccole comunità e la celebrazione eucaristica in gruppi (cfr. Notificazione sulle celebrazioni nei gruppi del "Cammino Neocatecumenale" in <u>L'Osservatore Romano</u>, 24 dicembre 1988) che permettono ai membri di porsi al servizio del rinnovamento della Chiesa.

Vari Fratelli nell'Episcopato hanno riconosciuto i frutti di questo Cammino. Voglio limitarmi a ricordare l'allora Vescovo di Madrid, Mons. Casimiro Morcillo, nella cui diocesi e sotto il cui governo sono nate, nell'anno 1964, le Comunità Neocatecumenali che egli accolse con tanto amore.

Dopo oltre vent'anni di vita delle Comunità, diffuse nei cinque continenti,

- tenendo conto della nuova vitalità che anima le parrocchie, dell'impulso missionario e dei frutti di conversione che sbocciano dall'impegno degli itineranti e, ultimamente, dall'opera delle famiglie che evangelizzano in zone scristianizzate d'Europa e del mondo intero;

- in considerazione delle vocazioni, sorte da codesto Cammino, alla vita religiosa e al presbiterato, e della nascita di Collegi diocesani di formazione al presbiterato per la nuova evangelizzazione, quale il Redemptoris Mater di Roma;

- avendo preso visione della documentazione da Lei presentata:

accogliendo la richiesta rivoltami, riconosco il Cammino Neocatecumenale come un itinerario di formazione cattolica, valida per la società e per i tempi odierni.

Auspico, pertanto, che i Fratelli nell'Episcopato valorizzino e aiutino - insieme con i loro presbiteri - quest'opera per la nuova evangelizzazione, perché essa si realizzi secondo le linee proposte dagli iniziatori, nello spirito di servizio all'Ordinario del luogo e di comunione con lui e nel contesto dell'unità della Chiesa particolare con la Chiesa universale.

In pegno di tale voto, imparto a Lei e a tutti gli appartenenti alle Comunità Neocatecumenali la mia

Benedizione Apostolica.

Dal Vaticano, il 30 Agosto dell' 1990, XII di Pon-
tificato.

Joannes Paulus PP. II

Pope should give us a more official support. Just as for Israel, so in the many times that the dark sea blocked our passage, to our astonishment the Lord has opened the sea before us and we have been joyful spectators of his gratuity.

When later we saw in our hands the letter of recognition of the Neocatechumenal Way that John Paul II had written to Monsignor Cordes, I could not help thinking of the words that Paul VI had said to me in the private audience that he had granted our team on the 12th January 1977. Looking at me intently (I remember well his penetrating blue eyes), after having asked: "Who is Kiko?" he put his hand on my shoulder and said to me, "Be humble and faithful to the Church and the Church will be faithful to you". I remember that he also gave us a medal and Carmen said to him that, instead of giving her a medal, she would prefer him to lay his hands on her, at which Paul VI, standing at his throne smiling, agreed, and making her kneel before him, imposed his hands on her.

It is surprising to see today how we have seen the words, "The catechumenate for adults is to be restored", which the Holy Spirit had inspired in the Council (*Sacrosanctum Concilium* 64), fulfilled through His work during these thirty years; not planned at a table, but in a history with facts and with persons, sustained and supported by the Bishops and above all by the Pope.

Everything has always so far surpassed us that we could do nothing but wait, day by day, to discern the footsteps of Christ which He was inviting us to follow. In this sense, today, seeing many 'Redemptoris Mater' seminaries for the New Evangelisation, that have come into existence thanks to the support of the Holy Father to come to the help of the dioceses which are in serious difficulty, and the thousands of vocations which are emerging from these small communities, we can only say with Saint Peter, after the miraculous catch of fish, "Leave me Lord, I am a sinful man".

KIKO ARGÜELLO and CARMEN HERNÁNDEZ

Rome, 15th of August 1992
Solemnity of the Assumption of the Blessed Virgin Mary

See translation of the letter on pp. 19-20.

Editor's note

The present collection does not contain all the speeches and words of Paul VI and John Paul II about the Neocatechumenal Way (for this, the publication edited by the Neocatechumenal Centre of Rome, The Neocatechumenal Way in the Speeches of Paul IV and John Paul II, *may be referred to). Here we report, usually in their entirety, the texts of around forty meetings held with the Neocatechumenal Communities (general audiences, particular audiences, visits to parishes), out of the more than sixty that have already taken place in the Vatican and the Diocese of Rome alone.*

The longest speeches have been subdivided into themes and distributed throughout the various chapters which make up the book. A mini title has been placed beside each passage, almost always taken directly from the Pope's words, and the source of the text itself is always indicated. At the end of each passage is an indication of where it continues or where it can be read in its entirety.

Most of the speeches, furthermore, were made ad lib and they retain all the strength and freshness of this spontaneity. This is why it seemed opportune to us, now and again, to complete the texts published by the L'Osservatore Romano *with additions reported faithfully from recordings of the various meetings.*

The appendix, as well as presenting a brief synthesis of the Neocatechumenal Way by its initiators, Kiko Argüello and Carmen Hernández, also includes texts of the Congregation for Divine Worship on the Neocatechumenal Way, the decree of erection of the 'Redemptoris Mater' diocesan seminary of Rome (with a brief presentation of other seminaries now in existence), the Letter of the Holy Father to the European bishops meeting in Vienna (1993), some statistical data about the Neocatechumenal Way in the Diocese of Rome and in the parishes of Spain, and the complete texts of some speeches of the Popes.

Letter of John Paul II approving the Neocatechumenal Way

To Our Venerable Brother
Monsignor PAUL JOSEF CORDES
Vice President of the Pontifical Council for the Laity
Appointed "ad personam" for the Apostolate of the
Neocatechumenal Communities

Every time the Holy Spirit germinates in the Church impulses for greater faithfulness to the Gospel, there flourish new charisms which manifest these realities, and new institutions which put them into practice. It was so after the Council of Trent and after the Second Vatican Council.

Among the realities generated by the Spirit in our days figure the Neocatechumenal Communities, initiated by Mr K Argüello and Ms C Hernández (Madrid, Spain), the effectiveness of which for the renewal of Christian life was acclaimed by my predecessor, Paul VI, as a fruit of the Council: "How much joy and how much hope you give us by your presence and by your activity... To live and to promote this re-awakening is what you call a 'post-baptismal' way, which will be able to renew in today's Christian communities those effects of maturity and deepening that, in the primitive Church, were realised by the period of preparation for Baptism" (Paul VI to the Neocatechumenal Communities, General Audience, 8th May 1974, in *Notitiae* 96-96, 1974, 230).

I too, as Bishop of Rome, have been able to verify the abundant fruits of personal conversion and fruitful missionary impulse in the many meetings I have had in the Roman parishes with the Neocatechumenal Communities and their pastors, and in my apostolic journeys in many nations.

These Communities make visible in the parishes the

sign of the missionary church and 'they strive to open a way for the evangelisation of those who have almost abandoned the Christian life, offering them an itinerary of a catechumenal type which goes through all those stages that the catechumens went through in the primitive church before receiving the sacrament of Baptism: it brings them back to the Church and to Christ' (cf. 'Postbaptismal Catechumenate' in *Notitiae* 96-96, 1974, 229). The announcement of the Gospel, the witnessing in small communities and the eucharistic celebration in groups (cf. Notification on the celebration of groups of the 'Neocatechumenal Way' in *L'Osservatore Romano*, 24th December 1988) is what enables the members to put themselves at the service of the renewal of the Church.

Many brothers in the Episcopate have acknowledged the fruits of this Way. I want only to recall Mons. Casimiro Morcillo, the then Bishop of Madrid, in whose diocese and under whose government the Neocatechumenal Communities – which he welcomed with so much love – were born in the year 1964.

After twenty years of the life of these communities, spread throughout the five continents:

– taking into account the new vitality which animates the parishes, the missionary impulse and the fruits of conversion which blossom from the dedication of the itinerants and, lately, from the work of the families which evangelise in dechristianised areas of Europe and of the whole world;

– in consideration of the vocations to the religious life and to the presbyterate which have arisen from this Way, and of the birth of diocesan colleges of formation to the presbyterate for the new evangelisation, such as the REDEMPTORIS MATER of Rome;

– having examined the documentation presented by you: welcoming the request addressed to me, I acknowledge the Neocatechumenal Way as an itinerary of Catholic formation, valid for our society and for our times.

It is therefore my wish that the Brothers in the Episcopate – together with their presbyters – value and help this work for the new evangelisation so that it may be implemented according to the lines proposed by its initiators, in the spirit of service to the local Ordinary and in communion with him in the context of the unity of the local church and the universal Church.

As a pledge of this wish of mine, I impart to you, and to all those who belong to the Neocatechumenal Communities, my Apostolic Blessing.

JOANNES PAULUS PP II

From the Vatican, 30th August, 1990,
12th year of the Pontificate.

BRIEF COMMENT FOR THE VATICAN PRESS OFFICE RELATING TO THE LETTER OF THE HOLY FATHER ON THE NEOCATECHUMENAL WAY

by Kiko Argüello

What is the Neocatechumenal Way?

In the early Church, in the midst of paganism, a person who wanted to become a Christian had to follow an itinerary of formation in Christianity that was called the 'Catechumenate' from the word 'catecheo' which means 'echo', 'listening'.

The current process of secularisation has brought many people to abandon the faith and the Church. Because of this a new itinerary of Christian formation needs to be opened up. The Neocatechumenal Way does not lay claim to forming a movement in itself, but to helping parishes to open up a way of Christian initiation to Baptism, in order to discover what it means to be Christian. It is an instrument, in the parishes, in the service of the Bishops, to bring back to faith many people who have abandoned it. Today in the West many dioceses are trying to carry out catechesis for adults. The Neocatechumenal Way is a theological-catechetical synthesis, a catechism, a catechumenate for adults, an itinerary of Christian formation for modern man.

In the early Church, the catechumenate was formed of a synthesis between Word (Kerygma), Liturgy and Morality. The early Church had above all a Kerygma, that is an 'announcement of salvation'. This announcement of the Gospel that was made by apostles like Paul and Silas, brought about a moral change in those who heard it. They changed their lives helped by the Holy Spirit who accompanied the apostles. This moral change was sealed and encouraged through the sacraments. Concretely, Baptism was given by stages. In this way the primitive catechesis was a 'gestation' to divine life.

When the catechumenate disappeared over the following centuries, this synthesis of Kerygma – Change of life – Liturgy was lost. The Kerygma as a call to faith that implied a moral decision no longer existed; it was transformed into a 'scholastic doctrine'. Morality became an 'internal forum' – a private act. The liturgy became the same for all.

The Neocatechumenal Way recovers this 'period of gestation', this synthesis between Kerygma, Change of life and Liturgy.

Why is it called Neocatechumenate?

Because the Neocatechumenal Way is essentially offered to those who have already been baptised, but who do not have an adequate Christian formation. *Catechesis Tradendae* affirms that the situation of many Christians in the parishes is of 'quasi catechumens'.

What is so newsworthy in this *Letter* of the Holy Father is that it recognises in the Neocatechumenate a Christian initiation for adults of a catechumenal nature, thus offering the dioceses a concrete instrument for evangelisation without making it into a religious order, a special association or a movement. Many times in the history of the Church the saints have tried to make the spirit of the Gospel come to life again in the people of God without necessarily encompassing it within a religious order. The time was not ripe. Today, after the Second Vatican Council, the current reality of atheism and secularisation puts the Church in a position where the renewal of the catechumenate is absolutely necessary.

With this *Letter*, the Pope validates 25 years of an experience which started in one of the poorest suburbs of Madrid, and which now extends to 600 dioceses, 3000 parishes and 87 countries through a total of 10,000 communities, and acknowledges the fruits of personal conversion and its missionary impetus. The renewal that has taken place in these parishes thanks to the Neocatechumenate has caused an extraordinary impulse for the missions, such that many catechists and even entire families have been ready to go wherever evangelisation is needed.

Another important fruit in the local Church is the flourishing, once again, of numerous vocations (in the first half of 1990 alone, more than 1500 young men from the Neocatechumenal Communities felt the call to become priests) and it has given rise to the birth of missionary diocesan seminaries that can come to the rescue of the many dioceses that find themselves in difficulty in this time because of a lack of vocations. The originality of these seminaries is that they involve a serious Christian initiation – the Neocatechumenate – in the formation of presbyters. Thus in a very short time, many bishops have decided to open these seminaries in their dioceses: in Rome, Madrid, Warsaw, Medellin, Bangalore, Callao (Lima), Newark (New Jersey, USA), Takamatsu (Japan) and many other countries where they have begun to function.

With this *Letter*, the Holy Father, having verified its fruits all over the world, formally acknowledges the Neocatechumenal Way as an 'itinerary of Catholic formation, valid for our society and our times' and hopes that all the Bishops together with their presbyters value and help this Way in their dioceses.

Rome, 24th September 1990

Chapter 1

Baptism and Neocatechumenate: "You are so necessary in the Church of today"[1]

A 'post-baptismal catechumenate'[2]

(Paul VI to the Neocatechumenal Communities, audience of 8th May 1974 – Text in Notitiae, 95-96, July-August 1974, p. 230, with some additional material taken from a tape-recording.)

We greet the group of priests and lay people who represent the movement of the Neocatechumenal Communities – here we see post-conciliar fruits! – gathered in Rome from many dioceses throughout Italy and other countries. They are here for a meeting on the theme of evangelisation in the modern world, the same theme to be examined by the next Assembly of the Synod of Bishops.

How great is the joy, how great is the hope, which you give us with your presence and with your activity!

Understand and develop the riches of your Baptism

We know that in your communities, you strive together to understand and develop **the riches of your baptism and the consequences of belonging to Christ. This task makes you aware that the Christian life is nothing other than a permanent coherence and dynamism which derive from having accepted being with Christ, and prolonging his presence and his mission in the world.**

1. John Paul II, during his visit to the parish of St Tarcisius (Rome, 3rd March 1985): "...Our age needs radical conversions like that of Paul of Tarsus. It is with great pleasure that I see you here and I think that you are very necessary in the Church of today" (cf. p. 45).
2. The titles given to these passages from the Pope's addresses and the sections of the text marked in boldface are the responsibility of the editor.

Whilst for you, this purpose is a conscious, authentic way of living your Christian vocation, it becomes an efficacious witness for others – you have an apostolate just because you are what you are – a stimulus for the rediscovery and the recovery of true, authentic and effective Christian values which otherwise might remain almost hidden and dormant, and almost diluted in ordinary life.

But no! You prove that they are true, you bring them to the light and give them a moral splendour which is truly exemplary – precisely because, with this Christian spirit, this is the way you live in your Neocatechumenal Communities.

To live and foster this re-awakening is what you call a kind of 'post baptism', which can renew in our contemporary Christian communities the effects of maturity and depth which were achieved in the early church during the period of preparation before baptism.

You do this afterwards. Whether 'before' or 'after' is secondary, I would say. The fact is that you aim at the authenticity, fullness, coherence and sincerity of Christian life. And this is a very great merit which, I repeat, consoles us enormously, and inspires our wishes, prayers, and most abundant blessings for you, for all those who help you, and for all those whom you can, with your greeting and message, greet on our behalf.

We are happy to know that you are the instigators of this reawakening of consciousness in many parishes. We are especially happy to know that in all that you do, you are extremely attentive to your dependence on your pastors and your communion with all your brothers. For this ecclesial sensitivity – which is always the guarantee of the presence of the Spirit – we give you our encouragement.

The Neocatechumenate is up-to-date

(*Paul VI, general audience, 12th January 1977* – Text translated from the original recording by Vatican Radio.)

The presence at this audience of a group noticeable because of its numbers – most of you here are part of this group – and because of the rank of the participants – your leaders, and above all the group of bishops whom you have brought with you – this group of the members of the Neocatechumenal Communities offers us, by your presence, the opportunity to draw two events of the Catholic Church to the attention of our visitors and to those listening. The

first is the Synod of Bishops three years ago, in 1974, on the subject "Evangelisation in our times": the way in which the Gospel is spread today. This was the theme of the 1974 Synod which provided the subject matter of our subsequent apostolic exhortation, "Evangelii Nuntiandi" of the 8th December 1975. If we had the foolish ambition of advertising our documents, we should almost like to recommend it to you because it is so full, it is a such a tribute to all that the Bishops said in the Synod. I have tried to interpret, to gather together, all their ideas, to organise them and to make them accessible in the simplest possible language, but also, most importantly, the clearest possible, so making us bold to recommend it to you, especially to you who want to be **Neocatechumens**, that is, to give instruction and evangelise the great crowds of people you succeed in reaching. I think it would be good for you and for your students, your disciples.

that on 'Catechesis': how to catechise young people and adults in our time

The second event is still in the future, and will take place this year, beginning on September 30th: the other Synod of Bishops. We will have about two hundred bishops here from all over the world, nominated by their respective episcopal conferences. What will the theme be? The theme will once again deal with evangelisation, but from another aspect, that is catechesis: how religion is taught, especially to children, to boys and girls, to young people and to adults too, at this stage of our civilisation, and how to become teachers. It is the bishops who wanted this theme, and we shall take it up again and develop it. **This shows how up-to-date you catechumens are.**

This shows an awareness that the fundamental mission of the Church is to spread the message of the Gospel, according to the last command given by Jesus at the end of his visible presence on earth – what were his words? "Go and preach!" *"Go and make disciples of all nations."* This awareness is keenly alive and at work in the Church today. How often it is said, when in looking at past history that has characterised the different periods of the history of the Church, "But what were they doing?" Either there was war between certain states, or there were dogmatic problems and so on, which were of little interest to public opinion or pastoral apostolate. The Church has been meditating again on her proper function and pastoral duties, and her first pastoral duty is to announce the Gospel and to go out to the world and say, "Look, I am bringing you the message, which the angels brought to the earth, 'Glory to God and peace on earth', and then the message of Christ to announce the Gospel, that is, the good news taught to us by Jesus Christ."[3]

The Church returns to its function: to announce the Gospel to the world

---

3. For the complete text see pp. 173-180.

The Catechumenate: preparation for baptism
The Neocatechumenate: after baptism

(Paul VI, general audience, 12th January 1977 – Text translated from the original recording by Vatican Radio.)

Catechumenate and baptism

The word 'catechumenate' refers to baptism. It was the period of preparation for baptism. Nowadays, baptism does not have the same development, at least in its didactic preparation. And so our visitors [the Neocatechumens] today say: We will carry out this preparation *after baptism.* The sanctifying grace received was not sufficient; on the contrary, sanctifying grace has done no more than light a fire which needs to spread itself into the whole of the baptised person's life. Saint Augustine says this: "If we cannot have the catechumenate beforehand, we will carry it out afterwards." That is, the instruction, completion and education, the whole of the Church's educative work, after baptism.

Today Baptism must be integrated with a subsequent initiation

The sacrament of Christian regeneration must once again return to being what it was in the consciousness and custom of the first generations of Christians. The praxis (the practice, isn't it so?) and norms of the Church have introduced the holy rule of conferring baptism on the newly born. What instruction do they receive? It is necessary therefore that the godfather should take the infant's place, speaking on its behalf. But the latter does not benefit from the attestation given by the godfather to the priest. What has happened is that the preparation has been liturgically concentrated in the baptismal rite. The liturgy in fact still bears traces of this preparatory initiation which preceded baptism, and which during the early times when society was profoundly pagan, was called the catechumenate. Later, the Church condensed this period. Why? Because all families were Catholic, all were good, all were Christian; the orientation of society was fundamentally Christian. The children would continue to learn 'along the way'.

But today our society is no longer uniform, homogeneous. It is pluralistic, and indeed in itself is full of contradictions and obstacles to the Gospel. In the social environment of today, this method needs to be completed by instruction, by initiation after baptism, into the proper life style of the Christian. This has to come after baptism.

An effective integration into the Church through a gradual and intensive evangelisation

This is the secret of your formula, which provides religious assistance, a practical training in Christian faithfulness, and effectively integrates the baptised into the community of believers which is the Church. They have already entered it from the supernatural point of view, but it was like a seed that has not yet had the advantage of developing.

Here we see the rebirth of the name 'Catechumenate'. This certainly does not intend to invalidate or to diminish the importance of the baptismal discipline as currently practised, but seeks to apply it according to a gradual and intensive method which recalls and renews in a certain way the Catechumenate of earlier times. The person who has been baptised needs to understand, to think over, to appreciate, to give assent to the inestimable treasure of the Sacrament he has received.[4]

What the Catechumens of the Primitive Church once did the Neocatechumenal Communities do now

(John Paul II: visit to the parish of St Timothy, Rome, February 1980 – Translated from the Italian edition of *L'Osservatore Romano*, 11-12th February 1980.)

The word 'catechumen' has almost disappeared

Catechumens, particularly in traditionally Catholic populations, are small children and babies. But they are not true catechumens because they are not capable of being prepared for baptism. The catechumens of the first centuries were a very important reality in the Church: **I believe that what they did for the faith in those days, the Neocatechumenal Communities are doing today.**[5] But they are doing this because they were baptised by others at the beginning of their lives. The essence of the catechumenate is the preparation for baptism. To be prepared, in the full meaning of the word, is to be introduced into the mysteries of the living God, because in Baptism you receive not only the name of Christian, but also a share in Christ himself, a share in the mystery of God living for men. The testimony that you have presented to me[6] proves that there is a moment of grace, a

4. For the complete text see pp. 173-180.
5. During his visit to the parish of St Anthony at Piazza Asti (Rome, 6th May 1979) the Pope had mentioned that the spirit of the Catechumens of the primitive Church must have been like that of the Neocatechumenal Communities: "And you explain all this with your Community, with your fraternal communion and with your joy, with your song, too, and certainly with prayer: because when the true reality of Baptism is discovered, the reality of the Grace of God, of our divine sonship, when all this is discovered, then we enter into profound joy and then also into a joy that can be communicated. I mean that one tries to communicate this discovery and this joy to others. I really think that the spirit of the groups of Catechumens of the primitive Church is the same spirit of the Neocatechumenal groups in the Contemporary Church. I hope that you will go on and also that you will pray sometimes for the Pope."
6. When the Pope meets the Neocatechumenal Communities in the Roman parishes, the parish priest usually presents the 'Way' to the Holy Father. Then the catechist who opened the 'Way' in the parish briefly explains how it began. After this, some brothers and sisters who were far away from the Church give their testimony. It is to these testimonies that the Pope refers here and in other speeches.

moment of enlightenment, a moment in which the living God is met, the God who seeks to live in our lives, to live your life. **This is very precious to your personal experience as Christians, but it is precious above all for apostolic formation.** This experience must be at the basis of the formation of every apostle – and that is to say, in the formation of every catechist. Because it is not sufficient to know the formulas of faith and theology, but it is necessary to enter into contact with the mystery of divine life opened to us all through Jesus Christ. **Only after such a personal experience can you give witness.** I hope that you will always deepen your faith, and have joy with you always.

The Neocatechumenate: a way to rediscover one's own Baptism

(*John Paul II: visit to the Parish of Our Lady of the Blessed Sacrament and of the Canadian Martyrs, 2nd November 1980 –* Translated from the Italian edition of *L'Osservatore Romano*, 3-4th November 1980, "The Pope resumes his visits to the parishes of Rome", with additional material from a tape recording.)

On Sunday 2nd November the Holy Father visited the parish of Our Lady of the Blessed Sacrament and of the Holy Canadian Martyrs, in Villa Massimo. The Pope celebrated the Eucharist in the church in the presence of Cardinals Poletti and Roy, of auxiliary Bishop Oscar Zanera and of the parish community.

The Pope then went downstairs into the crypt of the parish church, a very atmospheric place because of a large baptismal font set into the ground from which a spring of water flows out. At the opposite end the presidential chair is set in front of a panel painted with sacred scenes. In front of the chair is a large table beside which was shining the paschal candle. Around the table were at least five hundred people: the brothers and sisters of the Neocatechumenal Communities who have been following their Way in this parish for twelve years...

Fr Guglielmo Amadei introduced the eleven communities who are at present doing the Way to the Holy Father; the first was formed in 1968 and the last at Easter last year. Fr Amadei also underlined the great contribution that catechists from these communities had made to the pastoral programme of the parish – which is completely centred on evangelisation – and to other parishes in Rome, in Italy and many other countries in different continents.

Then Kiko Argüello spoke at some length of his spiritual experience and of the long journey to conversion:

'The Lord allowed me to have an experience of absurdity, of atheism, until he had mercy on me. He humiliated me to the point of making me sufficiently humble to ask him for help and afterwards he took me to live among the poor without my knowing what the way of the Lord really was. I went to live among the poor, the slum dwellers of Madrid, without knowing that God had a plan which today amazes me. I am astonished and frightened, because I know that probably this plan will not go ahead without very great suffering.'

Kiko then spoke of the great strength of the theological and catechetical synthesis which was necessary because of the humility of the people who listened to him and who were not able to understand abstractions. With the help of Carmen Hernández, and following the lines indicated by the Council, this ferment was transmuted into a way of faith, a progressive Catechumenate done in stages, in total obedience, which offers itself as a help to the parishes for the work of catechesis; to bring adults in the Christian community to fully relive the Gospel through the rediscovery of Baptism.

Deeply interested in the lengthy account of Kiko's spiritual experience and the origins of the Neocatechumenal Way, the Holy Father in his turn spoke at length, to deepen with sincerity and in a spirit of love the ecclesial sense of the Neocatechumenal Communities. Among other things he said:

Above all, I want to tell you that I love you, seeing so many of you meeting together, adults, young people, children, with your priests. I love you. I have followed with interest the information given to me by your presbyter. This is not the first time that I have heard him speak of his enthusiasm for the Neocatechumenal Movement[7], which being "way" is also movement. I have also listened with great interest to the testimony of your first catechist.

A way to discover faith

What can I tell you? Most importantly, **the word which came up most often was the word faith.** All of you are faithful, I mean you have faith. There is more to say: many have faith, but **you have followed a way to discover your faith,** to discover the divine treasure that you carry within you, in your souls. And you have made such a discovery, **discovering the mystery of baptism.** It is true that in the world there are a great many people who are baptised. Certainly they are still a minority among the people of the world, but they are many. Among these baptised, I don't know how many are aware of their baptism, not simply of

7. Carmen had the impudence, or the courage, to interrupt the Pope at this point, saying, "Father, it's not a movement, it's a way." The police and the Pope's entourage were alarmed but the Pope, smiling, answered immediately, "But if you're on a way, you move!" This distinction between movements, such as the associations fashionable at present, and the Neocatechumenate, as a post-baptismal Way, is clarified in the letter of approval of Pope John Paul II, as Kiko emphasises in his comment on the letter. Cf. also Appendix I, *The Neocatechumenal Way: a brief synthesis*, p. 127.

the fact of being baptised, but of what it means to be baptised, of what baptism means.

Now **the road or the way to discover faith through baptism is the road that we all find in the teaching of Christ, in the Gospel.**

Baptismal immersion and the death of Christ

We find it reflected too in a profound way in the letters of St Paul. He has shown us the immense depths of the mystery of baptism, comparing immersion in the baptismal waters with immersion in the death of Christ, a death which has brought us redemption, and a death which brings us resurrection. Thus the whole paschal mystery is summed up in the sacrament, I mean in the mystery, of baptism.

Look. To discover the dynamic depths of our faith is to discover the full meaning of our baptism. If I understand correctly, **your way consists essentially of this: to discover the mystery of baptism, to discover its full content,** and so to discover what it means to be Christian, to be a believer.

A discovery that has apostolic roots and that is original

This discovery is in the line of tradition, it has roots which are apostolic, Pauline, evangelical. At the same time, this discovery is original. It has always been so, and will always be so. Every time that a Christian discovers the depths of the mystery of his baptism, he is accomplishing an act which is completely original. It is not possible to do this except with the help of the grace of Christ, and the light of the Holy Spirit, because it is a mystery, because it is a divine, supernatural reality, and natural man is not able to understand it, to discover it, to live it. So it must be concluded: all of you who have had the grace to discover the depths, the full reality, of your baptism, ought to be very grateful to the giver of grace, to the Holy Spirit, who has given you such light, who has given you the help of the grace to receive this gift in the first place, and then to continue. Here we conclude the first part of the reflection.[8]

The way of the new man

(John Paul II: visit to the parish of Our Lady of the Blessed Sacrament and of the Canadian Martyrs, 2nd November 1980 – Translated from the Italian edition of *L'Osservatore Romano,* 3-4th November 1980 with additional material from a tape recording.)

Discovering Baptism as the beginning of

Here briefly is the second part: to discover baptism as the beginning of our Christian life, of our immersion in

8. For the complete text, pp. 180-183.

the discovery of the
sacramental dimension
of the whole of Christian
life

God, in the living God, and in the mystery of redemption, the paschal mystery, to discover our baptism as the beginning of Christian life, must constitute the beginning of the whole of our Christian life, step by step, day by day, week by week, stage by stage of our life, because Christian life is a dynamic process. Normally, one begins by baptising little children soon after birth, but then they grow. Man grows, the Christian must grow too. And so we must project the discovery of baptism on the whole of life, on all aspects of life. We have to see also, on the basis of this sacramental beginning to our life, the whole sacramental dimension of our life, because the whole of life has a multifold sacramental dimension.

The central point of such
an initiation is the
Eucharist

There are the sacraments of initiation: Baptism and Confirmation, through which one reaches the fullness, the central point of this initiation in the Eucharist. Moreover we know very well that the Fathers of the Church spoke of the sacrament of Penance as a new Baptism, as a second Baptism, a third, a tenth, and so on.

We can speak too of the last Baptism of human life, the Sacrament of the Sick. There are also the sacraments of community life: the Priesthood, Marriage. Christian life has a totally sacramental structure, and we have to frame the discovery of our own baptism against such a background, which is essentially sanctifying, because the sacraments make way for the Holy Spirit. Christ has given us the Holy Spirit in its absolute fullness. We need only to open our hearts and make way. **The sacraments make way for the Holy Spirit who works in our souls,** in our hearts, in our humanity, in our personality. He builds us anew, he creates a new man.

Way of faith, of Baptism
rediscovered. Way of the
'new man'

So **this way, a way of faith, a way of baptism rediscovered, has to be the way of the new man.** This new man sees what is the true proportion, or rather, the disproportion, of his created being, of his creaturehood, with respect to God the creator, and to the infinite majesty of God the redeemer, God the holy one and sanctifier. In the light of this, he tries to fulfil himself. Thus life takes on a moral aspect. This must be another, indeed I would say, the same fruit of rediscovering the sacramental structure of our Christian life, because sacramental means sanctifying. At the same time, we must discover the ethical structure, because that which is holy is always good, it doesn't have room for evil, for sin. Certainly the Holy One, the most Holy of all, Christ, accepts sinners, he welcomes them, but to make them holy. This, then, is the whole programme. So we have the second point, the second conclusion. Discovering baptism as the beginning of our Christian life in all its depths, we then need to discover the consequences, step by step, in our whole Christian life. So, to do this, we need to follow a way, **we must follow a way.**[9]

A way to live profoundly the mystery of being children of God

(*John Paul II: visit to the parish of the Nativity of Our Lord Jesus Christ, Rome, 14th December 1980* – Translated from the Italian edition of *L'Osservatore Romano*, 3rd-4th November 1980, with additional material from a tape recording.)

We have met together many times in the different parishes of Rome – the last time was in the parish of Canadian Martyrs. Here I have met and embraced many children, and this has made me think of the words of Christ who once said that we must all become like little children – even if we are fifty or sixty years old or more, like myself, we must be like children. We are speaking, of course, of supernatural filiation, which is initiated in us, and becomes rooted in us, at Baptism.

Living profoundly the mystery of divine sonship

You, whose spirituality as Neocatechumens is centred on the mystery of Baptism, must live profoundly the mystery of divine sonship, the mystery of being sons of God, the mystery of all that comes from this reality, baptism, which is the true power underlying divine sonship.

This, essentially, is what I wanted to say to you. But I am expressing it in a particular way to you because you are parishioners of the parish of the Nativity, where the mystery of the Son of God made man is at the centre of community life, and I am saying this because the feast of Christmas is approaching. I hope that you will walk always, and grow always, in that inner and supernatural reality of Grace, the Grace of being adopted sons of God, made like his only begotten Son, who became man in order to draw near us, to meet us, and to make us like himself."

Kiko then introduced to the Pope some itinerant catechists who, having had a formation in the parish of the Nativity, are now giving witness in different countries of the world. One of them, a young priest who had just returned from Latin America, spoke to the Pope of the dramatic situation facing missionaries and catechists, especially in Central and South America.

9. For the complete text see pp. 180-183.

"We need encouragement, Holy Father," the priest said, "because Central America is passing through a very difficult situation. We have returned, and like St Paul, we are wondering whether we act in vain, because we find ourselves in the situation of not knowing whether the Church is the Church of revolution, as many people tell us there, or whether it is to announce Jesus Christ..."

Before the young priest had even finished speaking, the Holy Father said in a strong, clear voice:

Announce only Christ!

"I will give you the answer immediately: Announce Christ! And Christ only." *A roar of applause supported the Pope's words.* "And may I add," *continued the Holy Father,* "that not a day passes when I do not pray for these countries, especially for those in great torment. Not a day passes when I do not follow the situation with faith and love." "You have to know," *concluded the Pope after pausing a moment,* "there they have a Mother who is very powerful!"

It is not enough to be Christian; one needs to become Christian every day

(*John Paul II: visit to the parish of St Francesca Cabrini, 4th December 1983* – Translated from the Italian edition of *L'Osservatore Romano*, 5-6th December 1983, with additional material from a tape recording.)

I am very happy to see you, and your families and your children. We are all children of God, we become children of God through Baptism, a great Sacrament, tremendous, I would say. It does not seem so because it is a very sweet Sacrament which works through water, with oil, with Holy Chrism (this morning I baptised a baby girl).

Baptism immerses us in the redemptive death of Christ so as to rise with him

And this Sacrament, Baptism, which is so sweet and which we usually confer on newborn babies, this Sacrament has tremendous depth, stupendous depth, because it immerses us in the redemptive death of Christ, immerses us, so we can rise with Christ and thus participate in his work. It is the only way to be children of God, the only sacramental way to be sons, to share in the life which Christ has brought us, showing it by his Resurrection.

The Catechumenate: a very ancient institution in the Church to prepare pagans for Baptism

What I say to you touches what is specific about your movement which is called Neocatechumenal. The Catechumenate was a very ancient institution of the Church. How many Catechumens passed through this ancient Rome of the Caesars, this Rome, this pagan Rome, and how many were prepared with the Catechumenate and the Baptism of adults! But today Baptism, the same Sacrament, has become the sacrament of little children, of newborn babies and this catechumenal way is deferred until after baptism: the Catechumenate thus becomes life-long; yes, we are Catechumens all our life long!

The institutional Catechumenate before Baptism is missing today

There is no institutional Catechumenate as it existed in the days of the early Christians, so the Catechumenate has become the task of our Christian life, of our life of faith. In fact, your movement, and here I welcome the one who inspired it (I know him well), your movement is centred on this process of becoming children of God, of becoming Christians. It is very important!

It is not enough to be Christian; we need to become Christian every day

Many people think, 'But we are Christian'; they say, 'we are Christian' without knowing this, because it is not enough to be Christian, you have to become Christian, to become Christian every day, to discover every day what *cristianus* means, *Cristo adscriptus*. For the first time in the city of Antioch they began to call the disciples of Jesus 'Christians', followers of Christ. This has to be discovered, to be discovered every day, to be discovered more and more, because the mystery of Baptism is so profound, it is a divine and at the same time a human mystery, the human being becomes the adopted child of God... enough!

In the parish you are a leaven that permeates with a new awareness

You reflect a lot concretely, you meditate a lot on this truth. I have to say that here in the parish of St Francesca Cabrini, that your movement here is leaven, leaven which must permeate the dough and the world of Christians in general. Not everyone is aware, not everyone fulfils it; here you are leaven, you must permeate this community, of about 20,000 people, permeate it with a new awareness of human dignity combined with the reality of divine sonship.[10]

To realise the baptismal dimension means to live authentically the identity of being a Christian

(*John Paul II: private audience for 2,000 priests of the Neocatechumenal Communities, the Vatican, 9th December 1985* – Translated from the Italian edition of *L'Osservatore Romano*, 11th December 1985.)

I have listened with great interest to the words addressed to me by Kiko Argüello in the name of all of you. He has

10. For the complete text see pp. 190-191.

described how all the Communities of the Neocatechumenal Way, throughout the various nations of the world, have committed themselves to continuous prayer and meditation for the Extraordinary Synod which is being celebrated twenty five years after the conclusion of the Second Vatican Council.

I encourage your experience based on the Sacrament of Baptism

Your spiritual participation in the preparation and your presence at the closing ceremony of the Synod have been a significant and solemn manifestation of your fidelity to Christ the Redeemer and to the pilgrim Church which transmits grace to men, especially in the sacramental signs which are a memorial of and make actual the efficacy of the Redemption.

In this audience I am glad to recall the many meetings I have had with your communities, particularly during pastoral visits in my diocese of Rome, meetings in which I have encouraged your spiritual experience, which is based on the fundamental experience of the Sacrament of Baptism, on the awareness that to realise the baptismal dimension means above all to live the authentic identity of being Christian. It means uniting oneself intimately to the Eucharistic Christ; it means loving concretely and effectively all men as brothers in Christ; it means making and directing one's moral choices in conformity and harmony with the baptismal promises.

Way of faith, of Baptism rediscovered
Way of the new man

"This way, way of faith, way of Baptism rediscovered," I said to your friends in the parish of Canadian Martyrs in Rome, "must be a way of the new man. The latter sees what is the real measure, or better, the nothingness of his created entity, of his creatureliness with respect to the Creator, to his infinite majesty, to God the redeemer, to the holy God who makes holy, and he tries to fulfil himself within that perspective" (*Insegnamenti* III 2 (1980), p. 1044).[11]

By means of your 'Way', one sees what a treasure the Catechumenate has been for the Church

(*John Paul II: visit to the parish of St Maria Goretti, Rome, 31st January 1988* – Translated from the Italian edition of *L'Osservatore Romano*, 1st-2nd February 1988.)

I thank you for this meeting, and for all the testimonies you have given. Listening to you and meeting you I always think of the catechumenate, and I think of it not only in historical categories.

11. For the complete text see pp. 191-196.

The Catechumenate of
the early and missionary
Church and the
rediscovery of such a
treasure

The practice of
Christians today seems
inadequate without a
prior Catechumenate

The disappearance of the
Catechumenate in its
primitive sense and its
substitution by the
catechesis of the Church
and Christian education
in the family

Certainly the catechumenate belongs to the history of the early and missionary church, but through your 'Way', and through your experiences one can see what a treasure the catechumenate has been for the Church as a method of preparation for baptism.

When we study baptism, when we administer this essential sacrament of our faith, when we read St Paul's words to the Romans, we see ever more clearly that its practice nowadays has become increasingly inadequate and superficial. If we consider the sacramental nature of baptism, and consider the baptismal promises which, in their content, constitute a completely new programme of life, the life of Christ, all this of course is practised and fulfilled in the liturgy of the Church today. But at the same time we can see how without a prior catechumenate, this practice becomes insufficient and inadequate for that great mystery of faith and God's love which is the Sacrament of Baptism: this immersion in the death of Christ and his resurrection; that is immersion in the very life of God, immersion in the Holy Trinity.

Naturally, there is an explanation for the circumstances which caused the catechumenate of the early, missionary Church to disappear with time, as baptism took place more and more in families where parents, urged on by faith, wished to have their infants baptised. Certainly these children could not be prepared for baptism with the methodology of the catechumenate. They were too young. Yet this methodology has been kept alive in mission countries. Sometimes it seems to me that the faith of those neophytes, of those new Christians of Africa, and of the other countries of the world, who have to undergo a catechumenal experience quite similar to the experience of the early catechumenate lasting for more than two years, is more mature. It seems to me that they themselves then become more mature Christians than we are – we who belong to nations, countries who boast of an old-established Christianity where the catechumenate, in its primitive and missionary sense, has disappeared. Of course that catechumenate didn't completely disappear. It has been replaced by a catechesis carried out by the Church, through instruction, teaching and through Christian education in the family. All this is an equivalent of the catechumenate in the early and missionary sense of the word. But this is something done after the sacrament. All of you belong to the category of Christians because all of you have received baptism as it is received today: in the family, in the parish, in the contemporary Church.[12]

12. For the complete text see pp. 196-199.

The word 'Way' is very appropriate.
The name 'Neocatechumenate' is also beautiful.

(John Paul II: visit to the parish of St Maria Goretti, Rome, 31st January 1988 – Translated from the Italian edition of L'Osservatore Romano, 1st-2nd February 1988.)

Reconstruction of the Catechumenate through the Neocatechumenal Way and the fruits of Baptism lived as once it was lived in the early communities

Through your Neocatechumenal Way (and I have to say that the word 'Way' is very appropriate[13]), one can almost reconstruct what was once the true catechumenate, and perhaps it can be made even deeper. For this is how we arrive at all the **fruits of baptism** being lived, just as they were lived by the early communities, by the early Christians, by the first generation of Christians who were ready to face everything, even martyrdom for Christ, and who led lives of great fidelity.

Of course, they were sinners too, because man, even after baptism, remains a potential sinner. However, there was a tremendous strength in this baptism, in this Christian life of the first Christians, which, in times of hostility and opposition, of persecution, of paganism, of a pagan and very worldly culture – we know well what the life of Rome was like in those early years of the Christian era – was able to give life to a Christianisation which spread not only among people, among families, but reached out to entire nations. Of course the more Christianisation increased in quantity, the more it began to decrease in quality.

In the countries where Christianity is long established we sense the exhaustion of our inner Christianity

Certainly today, especially in countries where Christianity is long established, the European countries particularly, we sense the exhaustion of our inner Christianity, of what should be the fruit of our baptism. Baptism is a sacrament that contains the programme of the entire Christian life. Of course, it is not the only sacrament, but it is the first and fundamental sacrament. We know very well that a building grows on its foundations.[14]

13. With regard to the name 'Neocatechumenal Way', Pope John Paul II , during his visit to the parish of St John the Evangelist, Spinaceto, Rome (18th November 1979), had already made this comment: "And the name is also beautiful: Neo-catechumenal, Neocatechumenal Communities. Because the name makes us think of the Catechumens who used to prepare for Baptism, and prepared for a long time, too, for months and years, especially during Lent, Then, after this preparation, they received Baptism with great fervour, with very great joy. There are the traditions of the *domenica in albis*, of white Sunday. They put on the catechumenal garments." (For the complete speech see pp. 59-60.)
14. For the complete text see pp. 196-199.

Chapter II

Church and secularisation:
"In this age we need to rediscover
a radical faith"[1]

Because this world is deaf

(Paul VI: general audience of 12th January 1977 – Translated from the original recording by Vatican Radio.)

The world of today
is deaf

This awareness of the fundamental mission of the Church to spread the gospel message is alive and working in the Church today, and – this is beautiful – it is the task of all ministers, that is, Bishops, priests, religious men and women, etc and the faithful! The faithful themselves become the voice which must propagate this message; the message of the evangelical announcement which today more than ever is worthy to be announced for two reasons which seem contradictory. One, we must announce it because the world is deaf, and so you have to raise your voice, to find a way so that it can be understood, and so you must insist, all must be called to a new school etc. The difficulty becomes something that provokes us, it becomes the incentive to become teachers of our catechism, that is to say of the truth of the Gospel to be announced.

A word is needed which
speaks of the meaning
of life:

And there is a second reason which is exactly the opposite of the first. He who knows how to see, to read, into the heart of the masses, the heart of the world, sees that deep down there is discontent, there is restlessness, there is need of a true word, a good word, **a word which tells the**

1. John Paul II – visit to the parish of Our Lady of the Blessed Sacrament and of the Canadian Martyrs, Rome, 2nd November 1980: "...in this age we need to rediscover a radical faith, radically understood, radically lived and radically fulfilled" (see following page).

38

We have the Word of
the Gospel

meaning of life! For the world of today no longer knows what it is, it no longer has the strength to define itself. Our world lives like a short-sighted person, or a blind man in the midst of darkness. We have the lantern, we have the lamp, **we have the Word of the Gospel, which becomes the light of the world.** The Lord told his apostles, "you are the light of the world". Well, if we are the light of the world, we must go towards these people who are lost, who are so angry, so cruel, who have become so disorientated, so without principles, without lines of conduct which are good and human; we must go towards them and say: "Look, this is the path, here is the way". And I repeat, the Church speaks for these two reasons, one being the difficulty and the other the opportunity of announcing the Gospel.

We are in a period
marked as never before
by the need for an
apostolic spirit

We are therefore in a marked apostolic, missionary, and didactic phase of the Church's life. We must all take part in it.[2]

The experience of a radical confrontation

(*John Paul II: visit to the parish of Our Lady of the Blessed Sacrament and of the Canadian Martyrs, Rome, 2nd November 1980* – Translated from the Italian edition of *L'Osservatore Romano*, 3rd-4th November 1980 with additional material from a tape recording.)

We live in times of
radical confrontation

My dearest ones, **we are living in a period** in which we are experiencing a radical confrontation – and I say this, because it is my experience over many years – **a radical confrontation that is everywhere.** There is no one single manifestation of this, but many throughout the world: faith and anti-faith, Gospel and anti-Gospel; Church and anti-Church, God and anti-God, if we can put it like that. An anti-God does not exist, an anti-God cannot exist, but an anti-God can exist in man, the radical denial of God can be created in man. We are living this experience in our history, and more so than in previous times.

We need to rediscover
a radical faith

In this age of ours, we need to rediscover a radical faith, radically understood, radically lived, and radically fulfilled. We have need of such a faith. I hope that your experience is born within such a perspective, and may lead towards a healthy radicalisation of our Christianity, of our faith, towards an authentic evangelical radicalism. This is why you have need of a great spirit, of great self control,

---

2. For the complete text, see pp. 173-180.

and also, as your first catechist has said, of great obedience to the Church. This has always been the case. This witness was given by the saints: by St Francis, by various charismatic people in different ages of the Church. This radicalism, I would say this radicalisation of faith is needed, yes, but it must always be situated within the life of the Church, and with her guidance, because the Church in her entirety has received the Holy Spirit from Christ in the persons of the apostles after his resurrection.[3]

The discovery of baptism is more profound when it comes from its denial

(*John Paul II: visit to the parish of the Immaculate Conception at the 'Cervelletta', Tor Sapienza, Rome, 7th March 1982* – Translated from the Italian edition of *L'Osservatore Romano* 8-9th March 1982 with additional material from a tape recording.)

The meeting with the Neocatechumenal Communities, the last of the visit, was introduced by a word from the parish priest, Don Riccardo:
"Holy Father, here you see a marvel that the Lord has done in this parish. I have already spoken about it yesterday, your Holiness, while we were having lunch with you.

Your Holiness, ten years ago, this parish was completely dead. Our Lord brought this Way here, and now there are six communities of young brothers and sisters. They have really won a place in my heart – and I had a hard heart – because I was the first one they converted. In 1972, the first community was born, and then another one every year.

Last year, Holy Father, the brothers in this first community went from house to house, announcing Jesus Christ and bringing peace. They knock at the door, and introduce themselves in the name of the parish priest. They announce eternal life, and they announce the forgiveness of sins, because, unhappily, people don't believe that God forgives sins – they think that God punishes. Among these brothers and sisters, there are many who are catechists for Confirmation and First Communion, and they also prepare couples for the baptism of their children.

The second community was born two years later, in 1974. They are at that stage in the Way in which they will begin to pray the Divine Office. They will begin to pray Lauds every morning. Among them too are many catechists for First Communion and Confirmation. They have many children, and we hope, Holy Father, that from among them

---

3. For the complete text see pp. 180-183.

there will come vocations, people who will continue Jesus Christ's mission as you are doing.

Then a third community was born. They are doing a scrutiny in which Our Lord will give them the grace to make a concrete sign, so that they are able to abandon themselves completely to God, instead of to the money and goods of this world. Among them too are catechists giving catechesis in the parish.

The fourth community was born last year, and is made up of two communities which were too small, and are now united – and they too have catechists. This year, we have again given this catechesis to adults and ninety people came twice a week for two months. Then they had a convivance, a two day retreat, and because there were so many, two communities were born. Holy Father, more than half of them had been far from the Church, many had political tendencies, some were Marxists. Our Lord has given them the grace of rediscovering the Church through this Way, and of seeing that only Jesus Christ can announce something good to us. The world proclaims many things as good and advantageous, but only Jesus Christ can give us Eternal Life.

I would now like our catechist, Giuseppe, who ten years ago brought the first message to us, and who is now married and an itinerant in the United States, to give his experience, and after that the responsible of the first community, Cesare."

Then Giuseppe, the catechist, who comes from the parish of St Luigi Gonzaga, spoke:
"Your Holiness, just a few words. I am happy about this visit. I came to catechise the first community here nine years ago. The ways of the Lord are truly incredible when you think that before following this way 15 years ago I was a Marxist, I had left the Church. I studied Hegel and Marx. I had done a thesis on Marx and I came to this very place here at Tor Sapienza. There is a factory near here, Voxon, where there are many workers. I came to preach violence, I came to invite people to rebel against injustice and to fight. And I have seen the mercy of the Lord who redeemed me from this great alienation. And he made me meet a way in my parish – my parish is that of St Luigi Gonzaga – he made me begin a way with brothers and sisters, and he made me return to the Church, he made me rediscover the Church. I did not understand what Bishops were, or the Pope; these were things which were very far away from me and I was hostile to them, because I had all the ideas of the world and through this way the Lord has brought me back to the Church, he has brought me to love my parish priest,

to have a sense of gratitude towards my parish priest for having allowed this way in my parish, this way which saved me from the terrible alienation in which I found myself. It has brought me to love the Church, the bishops, the Pope and to feel that the Church is my mother, who is bringing me to life and has made me rediscover the liturgy, which, like a mother, nourishes me with a bread which is the Body and the Blood of Jesus Christ."

Then Cesare, responsible of the first Neocatechumenal Community of the parish, spoke:

"Your Holiness, my name is Cesare, I am married with three children. I am very afraid... I too Father, had I not met this way ten years ago I don't know what I would be doing today. I too come from Marxism, I was on the extreme left, in the 'Magistero' movements, I was doing sociology because I thought that justice was needed in this generation. On entering this way I discovered true justice, which is the forgiveness of sins. I have discovered life in this Church which I have always judged, and I see that the Lord is revealing to me, and to these brothers and sisters, that this life is not just for me, but it is to be announced to this generation which is suffering. Going to people's houses with my brothers and sisters we see that this humanity has no hope and that the only hope can come from the announcement of the Gospel, can come from seeing a germ of life. And we are seeing how the Lord is blessing us in this parish. Many people who were far away from the Church are coming: people who are destroyed by drugs, people who no longer had any hope, destroyed marriages..."

At this point the Pope spoke as follows:

The most significant thing for you is: discovery

What is most significant, particularly in your communities in general, and in your community here, could be said in two words. One fundamental word which always comes up when listening to someone in the neocatechumenal way, is the word **discovery**.[4] Discovery is always something great. If you make some scientific discovery, if you discover a new continent, like Christopher Columbus did, then what a discovery that is. But without any doubt, all discoveries of a physical nature cannot be compared to those of a spiritual nature. For you, 'discovery' is the word which sums up each one of you and your community.

It is the discovery of the reality of baptism, which is a wonderful reality, an amazing reality. Even in theological terms, if we listen to what St Paul says in his letters, it is an amazing reality.

4.   The second word is 'itinerant', cf. p. 86-87.

Discovering one's own baptism	If we then take it existentially, as a way of being, the rediscovery of baptism is even more wonderful, more astonishing than baptism in general. It is a sacrament of the Church, yes, but I mean my baptism, my reality, the gift given by the Heavenly Father through Jesus Christ to me in person, the source of new life, divine life in me. We ought to speak at length about this, and look at the texts of St Paul word by word.
A more profound discovery when it comes from its denial	Let us return to 'discovery'. This discovery is all the more profound when it comes, as an affirmation, after a situation of contradiction, of negation. It could be said that the preceding negation makes the affirmation that follows it stronger and deeper. As there are ex-Marxists here, we might be inclined to think of dialectics, of Hegelism in fact, the yes and the no, the no and the yes. But this is now transcended, we pass from no to yes, and this "**yes**" is much more dynamic.
The example of St Paul	We have a wonderful example, the prime example. It is Paul who discovered Christ, and in so doing, discovered his baptism – because discovering Christ means discovering one's own baptism. Paul discovered it after he had been a persecutor, an anti-Christ let us say. If not an anti-Christ, an anti-Christian, because Jesus says to Paul, "Why do you persecute me?", not "my brothers and my followers", but "me". So the first thing: the discovery is a gift from God, a grace, and a grace cannot be explained. It is to discover one's own faith, one's own Christianity, one's being as a Christian – from this starting point one begins to see all the other elements. There is a new life, a new vision of life. All the elements, all of life, look different. It is a new world. In today's liturgy, we contemplated the Transfiguration: a new world.[5]

The evangelisation of those environments which have become almost dead and impervious to the Gospel is typical of your Communities

(*John Paul II: private audience for Bishops and parish priests attending the convention on 'Penance and Reconciliation', Rome, 10th February 1983* – From the English edition of *L'Osservatore Romano*, 7th March 1983.)

About two thousand priests from five continents and about sixty bishops, also from all over the world, met the Pope this morning, Thursday 10th February in the Paul VI Hall. The priests and bishops are taking part in a meeting organised by the Neo-

---

5. For the complete text see pp. 183-185.

43

*catechumenal Communities on a theme of great contemporary
importance in the life of the Church: 'Reconciliation and Penance in the mission of the Church'. Some of the reflections which
have come out of the meeting, which will end this evening with a
solemn celebration, were presented to the Pope at the beginning
of the audience by a Bishop and some priests. The Holy Father
gave the following address to the crowded gathering which had
been introduced by Kiko Argüello:*

Dear Brothers! I am happy to have the opportunity today
to meet a group of members of the Neocatechumenal Communities gathered in Rome to meditate together on Reconciliation and Penance in the mission of the Church, which
is the theme of the next Synod of Bishops.

I greet the bishops, pastors and priests here present, who
have come from all the continents for this occasion.

I would like my words to be a reflection on the spiritual
and ecclesial experience which you are intent on doing, that
they may be for you an incentive towards an ever greater
commitment in offering, within the context of the modern
world, a clear and genuine example of profound Christian
faith, lived constantly in intimate, docile and happy union
with the pastors of the Church.

Your witness is meant to be fundamentally one of announcing the Gospel message, which has as its centre the
proclamation that Jesus of Nazareth is the Messiah, the
Lord, the incarnate Son of God, who died and rose again
for our salvation. Evangelization – said Paul VI – will
always contain – as the foundation, centre and the same
time summit of its dynamism – a clear proclamation that in
Jesus Christ, the Son of God made man, who died and rose
from the dead, salvation is offered to all men, as a gift of
God's grace and mercy (Apostolic Exhortation *Evangelii
Nuntiandi,* 37).

The Neocatechumenate
for the evangelisation of
environments that are
deaf and impervious to
the Gospel

One of the typical manifestations of your communities
is precisely the evangelization carried out in countries and
environments which either have never heard the Christian
message or have become almost deaf to this message, because of the prevalence of ideologies, conceptions, of refusal or indifference to the question of God itself. This is
why you intend to prepare and train catechists, who will
have to strive first of all to study thoroughly and live personally the mystery of Christ. "Catechising" – I wrote in
the apostolic exhortation about catechesis in our time – "is
in a certain way to lead a person to study this mystery in all
its dimensions... to reveal in the Person of Christ the whole
of God's eternal design which is fulfilled in him... The
definitive aim of catechesis is to put people not only in

touch but in communion, in intimacy, with Jesus Christ: only he can lead us to the love of the Father in the Spirit and make us share in the life of the Holy Trinity" (Apostolic Exhortation *Catechesi Tradendae,* 5).[6]

Our age, in which so many have lost the faith, has need of radical conversions like that of Paul

(*John Paul II: visit to the parish of St Tarcisius, Rome, 3rd March 1985* – Translated from the Italian edition of *L'Osservatore Romano*, 4-5th March 1985.)

I know you. I meet you in different parishes of Rome, I also meet you in different countries of the world. It is very easy to identify you, because when you start playing the guitars and singing that characteristic Neocatechumenal song, in whatever corner of the world, the Pope immediately knows who it is and rejoices. He rejoices everywhere and he rejoices in this parish too. I have spoken to the various Neocatechumenal Communities many times, in different parts of Rome, and by now I know well that there are two elements which characterise your charism.

The enthusiasm of faith

The first is an enthusiasm for the faith. An enthusiasm for the faith rediscovered. Of faith rediscovered also in those who always had it, perhaps had even lived it, practised it; in those who were, more or less, good and honest Christians. Once it has been rediscovered, faith – rediscovered in all its significance, in its mystery, in its supernatural greatness – creates enthusiasm. This enthusiasm of faith is so necessary in our age, in this age which is cold and indifferent, this age which does not want to commit itself, which says of the truth, of faith, of God, of Christ: Who knows if this is true, if this could be true? So this enthusiasm is needed, this personal conviction which is the only thing that is able to convince others.[7]

6. For the complete text see pp. 185-189.
7. In the parish of St Basil (Rome, 10th March 1979) the Pope had already spoken about the 'dynamism of faith' – precisely about the rediscovery of Baptism: "Of all the words which you have used, the most important is 'to rediscover'. Many people think they know it all: the Church, Christ, the Gospel, God; they know it all, there's nothing to discover. They learnt it at school and that was enough. Later you forget it but you know it all. Instead there is everything to discover, everything to rediscover. It is only faith that knows how to discover itself, its content, its fundamental attitude, that is, a dynamic faith. And the Church, the people of God, needs this dynamic faith, that tries to discover, that knows how to discover itself.

So I hope that you will go ahead on the road that you have started, that of always discovering more the mystery of the Church, the mystery of Christ, the mystery of God. So this discovery brings us also to ourselves; for the mystery of Christ, the mystery of the Church finally explains us to ourselves. And I cannot live without the Church, without understanding what I am, without understanding myself. This is a happy endeavour, very positive and I hope you will persevere" (cf. *L'Osservatore Romano*, 11-12th March 1979).

Then, the second thing which I think is part of your charism is radical conversion. I have listened to your witnesses, especially the first, and I was greatly moved and immediately thought: what more do we want, we have another testimony of Paul of Tarsus. He was someone who was against, who quite simply wanted to kill Jesus, to destroy Christianity. Then suddenly he found Jesus risen and became his disciple, his most zealous, his most effective apostle. So I think our age, in which so many people have lost faith and have set off on other ways, following ideologies and philosophical systems and finding associations and organisations which offer anti-religious programs, needs radical conversions like that of Paul of Tarsus.

It is with great pleasure that I see you and I think you are very necessary in today's Church, in today's world. You must continue to cultivate your charisms and deepen your identity, always keeping very close to the pastors of the Church and always following that special grace which belongs to the identity of the Neocatechumenal Communities.

Many Christians don't even know what faith is, what a treasure they carry within them

(John Paul II: visit to the parish of St Felix of Cantalice, Rome, 4th May 1986 – Translated from the Italian edition of L'Osservatore Romano, "With Mary, model of your way to Christ" by P. Brocato and M. Ponzi, 5-6th May, 1986 with additional material from a tape recording.)

The presence of the Neocatechumenal groups is encouraged in the parish. The Pope had a special meeting with them, during which, after having listened to the testimony of one of the catechists of the community, he spoke about the many meetings with groups of Neocatechumens he has had in all the parishes of Rome and in his visits to other cities in Italy and throughout the world. These groups, said the Pope, have something that distinguishes them immediately from others...

Giacomo, a catechist of the Communities in the parish, then spoke:

Your Holiness, I am speaking because I am the catechist of these brothers and sisters. The first thing I want to say is that I am very happy to be here with you, in the grace that the Church gives us in fullness, with sweetness. I say this because I am violent by nature and I had a very troubled childhood, with a lot of suffering, and because I was not in the Church this gave me an image of a God who was a justice-maker, who somehow or another had to make up to me for what I had suffered. This made me suffer a lot and I grew up in a way that was completely wrong, becoming one of those Christians who give scandal because they preach what they do not practise. When I became aware of this situation, that I was a scandal for others because I had made violence my creed, I was already married and had two children and I was afraid of myself, Father, and even thought about taking my life. I asked the Virgin Mary, to whom I was devoted, to help me, to make some sense out of what I was doing because I was completely lost. One Sunday, when I went to Mass, there was a layman, bearded like me, who announced the pardon and the mercy of Jesus Christ for violent people like me, Father. Even for violent people like me the Lord had a way to turn back to love and forgiveness. So, Father, I have been in this Way for fifteen years and the Church is sending me into the world to announce forgiveness and mercy.

The Pope addressed these words to the Neocatechumenal Communities present:

Thank you for this testimony. It is not the first time that I listen to the testimony of one of the Neocatechumenal Communities and I am always very moved. But especially when I was coming in and I heard the song 'Mary, blessed Mary', then I understood immediately who was singing, because with this song I recognise you everywhere: in the middle of the African continent or in India, everywhere in the world you make yourself known with this song 'Mary, blessed Mary, you have believed in the word of the Lord.'

A way of faith rediscovered

It characterises your Way, the way of all the Neo-catechumenal Communities, it characterises each one of you because this way is the way of faith, of a faith that sometimes has been completely rediscovered, rediscovered in a profound conversion, as can be heard in different testimonies. Sometimes it is a rediscovered faith in the sense that it has been deepened, rediscovered in its profundity, for faith has a tremendous depth, an immense depth, of which we believers are not always aware. The profundity of faith! Faith is the participation in the knowledge of God himself. God allows us to know him, almost with his own knowing. Faith prepares us for the vision of God, for the beatific vision of heaven. So, throughout our lives, faith has always to be rediscovered, and this reality of faith, this profundity of faith is often neglected even by believers, by Christians. They do not know what it is, what it is that, being Christians, having faith, they carry within them.

A way of faith:
the particular charism
that you have as
Neocatechumens

So your Way consists of this: the rediscovery of faith either almost completely or in the sense of a deepening of what you already had before. And this is where this song 'Mary, blessed Mary, you believed in the word of the Lord' comes in.

A fuller, more perfect faith than Mary's cannot be imagined. This is the height of faith which can be seen above all at the moment of the Annunciation. We can say that it is an incredible faith because it takes a paradox to express this faith of Mary. And when the Virgin went to Elizabeth, Elizabeth expressed this, saying, 'Blessed is she who believed in the word of the Lord.' The faith of Mary is certainly an example of the faith of all believers, of all those who rediscover faith, who deepen their faith, and especially of all of you whose task is this way of faith; I would say it is the particular charism that you have as neocatechumens.

That is why meeting your groups always gives me joy, because together with the parents, the adults, I find many children. They say that the Neocatechumens have big families, they have children, indeed lots of children; this is also a proof of faith, of faith in God. To give life to men you need to have faith in God.

The crisis of the family
comes from lack of faith.

To give life to a man
you need to have a
profound faith in God.

If today we are living this great, so-called demographic crisis, this crisis of the family, this crisis of paternity, of maternity, a great and profound crisis, it is a consequence of a lack of faith in God. This cannot be changed, transformed, improved, without a deep faith. You need faith in God to give life to men. I wanted to add this to what I said before to confirm this aspect of your way too. May God bless you, the Father, Son and Holy Spirit; may he bless your families.

The Neocatechumenal Way
as a reply to the weakness of today's Church

(*John Paul II: visit to the parish of St Maria Goretti, Rome, 31st January 1988* – Translated from the Italian edition of *L'Osservatore Romano*, 1st-2nd February 1988.)

It is often said, and often we read too, that baptism, **our baptism, must last our whole life long**, must bear fruit throughout our life. But in our environment, in our countries, in our traditionally Christian society, often we see the opposite; in Rome, too, we see this. We are living in a period of dechristianisation. It seems that the faithful, those baptised years ago, are no longer mature enough to oppose secularisation and the ideologies which are contrary not only to the Church, to the Catholic religion, but also to religion in general; they are atheistic, indeed anti-theist. You, with your Neocatechumenal Way, in different environments, try to rebuild what has been broken down: you seek to rebuild it in a more authentic way, that, I would say, approaches the experience of the early Church.

The Neocatechumenal Way as a reply to the weakness of today's Church

The Neocatechumenal Way: it is longer and more demanding than the missionary Catechumenate in order to go on producing fruits

This is how I see the origins of the Neocatechumenate, of its way. Someone – I don't know if it was Kiko or someone else – asked himself: "Where did the strength of the early Church come from, and where does the weakness of today's Church – a Church with much greater numbers – come from?" I believe he found the answer in this Way.

I hope you will continue in this Way, to continue to accept all the demands which it makes, because it is not a short Way. If you consider the missionary catechumenate, it sometimes looks hard – four years! You are more demanding; yours lasts seven years or more! So then I hope that you will continue always to be demanding in your Way, and I hope above all that you continue to produce all these fruits, because among your communities it is evident how all the fruits of the Holy Spirit grow from baptism, all the charisms of the Holy Spirit, all vocations, the whole authenticity of the Christian life in marriage, in the priesthood and all the various professions, finally in the world.[8]

Your communities are the places where a 'doubting Thomas' becomes a 'believing Thomas'

(*John Paul II: visit to the parish of Mary, Mother of the Redeemer, Tor Bella Monaca, Rome, 10th April 1988* – Translated from the Italian edition of *L'Osservatore Romano*, 11th April 1988.)

"We heard in today's Gospel that Thomas was looking for signs so that he could believe that Jesus really was risen. Well, I think that for Tor Bella Monaca a sign that Jesus is risen is these brothers and sisters, their faith and their enthusiasm in the faith", *said the parish priest, introducing the two Neocatechumenal Communities, gathered in the church.*

"We are worried about pastoral programmes for adults", *went on Don Mario.* "Many people are far away from God, from the Church but I see that through the Neocatechumenal Way a net has been thrown wide and we see that many people are caught in this net and begin a way to look for the Lord."

8. For the complete text see pp. 196-199.

After having listened to some testimonies, the Pope addressed the following words to those present:

Dearly beloved, I greet you all. I greet the parents, I greet the adults, the young people and the children, of whom there are many, as is always the case in your communities. I thank the Lord for this growing life.

I meet you often, I met you on Palm Sunday afternoon. I listened to many testimonies and then I tried to speak at length. Today I meet you in this parish and I have to say that I rejoice because of this meeting and for this parish that you have found. You are trying to go on with your presence, your witness, your mission.

Stay always in the
Cenacle

Today we listened to a passage from the Gospel that is very interesting because there is the figure of Thomas, the unbeliever, who was converted to the Risen Christ in the Cenacle. I thought about you, because your communities, as many people have told me, are places, milieu, in which the conversion of the unbeliever, of a doubting Thomas who becomes a believing Thomas and cries out 'Lord', is repeated. I think that this is the Grace of the Cenacle. You must always be in the Cenacle.

**Your charism is that of Mary:
to walk in faith and give witness that there is a new life**

(*John Paul II: visit to the parish of St Cyprian, Torrevecchia, Rome, 22nd January, 1989* – Translated from the Italian edition of *L'Osservatore Romano*, 27th January 1988.)

The strongest religious experience among those that exist at the moment in the parish of St Cyprian is that of the Neocatechumenal Way, begun in 1981. The Pope dedicated the last meeting of his visit to the members of the five communities, about one hundred and fifty brothers and sisters. Claudio, who started the Way at St Cyprian, announced, "Your Holiness, after your Mass in the parish a new catechesis will begin. We hope that this coming of Peter among us will move many people to want to know Jesus Christ. As it says in this leaflet, Father, we were blind, lame, far away. I was far away from the Church. In this Church we have come to know, as the Word of today says, freedom for all the prisoners of anguish, of fear, of death. We were blind in that we did not see the love of God in our lives. We thank Peter who has come today to confirm us in our faith."

The testimony of the parish priest, Mgr. Pieraccini, was vivid and touching:

"I began this way in 1971 when I was in the parish of St Eugene. It was a time of great crisis because I thought of myself as a very good priest, very intelligent, successful. And I was proud, presumptuous. I see it clearly now but then it was as though I was blind. I found myself in a situation of great crisis, of great depression.

And this Way appeared, this movement, these catecheses, which came to make me able to abandon myself again to God, to re-awaken in me the confidence that God loves me, as I am. Despite my weakness and my sins, this love opened my eyes and made me see the signs of God's love for me. And this began to change my life and give me peace. Then I had to leave that parish to come here. I found a bigger parish, when I was getting older, was already old, but even staying here is something that I do day by day with joy, with happiness.

I have to say that in this Way you really do discover the joy of being with the Lord. I've also seen something else in all these years: how this way of preaching the Gospel attracts the people who are far away and brings them close to God."

Much struck by these testimonies, the Holy Father addressed these words to the communities:

This word that I used as word of life for the Marian Year and for the encyclical *Redemptoris Mater* is always in my mind. I repeat this word addressed to Mary: 'Blessed are you because you believed in the Lord', because without a doubt it is central in the way of the Virgin. I organised all the Marian encyclical around this word. In this way it can be of use to the Church and perhaps also for our separated brothers, because Mary goes before us in the way of faith.

When I meet you I always have a moment of surprise because so many of you say that you come from another shore where the Christian life is not led, indeed where God is denied, and where there is a search for another programme of personal and social life. And then they found this Way.

They set off along this road and they say, 'We have found joy, we have found peace.' Dear ones, you are walking within this parish. You walk in the **contemporary world**, this world of the daily routine, very rich and opulent, enjoying progress and secure of itself because of its riches and inventions. You walk in this world where at the same time it is difficult to walk. I think that the special charism of this movement, of this Way, is precisely that of walking with our contemporaries, with these people who are rich and poor at the same time. It is to go among them

I think that the special charism of this movement, of the Way, is precisely that of walking with our contemporaries, with these people who are rich and poor at the same time.

and to bring the testimony of another way, another life, another perspective.

Your charism is that of Mary: to walk in faith and in faith to bear witness to everyone

This is the **way of Mary, the way of faith**. You walk with her along the same way. Think always that you are walking with Mary, who walks with everyone because she is Mother. She walks with the Church, with Christianity, with the Christians who find it difficult to be united in a world divided between East and West, North and South, rich and poor. Your charism is that of Mary: to walk in faith and in faith to bear witness to everyone, the witness to another possibility, to another kind of self- fulfilment. Man tries to find fulfilment and does not succeed. You need to witness to this man to the fulfilment that Mary found in Christ. **He is the true self-fulfilment of man**. Because he says, 'I am the Way, the Truth, the Life'.

I hope that you will go on in this parish, in this vocation and in this Way.

Chapter III

"Rebuilding the parish, basing it on the Neocatechumenal experience"[1]

The necessity of a gradual and intensive evangelisation: a pastoral work for adults in the parishes

(*Paul VI: general audience, 12th January 1977* – Translated from the tape recording by Vatican Radio.)

Here we see the rebirth of the name 'Catechumenate'. This certainly does not intend to invalidate or to diminish the importance of the baptismal discipline as currently practised, but seeks to apply it according to a gradual and intensive method which recalls and renews in a certain way the Catechumenate of earlier times. The person who has been baptised needs to understand, to think over, to appreciate, to give assent to the inestimable treasure of the Sacrament he has received.

A need that is understood in the parishes

We are happy to see that this need today is understood by the institutional church structures: the parishes, the dioceses in particular, and by all the other religious families. In this area of structures, as I have said, the parish is fundamental.

Here we see a catechesis taking shape, which is subsequent to the one that baptism did not have. "Pastoral work for adults", as is said today, is taking shape, creating

---

1. Cf. John Paul II during his visit to the parish of St Maria Goretti, Rome (31st January 1988): "I think there is a way of rebuilding the parish basing it on the Neocatechumenal experience" (cf. p. 55).

While in other chapters the chronological order of the various statements of the Popes has been respected, in this chapter they have been arranged according to theme because of their fragmentary nature.

new methods and new programmes, and also new ministries. What a great need there is for people to help. And so we see catechists, sisters, and families too, who are becoming the teachers in this evangelisation that takes place after Baptism. New subsidiary ministries are supporting the ever more demanding roles of the priest and the deacon, in teaching and in participating in the liturgy. New forms of charity, culture and social solidarity are increasing the vitality of the Christian community and, before the world are becoming its defence, its apologia and its attraction.

Many are attracted towards the Neocatechumenal Communities because they see Christ alive in them

Many people are attracted to these Neocatechumenal Communities, because they see that there is a sincerity, a truth in them, something alive and authentic, Christ living in the world. May this happen with our Apostolic Blessing.[2]

Through your community the parish priest is in love with the parish

(*John Paul II: visit to the parish of the Immaculate Conception at Cervellatta, Tor Sapienza, Rome, 7th March 1982* – Translated from the Italian edition of *L'Osservatore Romano*, 8-9th March 1982, with additional material from a tape recording.)

The parish priest should always be one of us

I think, first of all, something must be said about your parish priest. I think that the parish priest, like any other priest, **should always be one of us**. And your priest is this; he is not the only one, but I see him so more than others, here too in this environment, one of us. And there is another thing: to say that a parish priest is in love may seem like a contradiction.

Through your community he is in love with his parish

But I tell you that **he must be in love** and I see that he is in love, in love with all the groups, but perhaps a bit 'more' with your group. This could have led to favouritism, but it has not. I see this because it is fairly clear, and it seems to me that through your community, he has fallen in love with the whole of his parish. And the parish is larger than your community but that's the way Jesus arranged things. He spoke to us of **leaven**: the dough and the leaven, and the leaven is always a part, something small, and the mass is the mass – but it needs leaven.

I think that the parish priest and his collaborators have found a leaven in your community, which I have also seen

2. For the complete text see pp. 173-180.

in other groups, but perhaps in your group in a special way. He has "walked in this Way" as you say in your language – I already know you a little from meeting you in several parishes in Rome – and not always in parishes, but mostly in parishes. I think that your community in this parish is very well organised. It is growing together with the parish priest and together with the parish. As he said, ten or fifteen years ago he saw the difficulties of this parish, what there was and what was missing, and together with you took on the appropriate apostolic commitments.[3]

There is a way to rebuild the parish by basing it on the neocatechumenal experience

(*John Paul II: visit to the parish of St Maria Goretti, Rome, 31st January 1988* – Translated from the Italian edition of *L'Osservatore Romano*, 1st-2nd February 1988.)

You need courage to take your experience, your witness, into the more dechristianised environments of the world. But this is providential, because such environments cannot be approached in any other way; those human communities so destroyed, so disintegrated, so far, not only from faith, but from being human. They can only be approached with a great experience of faith, with a deep conviction, with a life entirely permeated by the Holy Spirit. I hope that you may receive all these fruits in this parish, which seems to me to be based on the Neocatechumenal experience.

The Neocatechumenal Way, a method for the rebirth and growth of the parish like a renewal of the primitive community

I think there is a way **to rebuild the parish on the basis of the Neocatechumenal experience**. Of course this method cannot be imposed on everybody; but if there are many candidates, then **why not? It is authentic and is consistent with the very nature of the parish, because just as each one of us Christians grows from baptism, so does the Christian community grow naturally from baptism.** The Church grows from baptism; she grows in the **Eucharist**, yes; but she grows from baptism, for there is **no Eucharist without baptism**. The parish is a basic community in the Church. It can grow authentically on the experience and on the basis of the Neocatechumenal experience; it would be like the renewal of the early community that grew out of the catechumenal experience.

---

3. For the complete text see pp. 183-185.

May the Lord bless you, my dearest people, may he
bless your families, bless your candidates for the priesthood and the seminarians from 'Redemptoris Mater', bless
your young people and your children who, thanks be to
God, are numerous. They are also a cause for great hope
because the world, secularised, dechristianised, agnostic,
which no longer has faith in God, is losing faith in itself, is
losing faith in man. How else can the falling birth-rate be
explained? Indeed, how else to explain the anti-birth
mentality of communities, of nations, of groups, and of
political circles? The explanation is in the lack of faith in
man.

The lack of faith in man
derives from a lack of
faith in God

**But this lack of faith in man derives from a lack of
faith in God**. Man has his dimension, his origin, and this
origin of his is God himself because man has been created
in God's image and likeness. This explains who man is,
how he can live and how he can die. You need courage to
live in this world and in this meeting with these families
and these itinerants I see a sign of Christian courage.[4]

The parish is built on faith:
on Baptism which prepares us for the Eucharist

(*John Paul II: visit to the parish of St Ann, Casal Morena, Rome,
2nd December 1984* – Translated from the Italian edition of
L'Osservatore Romano, 3rd-4th December 1984.)

You have given me a good introduction to what your
community is in this parish, first through the parish priest
and then through your representative.

I see that this parish is also being constructed in the
sense of the building, of a material complex. But we know
well that **the parish is built above all, on faith, on Baptism which prepares us for the Eucharist**[5]: this is the
spiritual building. Baptism also means catechumenate and

---

4. For the complete text see pp. 196-199.
5. The Pope had already noted the great importance the Church gives to the
building up of the ecclesial community in faith when he spoke to members of
Neocatechumenal Communities from South America who were in Rome for an
international convention in connection with the Synod on the Family, 16th October
1980: "Present in this audience is a group of priests, married couples and catechists
from Neocatechumenal Communities in various countries of Central America. I
greet you with affection, beloved brothers and sisters, who are dedicated to a task to
which the Church gives great importance: **the building up of the ecclesial community in faith by means of a solid, systematic and progressive catechesis.** Dedicate
yourselves generously to this work which is so necessary and be faithful to the
personal experience of the Christian message and in your testimony to others. I bless

Neocatechumenate, it means that you must always return to that way which once prepared our forefathers, the first Christians, for Baptism, to become sons of God and co-heirs of Christ.

Neocatechumenal Community: to rediscover the newness of Christian life

In fact 'Neocatechumenal', as a temporal reality, means a community which rediscovers in the parish the newness of the Christian life, its **freshness,** its **originality**, because this is life in its full sense, divine life. This is the life that lies ahead of us for the whole of eternity, not just the life of these years here on earth. Life with God, life as children of God, given life by the only begotten Son of God who is the Word, the Word incarnate and born of the Virgin Mary, Jesus Christ.

May you be the good leaven of the newness of Christian life in this community of Saint Ann. My heartfelt blessing.

Living the joy of rediscovering Baptism in community

(*John Paul II: visit to the parish of St John the Evangelist, Spinaceto, Rome, 18th November 1979* – Translated from the Italian edition of *L'Osservatore Romano*, 19-20th November 1979 with additional material from a tape recording.)

The Holy Father's conversation with the representatives of the Neocatechumenal groups who are following their way of faith with the people of Spinaceto was particularly deep. Here, too, at St John the Evangelist as in the parish of St Luke, which the Holy Father visited two Sundays ago, it was the Neocatechumens from the parish of Canadian Martyrs who introduced the Way *of faith. One of the catechists, Giampiero Donnini, spoke to the Pope on behalf of everyone.*

"Holy Father, we are truly happy and thank the Lord for your presence here, because these communities, which have been

your search for intimate communion with your pastors, your work, people, families and ecclesial communities." (Translated from *L'Osservatore Romano*, 10-11th May 1982.)

Speaking on the same subject during his visit to the parish of St Mauro, Abbot (Rome, 9th May 1982), the Pope said, "We are in a chapel which takes the place of the parish church. In visiting the parish the necessity of having a church comes to mind spontaneously. The church does not yet exist, the church as an building. But the Church is already being built. The spiritual Church is being built through the Word of God and the Sacraments. It is being built through the Word of God whose ministers, the servants, the apostles, are you catechists. It is being built with the Sacraments beginning with Baptism and you, the Neocatechumenal group, are witnesses of the power of the Sacrament because it is not just a matter of an idea but of a person who lives and gives life: this is the Sacrament. The Sacrament brings us life, the Word of God brings us light and the Sacrament brings us divine life: divine light, divine life. So the Church is being built thanks to your apostolate. May you be the leaven in this construction of the living Church of St Mauro. I bless you from my heart." (Translated from the Italian edition of *L'Osservatore Romano*, 10-11th May 1982.)

walking in the parish since 1974, are opening a way of evangelisation within the interior of the parish, something you spoke about in your Apostolic Exhortation *Catechesis Tradendae.* They are doing a double service, within the parish, so that the parish can renew itself, to begin to welcome people who are far away from the Church; to welcome above all the atheists, the Marxists, the drug addicts, people who are, as you have said this evening in your homily, desperate, empty, for whom life has no sense. Father, we are discovering a wonderful thing: that Jesus Christ is alive and that he is risen! And that Jesus Christ risen and alive, is in his Church, with the power to overcome death in us. We are seeing, Father, for example, starting from our own marriages, that God has truly rebuilt them from nothing. We were divided, and the Lord has made us understand that conversion, as you reminded the Cardinals in your recent speech, is the fundamental work of the Church today: conversion in the light of the Second Vatican Council. We are working in this direction, Father, in this parish. We are helping the parish priest who called us in 1974, not looking for a new movement but to serve the parish so that it would be prepared to welcome the faraway people, the people who have no more hope, and who are asking what is the meaning of their lives. In this way, they are given the opportunity to rediscover their baptism, to see that baptism is not only something written down in the register, but that it is the power of God who is regenerating us to a new life, to the life of sons, as you have said so many times, to this change of nature.

Another thing Father. We find ourselves, as you say in the *Catechesi Tradendae,* giving a very important service. The diocese of Rome, I'm speaking of your diocese as Bishop, and we thank the Cardinal Vicar who is here; your diocese of Rome is actually carrying out this renewal. God has inspired some itinerant vocations and there are more than one hundred people, including married couples with children, also priests and young men and women, who are devoting their lives to the Gospel throughout the world to help the parishes in this renewal. Today the liturgy is very important as a moment of catechesis, of evangelisation – for without the liturgy, evangelisation is dead and the community doesn't grow. How can the Church grow without the Eucharist? How can the Church grow if there isn't a moment when we can come before Jesus Christ, and make Passover with him, experiencing that he comes to take us from our situation of death and sin, and bring us to the Father? That's why we need, Father, we need a special audience with you, if you grant one to us, the five of us who are looking after this way in Italy, to submit to you this experience of evangelisation, to share with you the joy and also the problems that we inevitably experience, because it is most important for us to be in communion with you and to have your blessing."

After having thanked Giampiero, the Holy Father wished to give emphasis to the great spiritual and evangelical content of the work being carried out in this direction in the Parish:

All the things you have said give me consolation because they show that the Church in your parish and also in the whole city of Rome, the Roman Church, by means of your communities, is a living Church. It is not only an administrative reality, even if with very great traditions, but a living reality. This living reality is made up of each one of us when enlightened by the grace of faith. Faith – so many have faith. I think that there are few in the world who have no faith at all. They always have something. But there are degrees in the intensity of faith, of its roots in our personality. So we need to make sure that these roots of our faith, of our personality, of our conscience, of our soul are always deeper. In this way faith, built in each one of us, strong in each one of us, so aware, so personal, becomes apostolic. I think that this is the vital sense of your Neocatechumenal Communities.

The Neocatechumenal Communities make us think of the Catechumens of long ago who were prepared for Baptism

The name is beautiful too: Neocatechumenal, Neocatechumenal Communities. Because the name reminds me of the Catechumens in the past who once prepared for Baptism over a long period of time, for months, even years, especially during Lent, and then, so prepared, they received baptism with great fervour, with great joy. This was the tradition of *domenica in albis,* "white Sunday" when they wore the catechumenal robes. Nowadays, in a certain sense, we lack this, because Christians are baptised as little children, when they are two weeks or a month old, depending upon the parents.

Nowadays that preparation is missing

We miss a little that institution of the early Church, that preparation that makes us live baptism. Baptism has become something that is done, not something that is matured.

The Neocatechumenate seeks to complete what is missing: to rediscover Baptism in a process within a community

So the Neocatechumenal Communities seek to complement, to complete, what we lack. Mature men and women like you go back towards the moment of their Baptism, to re-live this again, to prepare again what already exists in everyone of us. We are baptised, the reality of baptism exists in everyone of us, **but we need to see again what baptism is,** its true dimension, its supernatural, divine, sacramental dimension with all its richness, with all its consequences. **I think this is a good way to do it!**

Furthermore, you do this, you live this, in the communities. It is not a process that takes place in solitude, it is a process of the community, a process that takes place together. You live the joy of rediscovering baptism, its true meaning, its full reality: together, you do it together!

And so the spirit that animates everyone of us, transmits itself to the others, and there is a sharing of experiences, a sharing of enthusiasm and joy. This expresses itself in the prayer too, this expresses itself in the songs. These communities sing – and how they sing!

For a parish, such a group is truly leaven

Then, certainly for a parish, such a community, such a group, is undoubtedly leaven; for, as you have said, there really are so many people who have come from far away, but also many whose lives were far away from the Church, living in the different ideologies, living with different pre-occupations. These people need others who, aware of the significance of Baptism, live beside them to bring them to understand. They are baptised too, the great majority of them. I do not think there are many people in this parish who are not baptised. But once baptised that Baptism became more or less dead; it is as though dead! Others are needed, co-parishioners, to come and bring that Baptism to life in their friends, in their neighbours, and so on. Then this really is leaven.

to ferment the dough

And the leaven has to permeate the mass, as Christ says in the Gospel.

Created to be community

(*John Paul II: visit to the parish of St Luke the Evangelist, Rome, 4th November 1979* – Translated from the Italian edition of *L'Osservatore Romano*, 5-6th November 1979.)

The Community is always formed from within by means of the Holy Spirit who creates communion

The group or rather the Community is always formed from within, inside, and it is within that the Holy Spirit touches each one of us, what each one of us is, his personal intimacy, his spiritual intimacy, but it does not touch any of us separately, individually, because **he created us to be community,** to live in communion. He touches each of us to rebuild us in communion and this is how all these communities within the Christian communion can be explained, communities like yours, for there are five Communities.

We have to discover what we have inside, then we can give

I think that there is a rule, a simple rule: to give, one must have something, not in a material sense, but in a spiritual sense. To give, you must have something inside that is not material, but spiritual, and this invisible thing must be discovered.

I think that this is the rule of your **Neocatechumenal**

movement: it is about discovering, rediscovering what you have inside. There are many baptised Christians, but perhaps they have not discovered their baptism. They have almost forgotten their baptism. They are baptised people, their Baptism is in the documents, it is found in the parish registers, and is even registered in their hearts – but this interior registration is nearly dead, not awakened. It must be discovered!

Itinerant catechists: the fruit of this discovery

When you discover you have it, **then you must give it.** When you discover it, you cannot help but give it, because what you are discovering impels you to give it. In this way, all the Apostles were born, all the Apostles were born in this way, I think that if there are now **itinerant catechists,** if the Pope too has become *itinerant,* this is also a fruit he has discovered. Once you have discovered this richness, this mystery, this mystery of Christ, this mystery that makes up our own personal, spiritual and Christian identity, you cannot help trying to give it to others..

I am very happy with this meeting. I hope you will continue. To continue means **to follow the Holy Spirit and to follow also your vocation.** Discovering this mystery of Christ living within us, we discover also our own vocation.

In the Sacraments, particularly the Eucharist, the aspect of experience is important

(*John Paul II: visit to the parish of St Remigius, Colleverde, Rome, 8th June 1990* – Translated from the Italian edition of *L'Osservatore Romano*, 15-16th June 1990. This is part of the address the Pope gave to the various parish groups.)

...Baptism as it is offered to children today is an experience that concerns the family more than anyone else, but to live this experience there needs to be a return. It is this return that the Neocatechumenal Communities encourage.

Become a catechumen

They say to everyone, 'You are a Christian, you need to go back to your Baptism, you need to be prepared once more for the Baptism you have received. You need to become a catechumen, and you need, with this catechumenate, to arrive at the experience of baptism that the first Christians had, that St Paul had'.

St Paul's words about Baptism are stupendous. Before everything else the Christian experience is the experience of Baptism which is what takes us towards all the sacraments, but above all towards the Eucharist. In the practice of the Christian life in the parish the Eucharist is the sacrament that is most lived and it is an experience that is lived also with the children who are preparing for First Communion. There is a preparation, there is a deepening, there is a sense of what the Eucharist is, in the species of bread and wine, of what Christ has left us as Eucharist: himself, as gift, as food. Certainly, the Christian experience is above all the eucharistic experience and if it begins with the experience of Baptism the latter brings us to the eucharistic experience.

I am grateful to the movements that cause the experience of the Christian life to grow

Experience is necessary. We can receive the sacraments without living them, without entering into the depth of the mystery that is being celebrated. There needs to be this experience, the experiential aspect of the Christian life and I am very grateful to all these movements that are causing the Christian experience and the different aspects of the Christian life of a baptised person to grow and be plentiful, that take people to the depths of the Christian life.

In this way man becomes more open to God, understands what is in and out of proportion, understands what radical conversion is, understands what sin is, what it means to be justified by grace, what is the abyss of mercy, of love, of the Trinity, of the gift of God. In all these experiences based on the sacraments there is always the experience of prayer. Prayer too can be a ritual, without any deep experience, superficial, that stays on the surface of our thoughts, our commitment, our personality. But if with prayer we enter more deeply into communion with God, prayer itself becomes abundant, something splendid, extraordinary. Our prayers need to become deeper, need to be alive. There needs to be an experience so that what prayer is, what it is meant to be, what God is offering to us through prayer, is not lost.

An experience that carries out what is essential

I thank God that there are these experiences in your parish, experiences that carry out what is essential for the life of the parish, for the parish is not just an administrative structure, but it is life, participation in the divine life, participation, through Christ and the Holy Spirit, in the life of the Trinity.

Your Neocatechumenal vocation is profoundly linked to the Word of God

(*John Paul II: visit to the parish of St Eligius, Rome, 26th April 1987* – Translated from the Italian edition of *L'Osservatore Romano*, 27-28th April 1987 with additional material from a tape recording.)

I want[6] to underline the characteristic of today's meeting which is taking place on the second Sunday of Easter, at the end of the Octave of Easter. For all Christians, for Catholics, perhaps especially so for Orthodox Christians, for all Christians, this really is the greatest of all solemnities, *solemnitas solemnitatum*. But it is not only a solemnity; it is the greatest mystery. It is the mystery in which our spiritual way begins and with which it finishes, towards which it is orientated.

You members of the Neocatechumenal communities are orientated towards the Paschal mystery

As members of the Neocatechumenal Communities, you are especially orientated towards this paschal mystery, through the sacramental reality of Baptism. And at Easter we live Baptism together.

You only need to look at the liturgy of the Paschal Vigil, all this liturgy as it has been celebrated for centuries, especially in the first Christian generations and as it is still celebrated today in St Peter's. It unites these two dimensions: the paschal and the baptismal.

Because what corresponds to the paschal reality is our life, and above all – I shouldn't say above all, but first of all – Baptism. And your vocation is to live Baptism more deeply, to deepen the baptismal mystery which is the point of departure, the foundation of our Christian life, of our being Christian.

So I hope that you will go on in your way that is the Neocatechumenal Way, which at the same time is also a way where the Word of God is lived intensely. They go together: **Sacrament, Baptism and Word of God**.

The challenge of the Word of God

We can say that the Neocatechumenal Movement has accepted this great challenge of the Word of God. To contemplate this Word, deepen it, read it (in the deep sense of the word 'read' – 'read' means precisely to deepen) to read means to go right to the depths of what is meant, to the essence of what is signified. So, your Neocatechumenal vocation is very much linked, profoundly linked, to the Word of God. Live the Word of God and make the Word of God live for others.

A good formation for being a catechist is to be a Neocatechumen at the same time

And so you are often catechumens and catechists at the same time, and this is right. It can be said that a good formation for being a catechist is to be a Neocatechumen too, to live this Neocatechumenal Way. Because the truths of faith cannot be interpreted only intellectually, with speculative notions. Yes, with these too, but above all these truths have to be lived with the grace of God, with the light of the Holy Spirit.

---

6. For the beginning of this speech see p. 70.

Well, that will do for now, so as not to go too much into matters that concern your specific Neocatechumenal meetings.

I wish you a happy Easter, *Christós Anésti,* as the Greek says, or *Christós Vascrés,* as in Russian. This expresses the centre, the nucleus, of our Christianity.

I hope that you will always be nearer and nearer to this nucleus of our Christianity and that you will bring others, even those furthest away, to this central nucleus of our Christianity.

A deeper understanding of the Word of God and the teaching of the Magisterium by the individual and the community

(John Paul II: private audience for Bishops and priests attending the Convention on 'Penance and Reconciliation', organised by the Neocatechumenal Communities, Rome, 10th February 1983 – From the English edition of *L'Osservatore Romano*, 7th March 1983.)

In your communities you want to investigate, not only on a theoretical level, but in a totally special way in its vital dimension, the significance, the value, the richness, the demands of Baptism, the sacrament which is the necessary condition for salvation; which unites one with the death, burial and resurrection of the Saviour; which makes one live Christ's life itself, which makes the baptized person a temple of the Spirit, an adopted son of the heavenly Father, a brother and heir of Christ, a member of Christ's Body, which is the Church. Such thorough study is directed to the rediscovery and evaluation of the riches proper to Baptism, received usually in infancy, and to which, therefore, it is necessary to refer not as a purely juridical fact, but as the true founding moment of the whole Christian life.

Cultivate a baptismal spirituality

By cultivating what we could call a baptismal spirituality, you intend to animate, direct, enrich your pilgrimage of faith, which is the logical development of the intrinsic demands of the sacrament, so that your witness will be always more authentic, sincere, consistent, active and so that you can always be more willing to respond readily to the divine call.

Such readiness must be manifested in the continual meditation on and attention to Sacred Tradition and Sacred Scripture, which form "one sacred deposit of the Word of God, which is entrusted to the Church" (Dogmatic Constitution *Dei Verbum*, 10).

The Word of God and
the Magisterium of
the Church

From this follows the need for a constant and serious work of personal and community investigation of the Word of God and of the teaching of the Magisterium of the Church, through participation in serious biblical and theological courses. Such a commitment to study and reflection is shown to be more than ever necessary for those who, having to fulfil the role of catechist, have the duty to feed their brothers and sisters with solid spiritual food. Always keep in mind the solemn and strong statement of the Second Vatican Ecumenical Council: "**The Church has always venerated the divine Scriptures just as she venerates the Body of the Lord**, since, from the table of both the Word of God and of the Body of Christ she unceasingly receives and offers to the faithful the bread of life, especially in the Sacred Liturgy" (Dogmatic Constitution *Dei Verbum*, 21). From Christ the Word to Christ the Eucharist, because the Eucharistic Sacrifice is the source, the centre, the culmination of the whole Christian life.

Celebrate the Eucharist and, above all, Easter, with true piety, with great dignity, with love for the liturgical rites of the Church, with precise observance of the norms established by competent authority, with the desire for communion with all the brethren.[7]

Daily prayer, which becomes a dialogue with the Father; and conversion as the way of return to the Father

(*John Paul II: private audience with Bishops and priests attending the convention on 'Penance and Reconciliation' organised by the Neocatechumenal Communities, Rome, 16th February 1983* – From the English edition of *L'Osservatore Romano*, 7th March 1983.)

Your willingness to respond to the divine appeal likewise must be manifested in continual, untiring daily prayer, an expression above all of adoration which man, fragile, weak, aware that he is a contingent creature, offers to God, the Transcendent, the Infinite, the Omnipotent, the Creator, but also the loving and merciful Father; prayer that therefore also becomes intimate and affectionate dialogue between Father and Son. Prayer which becomes the suppliant chorus in the Pater noster, taught to us by Jesus himself: prayer which becomes the solemn and conscious profession of Christian faith in the Creed or Apostolic Symbol;

7. For the complete text see pp. 185-189.

prayer which finds in the Psalms the various and complex inner nuances with which the one who is praying – the People of the Promise, the new Chosen People that is the Church, the Christian in various spiritual situations – can turn to God, his hope, his rock, his salvation: "If the Psalm prays," St Augustine suggests to us, "pray; if it laments, lament; if it exults, exult; if it hopes, hope; if it fears, fear. All the things which are written here are our mirror" (*Enarr. in Ps. XXX*, II, s. III, 1: CCL 38, 213).

4. Your willingness to respond to the divine appeal is manifested in fulfilling, day after day, the compelling word of Jesus: "Turn away from sin and believe in the Good News" (Mk 1: 15). This conversion, this "change of mentality", is above all the rejection of true evil, sin, which draws us away from God. This conversion is a continuous journey of return to the house of the Father, like the return of the prodigal son (cf. Lk 15:11-32). This conversion finds its salvific sign in the Sacrament of Penance or Reconciliation.

Freedom from sin is the fruit and the requirement for faith

Freedom from sin, I wrote in the Bull of Indiction of the Jubilee for the 1950th Anniversary of the Redemption, "is... a fruit and primary requirement of faith in Christ the Redeemer and faith in his Church... At the service of this freedom, the Lord Jesus instituted in the Church the Sacrament of Penance, so that those who have committed sin after Baptism may be reconciled with God whom they have offended, and with the Church which they have wounded" (Bull *Aperite Portas*, 5).

The ministry of reconciliation – this wonderful gift of the infinite mercy of God – is entrusted to you priests. Be ministers who are always worthy, ready, zealous, responsive, patient, serene, following with faithful diligence the norms established in this matter by ecclesiastical authority. The faithful will thus be able to find in this sacrament an authentic sign and instrument of spiritual rebirth and of gladdening interior freedom.

And all of you, brothers, celebrate the Sacrament of Reconciliation with great confidence in the mercy of God, in full adherence to the ministry and discipline of the Church, with individual confession, as repeatedly recommended by the new Code of Canon Law, for the pardon and peace of the disciples of the Lord, and as the efficacious announcement of the Lord's goodness to everyone.[8]

---

8. For the complete text see pp. 185-189.

Visit to the tomb of the first Apostle: an act of adherence to the successor of Peter, as a guarantee of fidelity to the Church

(John Paul II: audience with members of the Neocatechumenal Communities from four parishes in Madrid, Rome , 23rd March 1984 – Translated from the Italian edition of L'Osservatore Romano, 24th March 1984.)

Dearest brothers and sisters, I am happy to be able to receive this large group of yours this morning, made up of the members of the Neocatechumenal Communities from the parishes of San José, San Sebastian, San Rocco and the Virgen della Paloma in Madrid.

In giving you my best wishes, I should like to extend them to the members of other communities of your parishes, particularly to your parish priests present here who have helped you to a vital meeting with Jesus Christ.

I am grateful for this visit to the tomb of the first Apostle, which is intended to be an act of adherence to the Successor of Peter, as a guarantee of fidelity to the Church, and which is part of the itinerary of faith that you are following.[9]

I know that recently you have dedicated special attention to studying the articles of the Creed, for your own formation and in order to help other Christians and families.

For my part, I encourage you to root your life solidly in the faith received from the Apostles and taught by the Fathers of the Church and which must be the light which enlightens each step of your way towards the Father.

Faith received from the apostles and the Fathers of the Church

I am happy too that as part of the programme of your pilgrimage to Rome, there is a visit to a Marian sanctuary like Loreto, to place your life under the maternal protection of the Virgin Mary, the Mother of Christ and of the Church.

The pilgrimage to Loreto

She, in being the Mother of the Christ of our faith, was the first and the best imitator of her Son, and is a shining pathway which leads towards the centre of the mystery of Christ (cf. *Marialis Cultus* 25). By her example, she teaches us to give

---

9. On other occasions (private audience with communities from Spain and from Ivrea, Italy – 7th December 1986; audience with other Spanish communities – 5th December 1987), the Pope was to speak about this "faithfulness to Peter", about this "pilgrimage to the centre of Christianity in the 20th century; about your desire for union with and fidelity to the Church of Christ." The Pope said to these brothers and sisters, "The Neocatechumenal Way will bring you to meditate on and to experience deeply the truth of the Creed as the vital fluid of your Christian being and as something that calls you to witness to the greatness of baptism." (See *L'Osservatore Romano*, 6th December 1987.)

ourselves to the Church, so that the image of her Son is continually formed in men, brothers in the world of today. She who, by her life and her sacrifice collaborated lovingly in the work of Jesus (cf. *Lumen Gentium,* 60ff) wants to go on teaching us the value of every man and the deep reasons for loving them without distinction or reservation.

Mary, Mother and Teacher

So, welcome her as true Mother, as Teacher, as guide and example for your whole life. For this, far from obscuring the Christ-centred orientation necessary in your life, makes it easier. With these wishes I encourage you in your way, so that united with your bishops and priests, and in fraternal communion with the other recognised spiritual and apostolic movements, you may offer your generous contribution to the Church in the present time.

This is what I ask the Lord for you and at the same time I give you my solemn Apostolic blessing.

I want to thank you for these very beautiful religious songs which you have sung with great strength, with great enthusiasm

(*John Paul II: visit to the parish of Our Lady of the Blessed Sacrament and of the Canadian Martyrs, Rome, 2nd November 1980* – Translated from the Italian edition of *L'Osservatore Romano*, 3rd-4th November 1980, with additional material from a tape recording.)

This joy that surrounds you, that is in your songs, in your behaviour, may very well be a sign of your southern temperament, but I hope it is a fruit of the Spirit, and I wish that it may be so. Yes, the Church needs joy, because joy, with its different expressions, is a revelation of happiness. So, here man finds himself faced with his fundamental, we can almost say his natural, vocation: man is created to be happy, for happiness. If he sees this happiness, if he meets it in the expression of joy, he can start a way. Here I must say to you: the songs are good, your expressions of joy are good, but the Spirit is the one who initiates this way.[10]

(*To the cantors of the Neocatechumenal Communities, Rome, 31st March 1981* – Translated from the Italian edition of *L'Osservatore Romano*, 2nd April 1981.)

I would like to thank you for your visit, for all these very beautiful religious songs, and you sing with great strength,

10. For the complete text see pp. 180-183.

with great enthusiasm. I thank you for this visit and I bless you all, I bless your families and your children, those who took part in a very special and beautiful way in this evening.

(To the cantors of the Neocatechumenal Communities, Rome, 21st March 1982 – Translated from *L'Osservatore Romano*, 22nd-23rd March, 1982.)

Cordial greetings to the cantors-psalmists of the Neocatechumenal Communities who have come to Rome for a meeting to prepare for the liturgy of the paschal triduum. Dearly beloved, may your lives witness to the mystery of the risen Christ whom you are preparing to celebrate with your songs, as he who 'dying has destroyed death and rising has restored life' is exalted before the world by the harmonious accord between words and works.

(Visit to the parish of St Francesca Cabrini, Rome, 4th December 1983 – Translated from the Italian edition of *L'Osservatore Romano*, 5-6th December 1983.)

You do well, very well! Sing, sing! Because song always demonstrates joy, this discovery of the divine and the human reality. Baptism brings with it great joy which must be expressed in song. I have seen during my visit that the parish sings with great energy, with enthusiasm! **You must sing.** You must sing because this song brings with it a spiritual meaning, an inner meaning of our soul; in fact we almost do not have enough means of expressing this, this meaning, this mystery, this reality which is the fruit of our Baptism.

Dearest ones, thank you for your presence, for your animation of the life of this parish. I bless you with all my heart, your families, the different groups (because I have heard that you belong to different groups, twelve communities, like the twelve apostles). Your presbyters are amongst you; I have met your itinerants. I bless you with all my heart.[11]

(Visit to the parish of St Ireneus, Rome, 9th March 1986 – Translated from the Italian edition of *L'Osservatore Romano*, 10-11th March 1986, with additional material from a tape recording.)

I am always very happy to see you. Meetings with you are very joyful because of two things: one is the singing,

11. For the complete text see pp. 190-191.

singing full of energy, that resounds, resounds; and the other thing is the children, the little ones who, let us say, do their Neocatechumenal Way, thank God! They always give us great joy, all of us; it gives me great joy to see them.

(*Visit to the parish of St Eligius, Rome, 26th April 1987* – Translated from the Italian edition of *L'Osservatore Romano*, 27-28th April 1987, with additional material from a tape recording.)

Perhaps first of all I have the right to greet you on behalf of the many Neocatechumenal Communities I met, or at least I saw, in Latin America, in different places in the course of my travels, my journey. This began in Montevideo and then went through that very long country, Chile, and then to that other big country, Argentina. I often saw the sign 'Neocatechumenal Communities', in Spanish of course, So all those who greeted the Pope, welcomed the Pope, did **so with the same spirit** as the Neocatechumens do in the various parishes of Rome; the same songs, at least with the same melodies that are sung here, with the same themes. I think that I should take the opportunity of our meeting and at least refer to this because your movement really is very dynamic and wide spread. It feels its vocation, the call of the Lord to be present in the Church, where the Church is already established, where the Church lives out its established Christian, baptismal way, but also where the Church is often very weak, very small, in countries where the majority are non-Catholic, like the Scandinavian countries, for example.[12]

(*Visit to the parish of St Maria della Fiducia, Rome, 21st October 1990* – Translated from the Italian edition of *L'Osservatore Romano*, 26th October 1990.)

I want to underline two things. The first is this: you love to sing songs to Our Lady, to Mary, who, in the words of Elizabeth, believed in the Word of the Lord.[13] And we could

12. For the continuation of this speech see p. 63.
13. The Pope has often referred to this song to Our Lady, 'Blessed are you, Mary', and has often used it as a starting point for the reflections he gives to the communities he is visiting. He did this during his visit to the parish of Our Lady of Lourdes (Rome, 13th February 1983; see *L'Osservatore Romano* 14-15th February 1983): "I hasten to draw your attention to the words of the songs that you sang to welcome me. They are moving words: '...Mary, you believed in the Word of the Lord'. They are words that are central for expressing all the Mystery of Mary; the Mystery of Mary is in these words spoken by her cousin Elizabeth. Mary really is in these words, she who believed in the Word of the Lord with a unique faith. The Mystery that is revealed is also unique; a very great faith, a Marian faith is needed to believe in these

say that this is a word, a text that is emblematic for your movement, for your Way, because we mustn't say movement... Certainly when you are on Way you move too... Well, starting from this word which is truly inspiring, which also inspired the encyclical *Redemptoris Mater*, I hope that you will always walk in faith and bring the others to whom you are sent, **those near and those far away**, to walk too. Then I have something else to say. I know that the Neocatechumens love children. The Pope loves children too and so we always have something in common.

words and to accept what they contain. I think that Mary, she who believed in the Word of the Lord, is the one who offers a model, indicates a road for all of us, especially for all of you. For what does it mean to be a member of a Neocatechumenal Community; what does it mean to be a catechist? It means to have believed in the Word of the Lord, to have made this Word the content, let us say, the flesh of your life, the substance of your life, and so to have profoundly assimilated this Word of the Lord. We can say that the Word works in you and wants to be expressed as though it were a baby wanting to be born. This Word wants to be expressed, given, transmitted like this. And as the Apostles did, so these *itinerant catechists* and other apostles of our time leave their homes, their towns, their native land, their parishes and go looking for other worlds, other countries, other peoples, they learn other languages to bring other people, other communities to the Word of the Lord, in which they personally have believed. Dear ones, I hope that you will walk well on this road, walk well on this road in the parishes, also in the parish of Our Lady of Lourdes and as I did for the young people I want to entrust you to the Mother of Christ and of the Church."

The Pope also spoke about this song during his visit to the parishes of Our Lady of Mercy (Rome, 1st May 1983), St Ireneus (Rome, 9th March 1986, see pp. 78-79), St Felix of Cantalice (Rome, 4th May 1986, see pp. 47-48), St Lucia a Piazza D'Armi (Rome, 18th January 1987).

Chapter IV

The necessity of signs of faith: "Give your life! I see that in your Communities these words are made flesh"[1]

A mute Christian, a barren Christian, does not exist

(Paul VI: general audience, 12th January 1977 – Translated from the tape recording by Vatican Radio.)

We are all involved in the building-up of the Church

The building up of the Mystical Body of Christ on earth, in other words, our present Church, is the duty, as the Council (*Lumen Gentium* 33) says, not only of priests, bishops, etc, but of every believer. Each one must be a witness; he must be able to transmit the message with which he has been entrusted, if by no other means than by his example, and with its support. **A mute Christian does not exist.** A barren Christian does not exist, a Christian living only for himself does not exist. He must live for the community, for the Mystical Body which is called the Church.

We are seeing the flowering of new ways of announcing the Gospel

In this vision, it is clear and desirable that efforts should be multiplied to put this immense and urgent programme into practice: to evangelise, to catechise. There are many initiatives parallel, and somewhat similar, to yours. And there is a flourishing of works and means to give the proclamation of the Gospel a better diffusion and interpretation we might say.

We have observed how this multiform phenomenon of the Holy Church is not simply concerned with the scholas-

1. John Paul II: visit to the parish of St Aloysius Gonzaga (Rome, 6th November 1988): "So, give your life. I see that in your Communities these words are made flesh" (cf. p. 80).

tic and the didactic aspect of its activities. It is not simply the instruction of pupils by school teachers. Rather it is something wider, more pedagogical and vital, concerned with the style of life, in which the teaching of religious truth is parallel to scholastic teaching and, indeed, united to the profession of life, of which the teaching is the norm and principle.

In the second place we note how this task does not place a heavy and difficult burden on those who carry it out or on those whom it helps, even though it is difficult in reality. For what is one of the greatest difficulties which priests encounter? Well, it is that no one comes. 'How boring listening to preaching, listening to the lesson, learning the catechism, it tires me and I like going out, going to the cinema, playing, etc.' Somehow this Church which teaches becomes so boring – but it is not so! We say it to ourselves and we say it to our people. Anyone who understands the secret of the truth which our words contain becomes as if struck by this light, by this truth and is so transformed into apostle, priest, announcer, as much as the disciple who listens: "Oh! I didn't think it was so beautiful, ah, but it's true, but just look..." I repeat, a horizon of light and beauty that is almost unexpected opens up. The fulfilment of this difficult task becomes an honour, a fortune, it becomes a vocation that enobles and exalts.[2]

The Gospel makes those who preach it happy

(*Paul VI: general audience of 12th January 1977* – Translated from a tape recording by Vatican Radio.)

I would like to ask, if there are missionaries amongst you, why are you missionaries? It is because you are exalted by the sense of the Gospel, by what it means to announce the Truth, to announce the secret of life, God's plans, the hopes which do not die! But it becomes so beautiful that you cannot escape from it. And so we, too, become called to be apostles and announcers of this truth!

The Gospel makes its witnesses happy

Carrying out this duty of announcing is no longer boring, just as the task of listening is no longer tiresome. It contains in itself the replenishment of tiredness which it entails and makes its witnesses happy, it makes them secure, it makes them participants in the expectation of the goods of the Kingdom of God which they announce. In our place here at the centre of the Church, it is our duty to welcome

2. For the complete text see pp. 173-180.

many who come from far away, from the missions. And we welcome these people with great pleasure, and we let them speak so that we may hear their witness. Some have enormous difficulties, one does not know how they can live, what they live on, how they overcome illness, hostility, dangers, and so on, and yet – I tell you this because you, too, are happy – when they talk and define themselves, they express a happiness which has no equal with the happinesses of this world. And if we dare say, "But do you want to you stay here or to go back?" "Go back, go back!" they say. And they go in the midst of enormous difficulties because they are caught by the joy of the Gospel.

Therefore then, we say that they who with simple and generous hearts put themselves at the service of the Gospel, undergo, certainly through a secret but sure charism of the Holy Spirit, a psychological and moral metamorphosis, which transforms the difficulties into stimuli. I repeat what I was saying before, why do the missionaries return? Because there is so much to do, because there are those poor people to be consoled, because there is danger, "I have to go and cure the lepers, I must go and prevent these poor people from being overwhelmed by other social movements and becoming the slaves of intolerable situations." The difficulty, the obstacle becomes attractive. What once aroused fear, was boring, was tiresome, instead then becomes the force which attracts, which makes one committed, which binds, and which makes the apostle – let us say the great word, but said in a general sense, 'Martyr', that is to say, witness.

The Gospel transforms difficulties into incentives

And this phenomenon is tremendous. Whoever knows how to look at the phenomena of the Church – we have this responsibility and this good fortune – cannot but say: Thank you God, for giving this vision to me, of seeing so many who are enthusiasts of the Gospel, of the Gospel which is difficult, of the Gospel which is painful, of the Gospel which costs, of the Gospel which does not yield, of the Gospel which collides against all the mentalities and all the vices and obstacles of the world. The Gospel, I repeat, makes those who preach it happy and turns the difficulties into incentives, the dangers into attractions, and the defeats themselves – it seems a paradox – the defeats, that is to say, the failures into merits (...but I did what I could!) and thus into peace which descends serenely into those hearts which have not even had the satisfaction of the success of their labours.

Now we can understand the testimony which our visitors bear today, and which deals with the pivot of Christian life, which is Baptism.[3]

3. For the complete text see pp. 173-180.

The discovery of Baptism has to become leaven within us

(*John Paul II: visit to the parish of Our Lady of the Blessed Sacrament and of the Canadian Martyrs, Rome, 2nd November 1980* – Translated from the Italian edition of *L'Osservatore Romano* 3rd-4th November 1980 with additional material from a tape recording.)

This discovery must be like leaven in us which is fulfilled in the apostolic dimension

That discovery (of Baptism as the beginning of our Christian life in all its depth) must become leaven in us. This leaven shows itself, taking flesh and becoming alive, in the fulfilment of our personal Christianity, in the building up, if we can say that, of the new man. But this leaven also realises itself in an **apostolic dimension.** We are sent; the Church is apostolic, not only founded on the apostles, but permeated throughout her body by a spirit and charism that is apostolic.

Certainly, this apostolic spirit must always be co-ordinated in a social and communal dimension of the whole body, and for this reason, Christ has also constituted the hierarchy. The Church has her hierarchic structure, as the Second Vatican Council's fundamental document, *Lumen Gentium*, reminds us. This is about the leaven and the apostolate.[4]

The family is the domestic church because it transmits faith to the children

(*John Paul II: visit to the parish of St Mary of Mercy, Rome, 1st May 1983* – Translated from the Italian edition of *L'Osservatore Romano*, 2nd-3rd May 1983.)

The catechumenal and Neocatechumenal reality and catechesis go together. First you have to receive the catechesis, you have to become a catechumen in order to prepare for Baptism and then, once baptised, once confirmed, you receive the strength of the Holy Spirit to transmit the faith in which you were baptised. That means to do catechesis. But the first speaker has rightly underlined the Neocatechumenal nature of the group, because the traditional catechumenate, in the early Church, was later replaced by the Baptism of babies; and these babies cannot do the Neocatechumenal Way. They are too small, they do not have the awareness, the intelligence, the knowledge.

---

4. For the complete text see pp. 180-183.

Later, as adults, as young people, they can begin the way to discover **the treasure of our Baptism**. That is what you Neocatechumens are doing. You do it with great commitment, with great enthusiasm, and you do it in several parishes of Rome, and not only in Rome but in all the parishes of the world.

May you continue in this way, and be faithful to the Holy Spirit, may you carry his gifts and his light to others.

To the catechists I wish to say that they have taken on a task which arises from our **Baptism** and our **Confirmation**. When we become mature Christians we must bear fruits and these fruits of faith are borne by giving faith to others, enlightening the faith for others.

This task is clearly the main task of the parents, of the family. **The transmission of faith in the family** is always fundamental. It is said that the family is the domestic church because that is where faith is transmitted from the parents to the children and young people. Of course the catechists of the church must also do this, not only the parents and the family. The parish must have its catechists. The priests are catechists in the parish, so are the sisters who are trained for this task, but so too are many lay people who are first prepared and then commit themselves to this task of the apostolate; the apostolate of the Word of God.

You have sung so much about the faith of Mary who believed in the Word of the Lord. Truly Mary is the fullest example of faith; she is the fullness of faith and Mary is also the first catechist. If we look at her work as catechist which she carries out in the world of today, of all ages, we realise that it is immense. I hope you will look at the Mother of Christ, the first catechist, to imitate her in carrying out your task as catechists.

The Communities are the leaven which must make the dough of the parish rise, in a human and in a Christian way

(*John Paul II: visit to the parish of St Hippolytus, Rome, 12th February 1984* – Translated from the Italian edition of *L'Osservatore Romano*, 13-14th February 1984.)

I want to thank you for this meeting which concludes my visit to your parish of St Hippolytus. Greetings to all the groups, just as the parish priest has presented you. My greetings and best wishes to each one that you may discover your own Christian identity more and more, your own charism. Because just as the religious families have their own charism, for example, the Franciscan family, the Capuchins of the Franciscan family, so too the different groups of the Lay Apostolate have their own specific charism. May you find this identity of yours more and more and this charism that belongs to lay apostolic groups.

This parish of St Hippolytus is very big and numerous. There is a mass of people but also a mass of Christians because I think that the majority of the inhabitants are baptised.

Within the mass of men, of those baptised, there must be leaven too

Jesus has told us that the Church, the Kingdom of God is like bread: to make bread you need the mass of dough but you need leaven too.

Yes, I am convinced that all these groups, the Charismatics, the Neocatechumens, are the leaven which must make the dough of the parish grow, in a human way and in a Christian way. The leaven must penetrate more and more so that the dough can become more and more Christian, more and more aware of being Christian, more responsible about its Christian identity.

Christian witnesses of Christ: this is leaven. How beautiful if the leaven wants to spread itself until it reaches Turkey

Your Patron Saint, St Hippolytus, was a martyr. To be a martyr means to be a witness. **And Christians must be witnesses of Christ, of his Cross, of his Resurrection,** of his faith, of his hope, of his charity. This is what leaven is. And how beautiful it is if this leaven wants to spread beyond the limits of its own parish reaching as far as Turkey, as you were telling me, to carry the yeast of the Gospel to non-Christians as well, to places which are somewhat intransigent, which close in on themselves when faced by the gospel message. Some of your brothers and sisters want to go there, to be leaven in that dough, until the whole of humanity is reached by the evangelical leaven and becomes the Kingdom of God.

May you all, especially you Neocatechumens, proceed along this way with great joy and with great responsibility, seeking always to make more room for the charity of Christ Our Lord and Redeemer; to extend the spaces of the Kingdom of God which has its roots in this world, towards eternity, towards the house of the Father. And I hope that you may all grow in the Kingdom of God, which at the same time is found within us, in the heart of each one of us and in that of Christ, and which has its external dimension in the dimension of the family. You are a portion of the Kingdom of God then, the parish of St Hippolytus. I hope that you may live Christian joy, Christian responsibility, the faith, hope and charity which anticipate divine life in this world.

This is your charism:
courage in manifesting your faith

(John Paul II: visit to the parish of the Great Mother of God, Rome, 11th November 1984 – Translated from the Italian edition of *L'Osservatore Romano*, 12-13th November 1984.)

You, in your journey of faith have discovered two things: the first is Baptism, since the term 'Neocatechumen' refers to this sacrament, in which the munificence of the divine life is hidden, the life offered to us by the Father with Christ in the Holy Spirit; the second discovery is the courage to live it.

Faith must be confessed, manifested, it must be taken to others, taken to the world. You have this courage of faith which is so often missing in Christians, and in those who are baptised. This more than anything is what is missing from everyday Christian life. You have that **charism of courage which is to manifest faith.**

I hope that you work well in deepening this charism and that you do good apostolic work in the parish of the Great Mother of God. May you find much joy in this vocation, much joy in your families, much joy in your children whom you love in a special way and to whom you give your whole life. May you receive great comfort from these children. They are the hope of the generations to come.

With these wishes I bless you with all my heart together with those close to you and with all the people to whom you go in your itinerant apostolate.

Faith received and transmitted

(John Paul II: visit to the parish of St Ireneus, Rome, 9th March 1986 – Translated from the Italian edition of *L'Osservatore Romano*, 10-11th March 1986, with additional material from a tape recording.)

So, dear ones, when I hear this song, this song to Mary, 'Mary, you believed in the word of the Lord', I know immediately that here there is a Neocatechumenal group. I hear this song everywhere, everywhere. I hear it in different countries and continents. In India recently I heard these songs, the same tone, the same melody, the same words: this invocation to Mary, who believed, and so became the first believer; we could say the leader of the chorus of all the believers. She believed, in the fullest and the most fruitful sense. 'Mary, you believed in the word of the Lord': this is how her relative Elizabeth blessed her, her cousin blessed her with these words. And with these words we bless her, the Church blesses her, all the Church and especially you Neocatechumens. Because for you the way of faith is the essential thing, the way of faith, that way which has its sacramental beginning in Baptism, that way which continues throughout the life of man, the life of each one of us.

'Traditio' and 'Redditio'; faith received and transmitted

As you have rightly said, especially in the first speech, this way has its own rhythm. This rhythm is expressed in these two words: **Traditio and Redditio**. Faith has to be transmitted and it has to be received, accepted, and this is done with Baptism and then in a Christian education. It is done by means of different people, different messengers of God, as for Mary it was done through the angelic messenger, Gabriel. It happens through Jesus Christ, who is the first, the consummate messenger of God for all humanity. It was done through the Apostles and is done through the Church. This first rhythm, this first stage is to receive the **Traditio**, it is the tradition: faith is handed on and is received. This then has to be followed up and continued with another stage: this is the **Redditio**. Once faith has been received it has to be transmitted because it is a good, a treasure, a treasure offered freely to us by God, not only to be hidden inside us to be lived in an intimate kind of way, privately, but it is given, it is 'handed over' to be handed on to others. But to take it to others, to transmit it to others, needs great enthusiasm, great conviction of faith.

The force of giving witness

And so the Neocatechumens become **itinerant catechists,** bringing the gospel of Christ, bringing the witness of faith; not only words in an abstract sense, but words that are testimony, the Word of God testified to by the faith of the catechist. This is a power.

Well, I hope, dearly beloved, that this double rhythm of faith, **Traditio** and **Redditio**, will always make up the rhythm of your life, while you are in the Way, and also when, the Way finished, you go back, but go back as especially mature Christians, to the community of the Church, the community of the parish.[5]

Be leaven for the dough, in the churches, in the dioceses, in the parishes

(*John Paul II: visit to the parish of St Aloysius Gonzaga, Rome, 6th November 1988* – Translated from the Italian edition of

5. For the conclusion of the speech see p. 69-70.

L'Osservatore Romano, 7th November 1988: *"The dough of the world needs the Christian leaven. May the breath of the Lord transform you into this leaven"* M. Ponti *and* M. Carrara.)

In the work of the parish, evangelisation and catechesis have and have had a pre-eminent place with respect to other activities. There have been various programmes for the liturgical animation of the feast day Masses and of cooperation between the various parochial initiatives with Parish Days. Particular attention has been given to looking for the 'far away', through home visiting. Preparation for Confirmation has been concentrated on and there have been efforts to provide a post-Confirmation and a marriage preparation programme.

The members of the Neocatechumenal Communities offer a notable contribution, both demanding and fruitful, to this constant work. They have been active in St Luigi Gonzaga for almost twenty years and today the five communities made up of about a hundred and fifty adults and eighty children are present here. Several itinerant catechists have gone out from the parish of Parioli to different countries of Europe, Asia, Africa and America. The Neocatechumens welcomed the Pope in a large white and yellow tent set up in the courtyard of the parish complex. After a brief introduction by the parish priest, Kiko Argüello introduced the various communities.

After he had greeted with affection the many children present, the Pope said:

Give your lives. I see that in your Neocatechumenal Communities this word is made flesh

The evangelical radicalism that we find in different pages of the Gospels is expressed above all in these words: **Give your life**. Christ was certainly a teacher, a 'rabbi'; he taught but he said everything, and he said it fully, at the end, when he gave his life, with his death and resurrection. It is his last word and the most complete word. So, give your life. I see that in your Neocatechumenal Communities this word is made flesh. There are many who are ready to give their lives in different ways, many. The Holy Spirit knows this well.

Another thing is connected with the word leaven. We know well the parable in the Gospel that speaks about the leaven. Well, **you are leaven**, a leaven which causes the mass of dough to grow. The Church is the dough, the world is a bigger lump of dough. The Church is the dough too. But sometimes this dough is inert, insufficiently catechised, insufficiently fed by the sacraments, insufficiently aware of what baptism is. **Baptism**, we can say, is the first leaven in each one of us, that makes us live in our body, in our soul, in our person. We are never sufficiently aware of what our Baptism is. St Paul has left us some indications, perfect messages about what Baptism is. But we never reach full awareness of what it is, of its reality, of what it means. this is why leaven is needed so that awareness of what Baptism is – it is itself a sacramental leaven – can grow. But this needs a leaven that is also apostolic.

You make yourselves leaven for the mass of dough in the churches, the dioceses, the parishes

With this awareness as your basis, you make yourselves leaven for the mass of dough in the churches, the dioceses, the parishes and in such a way that a word which corresponds fully to what Christ wanted of the Apostles is fulfilled: go. He didn't say: take palaces, riches, houses... no. He said to them: go. In this way you too **are itinerants in conformity with the word of Christ**. The Pope too, despite his house, the Vatican, St Peter's Basilica, tries to be something of an itinerant.

I don't pretend to have exhausted this theme. But in these few observations you can already see yourselves, recognise your image, and find, too, encouragement to stay always what you are, what you want to be. But in these words see also my blessing and let us hope that this expresses and brings with it the grace of the Lord. May the leaven, the itinerancy, grow in the grace of the Lord.

Just now there was a catechist who said he had heard something speaking in his heart, in his conscience. Certainly he heard it because Kiko set it going, but only as a human instrument. Really it was the Holy Spirit that was working, the Grace of the Lord, the Holy Spirit beginning to blow. It was the Holy Spirit blowing and not leaving this man in peace. Because **Christ did not come to leave us in peace**. He came to bring us peace, the greatest peace to which the human person aspires: peace with God, reconciliation, but he did not come to bring us a comfortable life, tranquillity, no, certainly not.

Chapter V

Itinerant Catechists: "Jesus Christ is itinerant with you"[1]

Live fully the fundamental announcement of the faith

(John Paul II: private audience with itinerant catechists of the Neocatechumenal Communities in the Clementine Hall, the Vatican, Rome, 7th January 1982 – From the English edition of L'Osservatore Romano, 15th February 1982, with additional material from a tape recording.)

Kiko introduced more than three hundred catechists from seventy countries in the following words:

Beloved Father, present here are three hundred catechists from the Neocatechumenal Communities, who have founded the Way in seventy nations. They make up small teams of evangelisation composed of a priest and two lay people, like a small community, in the image of the Holy Family of Nazareth, which help to carry out the renewal of the Second Vatican Council in the parishes.

Father, I would like to introduce to you very briefly, the itinerant presbyters who have come from all nations, from Australia, Africa, etc...

The married couples, the families who have sold all their goods and go out with their children to announce the Gospel to help in the missions of the whole world. Stand up families and children.

There are also present single girls who have offered their lives to announce the Gospel.

---

1. Cf. John Paul II: private audience with itinerant catechists, Castel Gandolfo, 26th September 1984: "You say 'itinerants' and you are itinerants but this being itinerant means above all that Jesus Christ is itinerant within you and that he is itinerant with you towards others" (see p. 89).

And finally the young men who have offered their lives to announce the Gospel. Five of them have recently decided to enter the Seminary.

We have also seen, Father, that in those places where the Neocatechumenal Way has been going on for over ten years, vocations are beginning to appear. We are very happy about this. This year in Italy fifty-seven young men stood up to enter the Seminary and forty-two in Spain.

We met for three weeks near the Sanctuary of Loreto, reflecting on what God is doing in the different nations where we are carrying out our ministry of evangelisation. We went to kneel at the feet of the Virgin Mary to entrust our mission to her and to ask her, at the little house of Loreto, since our mission is that of founding in the parishes small communities like the Holy Family of Nazareth who live in humility, simplicity and praise, to ask her help to carry this out.

Our greatest desire, for which we asked the Virgin as a secret, has always been to be able to bring these brothers here one day, to bring them to where Peter is, the 'rock' upon which Christ founded his Church.

Since these brothers and sisters have to speak to many Bishops in many nations, since they are mounted on God's *Merkeba* of evangelisation, so we want to show our very great adherence to you by making some **gesture of adherence**.

I asked them first, 'Do you recognise that the Bishop of Rome, Peter, is the rock upon which Christ built his Church?' and everyone replied that they recognise him as such. Then I asked them: 'Do you promise obedience and faith to Peter and to all the bishops of the Church who are in communion with him?' and they promised it. Then I asked them if they were prepared to offer their lives to serve the Church by helping to carry out the renewal of the Second Vatican Council through this Neocatechumenal Way which we are doing as a means of renewing baptism in Christians. And everyone said yes.

So Father, in the name of everyone I would like – if you will allow me – to kneel in front of you, together with all these brothers and sisters, as a small gesture of complete adherence to Peter. Because one thing I said to them, Father, was that through my experiences in many nations and the sufferings I have had, *I have understood that God obeys his bishops,* God himself obeys them. This impressed me so much that I thought: *if God himself obeys them,* how can I, and all of us, not obey them?

So, Father I should like to kneel before you...

When Kiko had finished, the Pope spoke to the itinerant catechists as follows:

I am sincerely happy to meet you today, itinerant catechists from various Neocatechumenal Communities, and I wish to express to you my satisfaction and a word of encouragement for your catechetical commitment, so valuable to the ecclesial community.

You want to live the announcement of faith with a continual interior conversion

You intend to live fully the **fundamental announcement of faith,** that is, the joyful news that Jesus of Nazareth is the eternal Son of God, who became incarnate and rose again for our salvation. You wish to accept in depth the inseparable bond that exists between adherence to this proclamation of life and resurrection and **continual interior conversion**. This entails a change of mentality, of attitudes, of selfish, closed and self-sufficient behaviour, in such a way as to acquire a new perspective and a new vision – the one based precisely on the message of Jesus Christ – which demands a humble openness with regard to God and all brothers.

Sustained by the Word of God

In this **way of faith,** which certainly has its fatiguing aspects and its inevitable difficulties, the **Word of God,** Holy Scripture, is a support, a comfort, a light and guide for you. It must be examined, read, meditated upon and studied with the awareness that it is not just a book, but it is God himself who speaks, acts, challenges, involves, and calls to a careful listening which will lead to complete adherence to his will. And the Word of God, both that of the Old and the New Testament, makes you meet him of whom the Scriptures are full, that is, Jesus Christ, who by his incarnation, "has in a certain way united himself with each man" (*Gaudium et Spes*, 22).[2]

Love all men generously and in their situation

(*John Paul II: private audience with itinerant catechists of the Neocatechumenal Communities, in the Clementine Hall, the Vatican, Rome, 7th January 1982* – From the English edition of *L'Osservatore Romano*, 15th February 1982, with additional material from a tape recording.)

In your reflections together you have wished to meditate on the fundamental value of the **sacrament of Baptism** in the spiritual journey of the Christian, and in your life as Christians you want to relive the complex and rich experience through which the Church led her new children in the first centuries.

---

2. For the continuation of this speech see below.

| | Without falling into a facile archeologism which smacks of affectation, be aware that to realise the **baptismal dimension** means, in the first place, to try to grasp at its sources the **authentic identity of being Christian;** that is, to live the deep change which took place in our human reality with the infusion of divine grace – the having become living temples of the Holy Trinity, branches of the vine, which is Christ, members of the Mystical Body, of the total Christ, that is, of the Church. Writing of the marvellous supernatural effects of Baptism, St Fulbert of Chartres, bishop, expresses himself as follows: "We know with certainty that, sinners in the first birth, we are purified in the second; slaves in the first, we are free through the second; earthly in the first, we are heavenly through the second; carnal through the fault of the first birth, we become spiritual through the grace of the second one; through the former, sons of wrath, through the latter, sons of grace. Let anyone, therefore, who offends the dignity of Baptism know that he offends God himself... |

Revive the authentic identity of being Christian

Without falling into a facile archeologism which smacks of affectation, be aware that to realise the **baptismal dimension** means, in the first place, to try to grasp at its sources the **authentic identity of being Christian;** that is, to live the deep change which took place in our human reality with the infusion of divine grace – the having become living temples of the Holy Trinity, branches of the vine, which is Christ, members of the Mystical Body, of the total Christ, that is, of the Church. Writing of the marvellous supernatural effects of Baptism, St Fulbert of Chartres, bishop, expresses himself as follows: "We know with certainty that, sinners in the first birth, we are purified in the second; slaves in the first, we are free through the second; earthly in the first, we are heavenly through the second; carnal through the fault of the first birth, we become spiritual through the grace of the second one; through the former, sons of wrath, through the latter, sons of grace. Let anyone, therefore, who offends the dignity of Baptism know that he offends God himself...

It is therefore a grace of the doctrine of salvation to know the depth of the mystery of Baptism." (Eph 5; PL 141, 198f.)

United to Christ in the Eucharist

To realise the baptismal dimension means to unite oneself deeply with Christ in the **Eucharist,** the source and summit of Christian life and of the whole of evangelisation (cf *Lumen Gentium*, 11; *Presbyterorum Ordinis*, 5).

Loving everyone, especially the poor

It means loving all men generously, concretely, actively, especially those who are spiritually or materially poor and needy; it means restructuring one's whole **moral life** in consistency and conformity with the **baptismal promises**.

Way of the new man

"This way of faith, the way of Baptism rediscovered," I said to your friends of the Parish of the Holy Canadian Martyrs in Rome, 'must be the way of the new man. This new man who sees what is the true proportion, or rather, the disproportion between his created being, his creatureliness with respect to the Creator, to his infinite majesty, to God the redeemer, to the holy and sanctifying God, and in the light of this he seeks to fulfil himself" (*Insegnamenti di Giovanni Paolo II*, 111-2 [1980] p. 1044).[3]

---

3. For the continuation of this speech see below.

I entrust you to the Virgin Mary so that you may make a personal contribution to the fundamental work of catechesis

(John Paul II: private audience with itinerant catechists of the Neocatechumenal Communities, the Clementine Hall, the Vatican, Rome, 7th January 1982 – From the English edition of *L'Osservatore Romano*, 15th February 1982, with additional material from a tape recording.)

In this liturgical season of Christmas, the Gospels of Matthew and Luke present to us some persons whose behaviour towards the newborn Jesus is particularly exemplary for us: the mysterious Wise Men, with the richness of their culture, attentive and sensitive to the signs of transcendence; the poor shepherds, watching over the flock, ready and obedient to the call of the angels; Joseph, the just man, who in ecstatic sleep still listens to the will of the Eternal God; and above all Mary, the Virgin Mother, who entrusts herself to God completely, utters the *'fiat'* and conceives in her womb the Son of the Most High to present him and give him to men.

To her in particular, beloved brothers and sisters, I entrust your generous commitment, so that in perfect and harmonious adherence to the Church and always under the pastoral direction of the bishops, you may make a personal contribution to the fundamental work of catechesis, being careful not to transmit your own doctrine or that of another master, but 'the teaching of Jesus Christ, the truth that he communicates, or, more precisely, the Truth that he is' (Ap. Ex. *Catechesi Tradendae*, 6).

With these wishes and as a sign of my affection, I willingly impart to you the Apostolic Blessing.

The discovery urges us to transmit it: one cannot remain silent

(John Paul II: visit to the parish of the Immaculate Conception, Cervelleta, Tor Sapienza, Rome, 7th March 1982 – Translated from the Italian edition of *L'Osservatore Romano*, 8-9th March 1982, with additional material from a tape recording.)

Itinerants: apostolic way

There is also another word[4] which is heard more and more often in contacts with Neocatechumenal groups. It is

4. "What is most significant, of particular significance, for all your communities and for your community here, could be summed up in two words. One of these is fundamental and when I listen to a catechumenal group this word always comes up: 'discovery'" (see the continuation of this speech above, p. 42). The second word is 'itinerant'.

the word 'itinerant'. *Iter* means way or journey, as we know well, but here it means an apostolic way, and the itinerants are those who set off on a journey, begin a way to take their discovery to others. We find ourselves once again in the footsteps of the Apostles, of Christians, of all Christians, of every generation. Christianity – the Gospel – is not a theoretical method which can be transmitted as something abstract or something that can be deduced. Not at all. It is an existential system: you **must be** a Christian by conviction.

Discovery compels you to transmit

A Christian who has **discovered** the value of his Christian being, of his faith, of his divine sonship, of his likeness to Christ, has finally discovered the reality of Christ in him, he has discovered his Baptism. Then such a man is able to **transmit**, not only is he able, but **he is driven, he is driven; he cannot remain silent**, but he has to walk, he must walk, it is, we could say, a natural motion. There is a propulsion which is found within, and the movement follows, it is propelled. That is enough, no more. It's enough or we would go on too long.

Remain leaven in the parish

May you continue in this way in this parish well organised, well organised in the life of this parish. May you remain leaven, because it seems to me that this word – we are speaking of the way you are organised in the parish – is the most important: **be leaven**. The mass of dough is great, twenty thousand parishioners. I think that nearly all of them are baptised – so there are many baptisms to be discovered. Therefore be leaven, continue to be leaven. Enough. A blessing and then you can go home. Sing another song. For you, to sing means to pray. We can sing the Our Father together once, because the Pope knows it too.[5]

Jesus Christ carries out his itinerancy within you and then carries it out towards others

(*John Paul II: private audience with itinerant catechists of the Neocatechumenal Communities, Castel Gandolfo, 26th September 1984 – Translated from the Italian edition of L'Osservatore Romano, 'The Pope to the Neocatechumens: Jesus Christ is itinerant within you to go towards others'*, 27th September 1984.)

Last night the courtyard of the Pontifical Palace of Castel Gandolfo became a presbytery during the Pope's meeting with the itinerant catechists of the Neocatechumenal communities.

5. For the complete text see pp. 183-185.

There was the presidential chair, the crucifix hanging from the newly painted walls, the lectern with the book of the Gospel, the Cross, an ikon of Our Lady. And then carpets and flowers, gladioli of varying colours which gave the place a sacredness that was interspersed with prayers, songs, and silences.

Last night's meeting, which was the Holy Father's final appointment before returning to the Vatican today, was once again a meeting of prayer, of proclamation of the Word and of listening, of reflection and of proposal.

Kiko Argüello, who with Carmen Hernández is the initiator of the Neocatechumenal Way, presented in a calm and sometimes fervent tone the latest experiences of the itinerants who were present. For two weeks, two by two, these 'last ones', these 'children of the Kingdom' – Kiko said, turning to the Holy Father – had gone to visit the nations of the world, carrying only a poor and crucified Christ, stopping to announce the 'joyful news' to the poor, the alienated, to priests in the parishes of the great metropoli and those of the remote territories of Africa and Asia, to proclaim with faith that Jesus Christ is the Lord and Redeemer of man.

Kiko communicated to the Holy Father this communal experience of itinerancy, comparing it to that of the Apostles in the Gospel, who, having preached the coming of the Kingdom, returned home happy with an experience of the strength of the presence of the Lord. In the different countries of Europe, North, Central and South America, Africa, Asia, and Oceania (the initiator of the Neocatechumenal Way gave the Holy Father a very detailed picture of this itinerant experience of evangelisation), these new messengers of the good news both suffered and rejoiced in the cause of the Gospel.

A couple from Rome, a young seminarian from Barcelona, an Italian girl, a Polish girl, a Spaniard and a young Italian priest recounted, amidst the participation and emotion of those present, their 'itinerant experience'. It was, in essence, a public confession of the wonders that God works through his 'faithful' who immerse themselves in the world to shake it from its sleep and religious indifference.

From the great metropolis of New York to the 'favelas' of Brazil, from the island of Cuba to China, from Italy to Scandinavia, these were the stages of a gospel story of our own times, lived and testified to with the strength of faith and love. "They even took us for drug addicts," *said the young Polish girl in giving her experience,* "but then they understood that we had a Christian message to offer to everyone with respect and with love." *The testimonial-story also went into some of the details which reveal the power of God who guides those who entrust themselves to him with a sincere heart.*

After the testimonies, the Pope spoke:

...Well then, I'd like to give you one, two, maybe three conclusions. Let us see. The first conclusion is that in your experiences and your conclusions I heard the authentic spirit of the disciples of Christ, who trust totally in the Lord.

Itinerant with Jesus the itinerant

You say 'itinerants' and you are itinerants, but this being itinerant means above all that Jesus Christ is itinerant within you, and that he is itinerant within you towards others. The fact that you are itinerants is secondary, the main thing is that **he is itinerant**. He wants to be itinerant. He wants not only to be present in the Church but also to be itinerant in the Church. The Church must be itinerant, always walking. The Church is in motion, she is not only a Church already settled, organised, structured. The Church is walking towards people, towards communities, towards nations, towards believers and non-believers. These distinctions, these divisions are different for Christ to what they are for us – and this is the first conclusion.

Your itinerancy is one of real evangelical trust

Then there is this **truly evangelical trust** that characterises your itinerancy: to carry nothing, to have nothing, not placing one's trust in oneself, but trusting totally in Providence, in what the Lord will do. Then also the humility – [you said,] "The Lord saved me, he took me out of my sins, of my lack of faith and so I have lived a great grace, received strength from the Lord. I have personally lived this strength of the Lord, his power, and now I must walk announcing this power, indeed I must transfer this power to others." The Lord is powerful! You trust in the power of the Lord and want to experience this power for yourselves and also in others. The Lord is powerful in his death and his resurrection, powerful in his grace, powerful in the Holy Spirit.

I am itinerant too

Then the final conclusion is this: that I, since I became Bishop of Rome and Pope, in this age of itinerants, had to become itinerant myself a little. There is a parallel here, a similarity, but I must say that the journeys that I make are much less severe than yours. It's true that they ask a lot from us, we have quite a heavy day, but apart from that, we don't go on foot, – no, we go with Alitalia or Air Canada, then with a Popemobile. I don't think that you could accept this way of being itinerant – I don't know. But I ask myself: can I do it any differently? In all humility I confess to you that I can't do it differently. So, let the Pope be itinerant as he is, and you carry on being itinerants in the way you are.

...Now let us sing! You must sing something: the song you sing everywhere and shows that you are

Neocatechumens, 'Blessed are you, Mary, for you have believed...'

The Church is certainly itinerant; so too is the Pope

(*John Paul II: private audience with 2,000 priests of the Neocatechumenal Communities, 9th December 1985* – Translated from the Italian edition of *L'Osservatore Romano*, 11th December 1985.)

Among you I have found many priests, but also many lay people, many married itinerants. I must say to you that the first people who went to Bethlehem, who recognised the Mystery of the Incarnation, were itinerants: they were shepherds. Then Jesus himself became itinerant when he was thirty, beginning with the messianic declaration at Nazareth. As well as that, he made all his Apostles itinerant, sending them all over the world.

The Church is itinerant, on a way

The Church, too, is certainly itinerant, on a way, and we can say that the Pope tries more and more to be itinerant, even if with more 'sophisticated' and, perhaps, less authentic methods than yours, for you are poor itinerants, with no aeroplanes. But we hope that all of us, the Pope too, will always be, using all possible means, itinerants of the Gospel, that is, itinerants of the Mystery, of this Mystery that was revealed by the birth of Jesus, by the incarnation of the Son of God and then by his mission, by his death on the cross and by his resurrection. This is how a life was revealed to us, a new life, a divine life, eternal life.

Itinerants in this life

We are itinerants of this life. It would not be possible for us to be itinerants of this life, of eternal life, if the same life had not been given to us first. We already have this life and this life impels us, this life comes from Jesus Christ. This life comes to us through Jesus Christ in the Holy Spirit. He is the source of the divine life in creatures, is the source of divine life in us men. It is he who drives us. Jesus Christ the itinerant impels us, the itinerant of the Father, for it is the Father who sent him and made him itinerant among us.

So Jesus Christ the itinerant pushes us; the one who was sent, the missionary, because he is the Word of God in Mission, *missiones divinarum personarum* – so I learned from St Thomas. *Missio* means to be sent and therefore to be itinerant. Christ impels us in the Holy Spirit because the Holy Spirit is sent too, sent in a different way – not like Christ, not in a visible, incarnate, human form – a Holy

Spirit, not incarnate, but sent. It could be said that the mission of the Holy Spirit is even more penetrating, for it descends into what is the most intimate of man, of every creature. As St Augustine said, 'Intimior intimo meo'. This then is the mission of the Holy Spirit, of the Spirit that is sent. And you become itinerants with the strength of the incarnate Son who gave us an example of the visible mission. Thanks to the mission of the Son and Holy Spirit, with the life which comes through them from the Father, you become itinerant.

Alas for me if I do not evangelise

As St Paul says, the mission compels us; woe to me if I do not evangelise!

I wish you the joy of the Christmas feasts. I wish you the joy of the itinerant shepherds who found the way to Bethlehem. I wish you the joy that comes from those who convert. There are many among you who are converted, who have found Christ, who have rediscovered God, coming often from the opposite shore. I wish you again the joy that comes from the conversion of people, of souls. As Christ said, 'There is more joy in heaven for one sinner who converts than for ninety nine just men.' I wish you this joy and that in this way your itinerancy and your Neocatechumenal Way will be rewarded.

Once again I wish you 'Happy Christmas'. To make things more simple I say it in Italian but it should be said in many languages. I want to extend this wish for a Happy Christmas to all the Communities, to all the peoples from whom you come, to your parishioners, to your colleagues, to your families.

May Jesus Christ be praised.[6]

A missionary, itinerant, Neocatechumenal parish

(*John Paul II: visit to the parish of St Leonard Murialdo, 22nd March 1992* – Translated from the Italian edition of *L'Osservatore Romano*, 23rd-24th March 1992.)

Thank you for this presentation in words, but that is above all a presentation of persons. It can be seen that your parish is here in Rome, in this district, but at the same time it is in many places, in many localities, in many settings outside Rome. It is a missionary, itinerant, Neocatechumenal parish.

6. For the complete text see pp. 191-196.

I greet you all: Australians, Africans, French, Germans, Polish, Byelorussians...[7]

The Church of Rome, as you must know, is living today in a period of confrontation. Confrontation means – we can say – above all the application of Vatican II, above all of *Lumen Gentium* and of *Gaudium et Spes*. It is confrontation with the different realities which demarcate this city and Roman society and it is important for the future of the city, of Italy and also of the Church. But it is a confrontation in which the Church is confronted and in which in its turn it confronts in faith. With its faith of two thousand years Rome looks at the problems of our millennium, of the end of this second millennium. It looks in faith and tries to understand these problems even if they are difficult, even if sometimes they are in conflict with what faith tells us. It looks at these problems with courage because the Church must have courage. Christ told us, 'Do not be afraid,' and this is the key word of his messianic mission and of our apostolic mission. Do not be afraid. I say it also to you itinerants so that you may have courage. Sometimes I hear that you are afraid of some situation that you meet, that faces you and that you are facing. Don't be afraid, because it is always about the same thing: 'I am with you.' These are not only words but a reality.

With a blessing to all of you here – the few from this parish who are still in Rome – and to the many who are in the different continents.

7. The parish of St Leonardo Murialdo, where there are ten Neocatechumenal Communities, has many itinerants and families in mission in the continents and countries mentioned here by the Pope.

Chapter VI

"The family in mission is the image of the Trinity in mission"[1]

A profound faith is needed to walk as a family in today's world

(Celebration of the Eucharist with Pope John Paul II and handing over of the missionary crucifix to the first families in mission, Castel Gandolfo, 28th September 1986 – Translated from the tape recording by Vatican Radio.)

Kiko Argüello introduced the itinerant Catechists and the families who were present to the Pope as follows:

Dearest Holy Father, present here are the itinerant teams responsible for seventy two nations who have come from all over the world for a twenty day convivence to reflect together and above all to live together in communion. Also here are the twelve families who, after this convivence, will leave to evangelise in northern Europe, invited by the bishops of Hannover, Stockholm, Copenhagen and various other places. They will go with all their children. Here we have about seventy priests, forty eight families with more than two hundred children (an average of five per family), seventy four young men, twenty eight young women and also sixteen seminarians who accompany us. So here is nearly everyone who is carrying forward the evangelisation throughout the world through the Neocatechumenal Way.

We thank you, Father, for this meeting which seals the twenty years since the birth of the Neocatechumenal Way and the

---

1. From the homily given by John Paul II during the Eucharist celebrated at Porto San Giorgio, 30th December 1988: "With this great witness, the family in mission as image of the Trinity in mission, a socio-political, socio-economic programme should be carried forward" (cf. p. 203).

evatgelisation all over the world. And we are very grateful to the Family of Nazareth and to the Virgin Mary for this meeting.

At the end of the celebration the Holy Father addressed the following words to those present:

Dearly beloved, we have celebrated the most holy Eucharist, celebrated this most holy Eucharist contemplating the way of the **Holy Family of Nazareth** of Joseph, Mary and Jesus; of Jesus, Joseph and Mary. The Church tells us that this Holy Family is the model for all Christian families, for all the families in the world. Mary and Joseph, their lives centred on this mystery of the incarnate Son, show us this way of faith that must construct and fashion the life of every Christian family. We have prayed for all the families of the world. We have prayed especially for the families present here, for your way in the faith.

To realise the plan of God
– of love of life –
in today's world, a profound faith is needed

To walk as a family in today's world a profound faith is needed. You need a courageous faith to make present in today's world this plan of God for the family, this plan of love of life which is proper to every family, which is its vocation. You need great faith to walk as a family in the tracks, the footsteps, of the Holy Family; and to get others, other families, to walk.

Very dear brothers and sisters, together with my brother Bishops and priests, I hope that all of you may do this way of faith as families. I hope too that this way of faith may be an example, may be attractive to other families in today's world. For you, as for us the model and example is the Holy Family of Nazareth. I give you my blessing.

Mission is entrusted to the family first of all

(John Paul II: private audience, with the sending out of 35 families for the 'New Evangelisation', Castel Gandolfo, Feast of the Holy Family, 27th December 1987 – Translated from the Italian edition of *L'Osservatore Romano*, 30th December 1987.

My very dear friends, I thank you for your visit today to Castel Gandolfo, on a day during Christmastide that is very meaningful. The Holy Feast of Christmas is celebrated with great liturgical solemnity, and with great joy and public participation, but perhaps we are not sufficiently aware of what this Holy Feast of Christmas is.

The mission of
the Holy Family

The Holy Feast of Christmas is the beginning of a mission, a divine mission among men. God is born as son of man, from a woman; he is one sent by the Father, the heavenly Father, and is born to fulfil this mission. And then immediately after the Holy Feast of Christmas comes the celebration of today's feast of the Holy Family. And this is very significant; it means that this divine mission becomes human with the incarnation of the Word of God, **that this mission is entrusted in the first place to the family**.

I see in this meeting, and in the evolution of your Neo-catechumenal Way and in the missionary project entrusted to various families, (not to individuals but to whole families), I see this significant event which belongs to the History of Salvation, to the history of the divine mission among the whole human family, among men, among the human race, being put into effect.

Your families in mission with the Holy Family

And I hope that you will participate in this divine mission that was entrusted to the Holy Family with your families, above all with the life of these families, a life faithful to what God wants the human family to be and which he showed us in the Holy Family of Nazareth.

Then the mission is called *ad extra*; the mission is to go, to teach, to do what Jesus told the Apostles to do at the end of his messianic mission on this earth. But the Second Vatican Council says very well that those twelve were representatives of all of the new Israel, naturally including the family which is the basic cell of every people, of the old and of the new Israel. So their mission has to involve families; and we are trying to rediscover this, because perhaps it had become somewhat hidden, was not valued enough, not put into practice enough, even though there are in the Church many good traditions of the Christian family. But this missionary characteristic has a certain novelty.

Rediscovering the novelty of the missionary family

And the wind of your movement, or, better, of your Way, is precisely trying to rediscover this **new missionary aspect of the family**: the Church in *status missionis*, all of the Church being missionary, the family in *status missionis*.

I hope that you will walk (to walk also means to move), that you will walk well along this road that you have found in the Neocatechumenal Way. And I want to give a blessing to all of you who are here, to those who are preparing for a mission in faraway countries, or perhaps not so faraway, not always geographically far away, but very often spiritually far from faith, from the Christian vision of life.

The witness of the family for the far away

There, this is the mission of the families: to bring close a family that is far away, that has gone away from the faith, the presence of a family, the witness of families, the apostolate of families is needed.

Father, Son and Holy Spirit: Trinity in mission

(Celebration of the Eucharist by Pope John Paul II and sending out of families for the 'New Evangelisation', Porto San Giorgio, Italy, Feast of the Holy Family, 30th December 1988: from the homily. Cf. *L'Osservatore Romano*, 31st December 1988.)

The mystery of the Most Holy Trinity in mission

May Jesus Christ be praised.

Dearly beloved, we are living the Christmas period. In this period we live in faith the great divine mystery, the mystery of the most Holy Trinity in mission. It was known and confirmed that God was one and only one. We can also accept what Paul said when he spoke at the Areopagus, that God is that spiritual absolute in whom we live, in whom we move, in whom we have our being. But what was not known, and what many today still have difficult in accepting, was the profound reality of God Trinity in whom we live, in whom we move. And he, Trinity in mission, is not only an absolute being, above all others, but the Father in his infinite, inscrutable reality who generates, generates his Word from eternity without beginning.

And with this his Word he lives the ineffable mystery of Love, which is a person and not only an interpersonal relationship; it is a person, the generated Son, Spirit, Love breathed out.

Christmas: mission of the Son, sent by the Father to bring us the Holy Spirit

Every year the holy time of Christmas reminds us of this mystery of the Trinity in mission, here in the Night of Bethlehem, this mission of the Son, sent by the Father to bring us that Holy Spirit by whom he was conceived in the Virgin. He comes to bring us this Spirit. The night of Christmas is this night in which the reality of God-communion, the unity of the Divinity, absolute unity, unity of communion, comes close to our human mind, to our eyes, to our history and becomes visible. That is, the hidden mystery, the *Mysterium absconditum a saeculus* becomes visible, the mystery hidden from all time is revealed, becomes visible. By means of this poor reality of the birth of the Lord, of the Crib, of the Night of Bethlehem, of Mary and Joseph, the great mystery of the Trinity in mission is revealed. This is our God: this is our God! Ineffable mystery!

This is how we must speak, this is what we must confess, witness to, knowing our inadequacy in front of the inscrutable mystery of God, divine unity, unity of the divinity, and at the same time unity of communion. During this Christmastide Holy Mother Church has us celebrate today another human mystery: the Holy Family of Nazareth.

We contemplate this reality, this mystery of the Trinity in mission. During the Christmas period we contemplate it with a special depth and intensity and with intense joy because this mission – the Word sent to the world to speak in person of his Father, of the divine reality, he, the Word, comes in this night as a human baby, poor, stripped of everything; in this moment already stripped – he could not be born in any other way. No human richness could provide an adequate context for the human birth of the eternal Son of God. Only that poverty, that abandonment, that Crib, than Night of Bethlehem could do so. It was right that no lodging could be found in that little town.[2]

The Church: a big family in mission.
Every Christian family is in mission

(Celebration of the Eucharist by Pope John Paul II and sending out of families for the 'New Evangelisation', Porto San Giorgio, Italy, Feast of the Holy Family, 30th December 1988: from the homily. Cf. L'Osservatore Romano, 31st December 1988.)

Dearly beloved, we contemplate this divine reality, **the Most Holy Trinity in mission**, and at the same time we feel how inadequate to talk of this mystery are our human concepts, our poor human words. Nevertheless, he who was sent to us, the Word, comes to speak and comes also to make us speak. More than that, he sought out those people who were most simple to take up this Word, this divine Word; he sought out the most simple.

The Holy Family is this: the human family on a divine mission

We have to say that we are contemplating today the family in mission, because the Holy Family is nothing other than this: the human family on the divine mission. And here, this human family like a smaller community, shows itself to be, at the same time, like a big human community which finds itself on the divine mission: this is **the Church**. Particularly in the Second Vatican Council the Church has recognised her family and her missionary character. She is a great family in mission. Inside this great family-Church is every human family, every family community, as family in mission. A lot is talked about the family as a smaller, more basic society and all this is true.

And so, at the same time as mirroring the mission of the Word, the Son, the family mirrors the mission of the Holy Spirit, which is Love

But when we see the principle mystery constituted by the Trinity in mission we cannot see the family outside this: it, too, is in mission. And its mission is really fundamental, fundamental for the divine mission of the Word, for the divine mission of the Holy Spirit; it is fundamental.

2. For the complete text, see pp. 199.

The divine mission of the Word is that of speaking of the Father, of giving witness to the Father. It is the family which is the first to speak, the first to reveal this mystery, the first to witness before the new generations to God, to the Father. Its word is more efficacious.

And so every human family, **every Christian family, finds itself on a mission**. It is the mission of Truth. The family cannot live without Truth; more than that, it is the place where there is an extreme sensitivity towards the Truth. If truth is lacking in relationships, in the communion of persons – husband, wife, fathers, mothers, children – if truth is missing, communion is broken, the mission is destroyed. You all know well how subtle, how delicate, how very vulnerable, is this communion in the family. And so in the family is reflected also – together with the mission of the Word, the Son – the mission of the Holy Spirit which is love. The family is in mission, and this mission is fundamental for every people, for the whole of humanity; it is the mission of Love and of Life, it is the witness of Love and of Life.[3]

Holy Church of God, you cannot fulfil your mission except through the family and its mission

(*Celebration of the Eucharist by Pope John Paul II and sending out of families for the 'New Evangelisation', Porto San Giorgio, Italy, Feast of the Holy Family, 30th December 1988: from the homily.* Cf. *L'Osservatore Romano*, 31st December 1988.)

Holy Church of God, you cannot do your mission, you cannot carry out your mission to the world except through the family and its mission.

Dearly beloved, I came here very willingly. I accepted very willingly your invitation on the Feast of the Holy Family to pray with you for the most fundamental and most important thing in the mission of the Church: for the spiritual renewal of the family, of the human and Christian families of all peoples, of every nation, perhaps particularly those of our western world, which is more advanced, more marked by the signs and benefits of progress but also by the failures of this one-sided progress. If one is talking about a renewal, about a regeneration of human society, even in the Church as a society of men, one has to begin with this point, with this mission. Holy Church of God, you cannot carry out your mission, you cannot fulfil your mission in the world, if not through the family and its mission.

This is the main reason why I accepted your invitation to

3. For the complete text, see pp. 199.

be together and to pray together in this gathering made up above all of families, of couples, of children indeed of itinerant families.

The Family of Nazareth is also an itinerant family

It is a beautiful thing. We see that the Family of Nazareth was also an itinerant family. And it was so straight away, from the first days of life of the Divine Infant, of the Word Incarnate. It had to become an itinerant family, itinerant and also refugee.[4]

You, as itinerant and Neocatechumenal families, bring the witness of the family in mission

(*Celebration of the Eucharist by Pope John Paul II and sending out of families for the 'New Evangelisation', Porto San Giorgio, Italy, Feast of the Holy Family, 30th December 1988: from the homily.* Cf. *L'Osservatore Romano*, 31st December 1988.)

Many painful realities of our time – that of refugees, for example, or of emigrants – are already engraved, are present in **the Holy Family of Nazareth**. But for you this Family is above all an itinerant family because it goes everywhere: it goes to Egypt, it comes back to Nazareth, it goes back to Jerusalem with the twelve year-old Jesus, it goes everywhere, always as itinerant to bring a testimony of the family, of the divine mission of a human family.

I think that as itinerant Neocatechumenal families you do the same

I think that you as itinerant Neocatechumenal, families do the same thing: in yourselves you constitute the aim of your itinerancy which is that of bringing everywhere, to different environments, perhaps to the most dechristianised environments, the witness of the mission of the family. It is a great witness, great in human terms, great in Christian terms, divinely great, because such a witness, the mission of the family, is conclusively inscribed in the path of the Most Holy Trinity. In this world there is no other more perfect, more complete image than that which is God; **Unity, Communion**. There is no other human reality which corresponds more, which humanly corresponds more to that divine mystery.

Bearing witness everywhere, in the most dechristianised situations, through the mission of the family

And so, bringing as itinerants the witness which is properly that of the family, the family in mission, you bring everywhere the witness of the Most Holy Trinity in mission. And so you make the Church grow because the Church grows from these two mysteries. As the Second Vatican

4.   For the complete text see pp. 199.

Council teaches us, all the vitality of the Church comes finally, or principally, from this mystery, from this mystery of the Trinity in mission. Together with this you bring the witness of the family in mission which tries to walk in the footsteps of the Trinity in mission. And in this way also a message is brought, the message of Bethlehem, the message of Christmas, a joyful message.

We know that this message too, according to traditions and customs, is always linked to human families. It is the feast of the family. This feast needs to be given a deep breath of life, a full dimension, full in human terms, full in Christian terms, divinely full because this human mystery, this human reality of the family is rooted in the divine mystery, in the mystery of Divine communion.[5]

The family in mission: itinerant in order to bring the witness of Baptism

(*Celebration of the Eucharist by Pope John Paul II and sending out of families for the 'New Evangelisation', Porto San Giorgio, Italy, Feast of the Holy Family, 30th December 1988: from the homily.* Cf. *L'Osservatore Romano,* 31st December 1988.)

You are communion, communion of persons, like Father, the Son and the Holy Spirit

You are communion, communion of persons like the Father, the Son and the Holy Spirit.

You are communion of persons, you are unity. You are unity and **you cannot not be unity**. If you are not unity, you are not communion; if, instead, you are communion, you are unity. There are many families in this world of progress, rich, opulent, who lose their unity, lose communion, lose their roots. Here **you are itinerants** to bring the witness of these roots; this is your catechesis, this is your Neocatechumenal testimony: this is how the fruitfulness of Holy Baptism is spoken of. We know well that the sacrament of Matrimony, the family, all this grows in the sacrament of Baptism, from its richness.

To grow in baptism means to grow in the paschal mystery of Christ. Through the sacrament of water and the Holy Spirit we are immersed in this paschal mystery of Christ which is his death and his resurrection. We are immersed so as to find again fullness in life and this fullness of the person but, at the same time, in the dimension of the family – communion of persons – to bring to, to inspire with this newness of life different environments, societies, peoples, cultures, social life, economic life... All this is for

5.   For the complete text see pp. 199.

the family. You must go throughout the world to say to everyone that it is "for the family" not "at the cost of the family". Yes, your programme must be fully evangelic, full of courage, courage in giving witness, courage in asking, asking before everyone, above all before our brothers, before human beings, before our sisters, all these families and all these couples, all these offspring. But also before others. With this great witness, the family in mission as image of the Trinity in mission, must also carry forward a socio-political, a socio-economic programme, I would say. The family is involved in all this and can be helped, carried along, privileged – or it can be destroyed.

The family: there is no other dimension in which man can express himself as a person

You must, with all your prayers, with your testimony, with your strength, **you must help the family**, you must protect it against every kind of destruction. If there is no other dimension in which man can express himself as a person, as life, as love; it has also to be said there is no other place or environment in which man can be so destroyed. Today many things are being done to normalise this destruction, to legalise this destruction; a profound destruction, deep wounds in humanity. Much is being done to systematise, to legalise this. In this sense people speak about "protecting". But the family cannot really be protected without going to the roots, without entering into its deep reality, into its intimate nature; and this intimate nature is the communion of persons in the image and likeness of the divine community. Family in mission, Trinity in mission.

Dearly beloved, I do not want to go on, I do not want to prolong this. I leave you these reflections which come to me spontaneously. Today is the day on which above all else the Holy Family must speak to us and this is my humble prayer: that this Holy Family of Nazareth, through our assembly, through our songs, through our prayers and also through these my words, may speak to all of us.[6]

The work of those who consecrate all their physical and spiritual resources to evangelisation is marvellous

(John Paul II: private audience for the sending out of 100 families from the Neocatechumenal Communities for the 'New Evangelisation', Rome, 3rd January 1991 – Translated from the Italian edition of *L'Osservatore Romano*, 4th January 1991.)

6. For the complete text see pp. 199.

Introduction by Kiko Argüello:

Dear and most reverend Father, we have come just now from Porto San Giorgio, from the tent that you honoured and sanctified with your presence two years ago.

We have been there, one thousand people, four hundred families, for a week, preparing ourselves in a retreat of conversion. The families who were sent two years ago to the most difficult zones of Latin America were present. They were sent to the *pueblos jovenes*, the shanty towns of Guayaquil in Ecuador, and to many other places... Some were sent too to the fringes of Europe, such as Hamburg or to neighbourhoods of Amsterdam in Holland, to New York (the Bronx), and together we have seen something of their experience. They have all come with eyes full of light, of love, of the tenderness of Our Lord Jesus Christ who has been with us in the midst of very great suffering and has helped us very much.

They have all decided to return. They have told us many striking facts and of how God has tested and prepared them for the mission. In these years of 'incarnation' many went to these countries, to Japan for example, without knowing the language, and we have done this deliberately because we think that it is better to go being the last ones (someone who doesn't know the language is poor). And in fact, this has been very effective because the people round about gave things to these families, came to their assistance, gave them help, and this has made their mission easier, the mission to make present the immense mystery of the Holy Family of Nazareth. In many places these families have begun to give catecheses. They have been able to announce Jesus Christ and little Christian communities have been formed, with pagans. In China – Taiwan – a small community of eleven people including four catechumens was born in a completely pagan village.

Now we have very many requests from many Bishops, including Bishops who had already asked for families and after two or three years (some have already been on the mission for three or four years) have seen the fruits, especially in Latin America in the face of the 'sects'.

These families went to zones where there are no parish priests, where, because of the lack of clergy, there are no churches.

We have many requests, so many that we have had to make a selection. So we asked the first communities in Spain, where the families have an adequate preparation with more than fourteen years in the Way, and many, many families offered themselves. It is something surprising, that they are ready to go with their children where the Church thinks good. There, where the family is destroyed, they are ready to be the real presence of a Christian family, and we are surprised by this generosity of theirs because they know that they are going, many of them, to martyrdom, to very difficult situations. We have four hundred new families who offered themselves. We met with those who were already in mission and with other itinerants – a thousand people altogether.

The seminarians of the 'Redemptoris Mater' of Rome were also present and it was a marvellous preparation for them to hear these families, the difficulties...

Then, until last night, until almost three o'clock this morning, all of yesterday was taken up by looking at, evaluating every 'request'. To be able to send the families we asked for an official letter from each Bishop and that the Bishop also take some responsibility for helping them with the house etc.

At the end we chose one hundred families. Here are the brothers and sisters who have already been given a destination, who are ready to leave. Six families will go to Russia, to Moscow; four to Byelorussia; two to Georgia; two to Yugoslavia; six new families to Germany (to continue the marvellous work that these families are doing in Holland, asked for by the Bishop); two to England; two to France. Then in the United States the Bishops have asked for nineteen families, for the city outskirts, above all to begin work with the blacks, where the Catholic Church is finding itself in difficulties. For example, the Cardinal of Washington, the bishops of Dallas and San Antonio in Texas, have made requests. Then in Central America and Latin America, for example, for Chile, for Colombia (two families); another family for Ecuador, two for Venezuela; three in Mexico. In Asia: ten families for Japan; another five for nationalist China. In Africa, four for Zambia; four for Cameroon; then Ethiopia, Ivory Coast, Australia, etc. A total of one hundred and four families with a total of four hundred and nine children, and all young, some not so young. When these families have children of fifteen, sixteen years of age, we asked them for their opinion, if they were ready to go with their parents. In this we have seen an enormous generosity and how these young people love their parents... Good, about the mission: we have listened to the families who have come back. They said that the first evangelisers have been their children (in Japan, China, Holland) in their colleges, schools, with the mothers – it was beautiful! We could say that their children are the spearhead of the 'New Evangelisation' by families. The children also give witness to their friends, bringing their friends... for example, the families in Japan are always finding their homes invaded by Japanese children, friends of their children. And these children know the language already for they learn it very quickly. Through the children the families have got to know other Japanese families. What helps the evangelisation of these families is that none of them are Christian, they are all pagans which makes them very interested in, very struck by this way of 'living the family', seeing the family table like an altar where the father transmits, 'passes on', the faith to the children and where the marriage bed is also an altar where new children are given life. A new culture appears, that is also such a profound and marvellous reality that we are surprised. There, Father, I don't want to go on any longer but only to say that we have been very struck by the fact that so many wanted to go. Out of these four hundred families only one hundred can leave but all of them wanted to go.

And I said to them, 'But do you realise what you are doing: going to very poor, very difficult places?' But we were all moved by an ardour, by the desire for martyrdom, by a supernatural 'force' that was present in our midst...

After the conclusion of the Gospel of Mark had been sung, the Pope addressed those present in the following words:

In the light of Christmas we have met the Saviour; we have contemplated the marvels that God has done; we have been invited to welcome the gift of Salvation and to spread it among our brothers. Your commitment to evangelisation is born from this mystical embrace with the Word incarnate. This commitment is all the more urgent today because we are living times of profound social change. We find ourselves, in fact, at a turning point in history, projected towards a future laden with expectations and hopes but threatened by disquiet and fears that strike the human being at his deepest level. Man calls for peace, serenity; he asks for help and solidarity; he needs Love. He needs Christ.

You consecrate the whole of your existence to evangelisation

But what is marvellous, however, **is the work of those who, like you, consecrate every physical and spiritual resource to evangelisation.** You are sure that only Jesus can fulfil the expectations of the person and so you do not hesitate to leave everything and set off on the roads of the world, witnessing in this way to the living presence of the Redeemer among us and to the power of his Word that saves us.

Messengers of reconciliation and apostles of fraternity and service

Be grateful to Providence which has chosen you and listen constantly to the Spirit. Persevere in prayer and in the practice of virtue. Be **messengers of reconciliation and apostles of fraternity and service**. The Lord, who asks total availability from you, associates you in this way with the mystery of the Redemption of the world.[7]

---

7. For the continuation of this speech see the section below.

Your concern for evangelisation urges you above all towards families

(John Paul II: private audience for the sending out of 100 families from the Neocatechumenal Communities for the 'New Evangelisation', Rome, 3rd January 1991 – Translated from the Italian edition of *L'Osservatore Romano*, 4th January 1991, with additional material from a tape recording.)

I cannot but underline, with deep joy, that your concern for evangelisation urges you **above all towards families**. In this age, is it not that the family perhaps needs to be evangelised again so that it can rediscover its role as the primary cell of the Christian community, the domestic church, within which it is possible to live the primal experience of the meeting with God? How deeply can be felt the current social situation of the crisis of the family! It is not easy to think that there will be a better future when the home goes back to being the privileged place for the welcoming of life and for the growth of the person: a school of human wisdom and of spiritual formation.

With a joyful soul I greet the many families among you who are already in mission in the most dechristianised parts of the planet; I greet also the couples who are preparing to leave. **Yes, families evangelise families!**

May the Lord make you into his instruments everywhere; may his grace always accompany you.

I gladly hand over the cross to those who are called to be itinerants in the service of the Gospel, in other countries. Entrust yourselves to God and, resisting every difficulty, make yourselves 'ambassadors for Christ, ... as though God were appealing through us' (2 Cor 5:19).

Live in cordial obedience and filial communion with the Pastors, for you are members of a living body: the Church. It is they who invite and welcome you. You must show docility towards and confidence in them. It is through their directives that the will of the Lord is made known to you in your particular mission.

The new evangelisation demands a new enthusiam and renewed methods

The task which awaits you – **the New Evangelisation** – asks you to present with new enthusiasm and **renewed methods** the eternal and immutable content of the patrimony of our Christian faith. As you know very well, it is not only about transmitting a doctrine but it is to meet the Saviour in a deep and personal way.

I invoke Mary, the Mother of the redeemer, so that she may help you in this way. To her, Star of the New Evangelisation, I entrust each of you, your communities and all those whom you will meet.

While, in the name of the Lord, I exhort you to set off with courage and to be ardent witnesses of the Gospel everywhere, I bless you from my heart.

The Holy Father added spontaneously:

The Neocatechumenate embraces all of life, all the life of the family

Well, what I have said was a reply to your beautiful introduction which was realistic, in a Christian and Neo-catechumenal way. But introductions must always have a follow-up. Now we have this follow-up here in the Paul VI hall, but then there will be more follow-up in your journeys as itinerant families, families that carry out an in-depth evangelisation in **the Neocatechumenate, that embraces all of human life**, embraces all the life of the family that evangelises or that is evangelised.

And so I wish you a good journey: from the itinerant Pope to the itinerants!

Prayer for the sending out of the families for the 'New Evangelisation'[8]

Blessed are you, Holy Father,
Our God, Eternal King,
for in your infinite goodness
you sent your beloved Son into the world.

In his human growth,
you entrusted him
to the Holy Family of Nazareth,
where Mary, ever Virgin, and Saint Joseph,
her spouse, brought him up with care
so that he might come to maturity
and carry out your mission of salvation
for the whole human race.

You, in your divine kindness,
looking with love upon the lost faith
of so many of your children,
have raised up these families
through the Neocatechumenal Way,
so that following in the footsteps
of the Family of Nazareth
they may call mankind together
in a 'new school'
to a Way of baptismal growth.
Here, nurtured and looked after by the Church,
may they reach that maturity of faith
which allows them to live
according to your will.

(Extending his hands)
Father, send your Holy Spirit
upon these families
to sustain them among those nations
to which you are sending them,
so that in the midst of so many of the poor
they may overcome every temptation of the devil
and, full of joy, lead new sons
and daughters to you
who will sing your praises for ever.
Through Christ our Lord. Amen

8. This prayer was prepared by Kiko Argüello for the sending of the families by John Paul II at Porto San Giorgio, 30th December 1988.

Chapter VII

The 'Redemptoris Mater' Seminaries: "It does not surprise me that in your Way there are vocations"[1]

Tell them: 'The Kingdom of God is near'

(Eucharist of Pope John Paul II with a group of young men from the Neocatechumenal Communities preparing to enter the seminary, the Vatican Gardens, 3rd July 1983; from the homily – Translated from the Italian edition of *L'Osservatore Romano,* 4-5th July 1983, with additional material from a tape recording.)*

"The harvest is great, but the labourers are few. Pray then to the Lord of the harvest to send labourers to his harvest." This famous passage from the Gospel of Luke set out by the liturgy of the day was at the centre of the meditation and prayer yesterday, Sunday 3rd July, of the Holy Father together with about four hundred young men who had spent the previous week at Porto San Giorgio on a three day spiritual retreat on the theme of vocations. At the celebration of the Eucharist which took place in the early morning before the altar at the grotto of Our Lady of Lourdes in the Vatican Gardens, the Pope demonstrated his fatherly love and encouragement to those young men involved in a serious and conscientious vocational way. Among the young men – all of whom had begun to think about their vocation in the Neocatechumenal Way – were about fifty of the one hundred and fifty seminarians whom the Neocatechumenal Communities have up to now given to the Church in Italy. Moreover, among those young men who prayed yesterday with the Pope there are many

1.   John Paul II to the young men of the Neocatechumenal Communities journeying towards the priesthood. Vatican City, 31st March 1985. "And this is a fruit of meditation on and a deepening of the mystery of Baptism, so I am not surprised that there are vocations in your movement. It confirms that your movement is authentic and corresponds to its nature and its name."

others, more than sixty, ready to reply to the call which the spiritual retreat just ended has decisively clarified.

Around the great table, set out in the middle of the assembly, about thirty priests concelebrated with the Pope. Kiko Argüello – who with Carmen Hernández, also present, promotes and inspires the Neocatechumenal Way – led the assembly in song.

In his homily, the Holy Father addressed the following words to the assembly:

'The harvest is great, but the labourers are few. Pray then to the Lord of the harvest to send labourers for his harvest' (Luke 10:2). This affirmation, pervaded by trepidation and open to hope, dear seminarians and young men, resounds for us today gathered in front of this grotto of Lourdes, at the beginning of a celebration of the Eucharist which is taking place in very evocative surroundings.

The labourers are few:
a problem of yesterday,
today and tomorrow

The labourers are few: this was the problem facing Jesus in entrusting to his disciples the task of preaching the Gospel to the people; the same problem arises in our own day, ever present, ever pressing. Innumerable people, scattered throughout the whole world, are awaiting the word of salvation. So it's a problem of yesterday, of today, of always.

The peoples of the earth are continually increasing in number and they yearn, with greater or lesser awareness, to discover the fundamental values which give sense to human life. And how many, having welcomed the Gospel, run the risk of forgetting, besieged as they are on every side by alluring and often false prospects; they need someone, therefore, to help them to relive the word of Jesus. What is more, the truth that is to be communicated is so rich and vast that it needs to be deepened all the time in order to extract all its preciousness and to relish all its sweetness. These few points, inspired by today's Gospel, are enough to let us foresee how necessary it is to pray incessantly to 'the Lord of the harvest to send labourers for his harvest'.

A message of hope
and consolation

The message to be announced is above all a message of salvation for mankind: '**Tell them: the kingdom of God is at hand**' (Luke 10:9). The kingdom of God, which is the victory of his love over all sin and human misery, is already among you. It is, as well, a message of hope and of consolation, as the prophet Isaiah had foretold: 'Rejoice with Jerusalem... as a mother consoles her son, so will I console you... You shall see and your heart shall rejoice' (Isaiah 66:13-14). Man in fact is destined to realise in Christ the Redeemer the fulness of his own divine vocation. It is a message too of peace and of charity: 'First say peace to this house... heal the sick you find there' (Luke 10:5-9). The kingdom of God is being constructed in history, already offering on this earth its fruits of conversion, unity, love among men.[2]

Carry no purse, nor haversack, nor sandals

(*Eucharist of Pope John Paul II with a group of young men from the Neocatechumenal Communities preparing to enter the seminary, the Vatican Gardens, 3rd July 1983; from the homily –* Translated from the Italian edition of *L'Osservatore Romano*, 7th July 1983, with additional material from a tape recording.)

What should the **apostle** be like, with what kind of spirit will he carry out his mission? He should, in the first place, be aware of the difficulties and sometimes the hostile reality which awaits him: 'I am sending you out like lambs amidst wolves' (Luke 10:3). This reality is opposed to the work of the evil one.

Glory only in the Cross of Christ

That is why the apostle will strive to be free from human conditioning of every nature: 'Carry no purse, no haversack, no sandals' (Luke 10:4), he will rely solely on the **Cross of Christ** from where our redemption comes, as St Paul says in the second reading. To glory in the cross means to abandon every motive for personal boasting, in order to live only on faith and in rendering thanks for the salvation brought about the sacrifice of Jesus. What becomes crucified is the world of personal selfishness, of self sufficiency, of taking security in one's own worth.

Dear seminarians and young people, the mission of the apostle is a sublime mission, looking enthusiastically to the good of the whole world; it requires a great deal of generosity, which is far beyond the capacity of man. We must therefore turn towards heaven, invoking the divine assistance, which you can ask for with confidence through the intercession of the Mother of Jesus and our Mother.

I hope that you will be apostles who are full of joy

May you be apostles who are happy in exercising your mission, because you are aware, because you trust, because you are spiritually free. The disciples sent by Jesus 'returned full of joy' (Luke 10:17). You too, during these years of preparation for the priesthood, will learn the art of being joyful, not out of human motives, but based on the certainty that **'your names are written in heaven'** (Luke 10:20) because you have been predestined by the love of Christ Jesus. He has called you from your families, from the womb

2. For the continuation of this speech see the section below.

of your ecclesial communities, to make you his co-labourers, his priests, his administrators of his divine mysteries.

Joy is the work of the Holy Spirit in us (cf. Gal 5:22). To his interior guidance, to his powerful and unfailing support, you entrust your vocation so that it can mature *in pace et gaudio* to bear the abundant fruits of eternal life.

Vocations are a sure proof of the authenticity, the maturity, of every Church

(*John Paul II: private audience with young men from the Neocatechumenal Communities preparing for the priesthood, the Vatican, 31st March 1985* – Translated from the Italian edition of *L'Osservatore Romano*, "Young Neocatechumenal men with the Pope on the way towards the priesthood", by C.D.L., 1st-2nd April 1985, with additional material from a tape recording.)

Yesterday, Sunday afternoon, the Sistine Chapel, crowded as never before, came alive with a long meeting held between the Pope and one thousand, two hundred and seven young men involved in the Neocatechumenal Way, a way which will lead them all to the priesthood. In presenting the assembly to the Holy Father, Kiko Argüello, who inspired the Neocatechumenal way, affirmed that the young men had gathered in Rome for the international gathering of young people and for the special meeting reserved for young men in the Neocatechumenate who had discovered their vocation to the priesthood through the way itself. Although they came from about seventy different countries, most of the young men were Latin Americans who were happy to be able to show John Paul II how they had welcomed his invitation made in Peru, during his visit to the "Continent of Hope", to "Go, return to your own countries and evangelise".

The Rome meeting of the Neocatechumens was described by the young men themselves as "an immersion into Baptism" and was divided into the deepening of three fundamental aspects of the way of future presbyters, centred on the liturgy, the sacramental aspect; the Word, the presbyter, a spouse, with special reflection on St Luke chapter 9; the Church. Special mention was made of the rediscovery of the local Church.

It was Kiko himself who later explained to the Holy Father how the group was made up and the place of origin of the individual participants. There emerged a complete and detailed picture of the commitment undertaken by the Neocatechumenal communities throughout the world to bring to birth and deepen vocations of special consecration. And today there are many young men who reach the seminary thanks to the Neocatechumenal way. This was shown by two of those present who spoke of their own experience. One of them was from Santo Domingo and the other was from Munich in Bavaria. The Brazilian Bishop of Jundai, Roberto Pinarello de Almeida, on the other hand said that the seminary in his diocese had taken on the methodology of the Neocatechumenal way in the formation of seminarians. The 'tripod' of the Word, the Liturgy and Community is a very efficacious nourishment for the seminarian who puts himself at the service of the Church, for the Church.

These are the Pope's words:

I would like to sum up for you the thoughts which I have had during this meeting. I also have here a prepared text, but I won't read it because these thoughts which are spontaneous, sudden, are more to the point. We have done a little geography and statistics. We have been around the world, beginning with Mexico, the whole of Central America, the Antilles, Latin America, I was thinking that we would stay in these parts, but we left Latin America and went to Oceania, to Australia, Japan, China, Taiwan. And I don't know why we never went to that great country between China and Poland. Then we went to various European countries and I heard that Italy also is quite well represented, not just Spain. Poland a little less but there are also seminarians from that country, thanks be to God.

We are instruments of the Holy Spirit

While this geography and statistics was going on, I was thinking that we should always refer, even in statistical matters, to spiritual things, to the Holy Spirit: there is one statistic which is only recognised through its person and its mysterious working in the soul. We are all instruments, and sacramental, holy, instruments of its workings but what is important is its workings. The instrument is always of secondary importance, even thought it is necessary. It is necessary because the Church is not the heavenly Church, it is the Church on earth, it is the Church of men, and men are called to make up the Church. The call is needed, Christ did it that way, he called. He himself started to preach, to evangelise, but he soon called, from the very first days. This process of vocation, of the call, must be repeated. In fact, this process of vocation is a certain proof of the authenticity and maturity of a Church, both in a universal and a specific and local sense.

Vocations are a sign of the vitality of the Church

I remember that in the days of my youth and later when I was Bishop of Cracow, each parish evaluated itself according to the vocations it had, vocations to the priesthood and to the religious life. This was a sign of the vitality, a sign of the maturity of the Church.[3]

3. For the continuation of this speech see the section below.

The vocations that arise from the Neocatechumenal Communities are a guarantee of the authenticity of the Way

(John Paul II: private audience with young men from the Neocatechumenal Communities preparing for the priesthood, the Vatican, 31st March 1985 – Translated from the Italian edition of L'Osservatore Romano, 1st-2nd April 1985, with additional material from a tape recording.)

I am getting to know your movement, your Neocatechumenal movement, more and more and in different circumstances, always briefly, but from these fragments a whole is made up. I would like therefore to say what seems to me to be important.

Baptism, the first consecration

You are a Neocatechumenal movement, it means a movement that puts the sacrament of Baptism in the centre of what we can call your 'spirituality'. You put Baptism at the centre of your spirituality. What does Baptism mean? It means many things, but amongst these things which make up the whole of a great theology of sacred Baptism, there is one. It is the first consecration of the human person to God, in Jesus Christ: the first consecration. Of course, there are many, many people baptised in the world who have little or no awareness of this, which is the first consecration. If anyone then makes an examination, a deep and existential examination, a truly religious examination of his Baptism, he must, once at least, find himself confronted by this reality: I am a person consecrated to God! In this first, principal and fundamental consecration, it is easier to rediscover one's vocation whether it is to the priesthood or to the religious life. This does not in any way mean a lesser appreciation of the Christian in general, of the Christian vocation as such, of the vocation of all the laity, in fact you have as your guide a layman. St Francis of Assisi did not want to be a priest and only accepted ordination as a deacon. Every Christian vocation is marked, is signed, by this consecration of the person, of the man and the woman to God.

If this is understood, it is easier to understand that vocation in which man, starting with his initiative, of course guided by divine grace, offers himself to the service of God, of Christ, of the Church. He dedicates himself to complete and total service, in consecration in the priesthood and in consecration in the religious life. Two somewhat different but convergent consecrations.

It does not surprise me that in your Way there are vocations

And this is a fruit of meditation on and a deepening of the mystery of Baptism, so I am not surprised that there are vocations in your movement. It confirms that your movement is authentic and corresponds to its nature and its name. This then is the main thing I wanted to say to you.[4]

An itinerant vocation

(*John Paul II: private audience with young men from the Neocatechumenal Communities preparing for the priesthood, the Vatican, 31st March 1985* – Translated from the Italian edition of *L'Osservatore Romano*, 1st-2nd April 1985, with additional material from a tape recording.)

Now a third thing, related rather to this occasion. We are in the Sistine Chapel, renowned, above all, for the wonderful paintings like Michelangelo's *Last Judgement*. It is known too for an event: here in this Chapel conclaves are held and Popes are elected, the Bishops of Rome. The last time the Cardinals who were present in a greater number than ever before, elected an unknown Pope, but they elected a Pope who rediscovered an itinerant vocation. And so we are itinerants. And this is another aspect of your Movement.

The Church of the apostles was, of course, itinerant, and the most itinerant amongst the apostles was certainly St Paul.

The apostolic and itinerant Church. We are all pilgrims

But today also the Church is itinerant, all are itinerants, even those who never move house or move to another place in their lives, because we are all pilgrims, and pilgrim means something even more than itinerant. We are all pilgrims in the Holy Spirit, pilgrims going towards the Father's house. And Christ guides us through the Holy Spirit.

I would like to add yet another observation. Here in this Chapel many prayers are said, and around this Chapel, throughout the world, many prayers are said at the time of the death of a Pope and the election of his successor. I want to end this meeting by praying with you to the Holy Spirit for vocations which are so necessary to the Church. We, too, compile statistics related to the universal Church and we have to do so. In fact, yesterday with Monsignor Sostituto we were speaking with the representatives of the Statistics Office of the Church. The Church today must make great efforts in prayer, in contact with the Holy Spirit to stay alive, to keep up the number of vocations, because this number, in some countries of the world, in some churches

4. For the continuation of this speech see the section below.

is threatened, and in other churches has been insufficient for some time.

Let us end by reciting a mystery of the Rosary, a mystery of the Holy Spirit, the third glorious mystery, because here in this Chapel you ought to recite the mystery which refers to the Holy Spirit. We will recite it in Latin; you are seminarians, so you ought to know Latin.

You are here reflecting, praying and thinking about the mission of the Church in the world

(*John Paul II: audience with young people from the Neocatechumenal Communities, Rome, Palm Sunday, 27th March 1988* – Translated from *Avvenire:'E in 65 dicono "Eccomi"'*, by Giuseppe Gennarini, 29th March 1988.)

After twenty years of deep crisis, vocations are beginning to reappear in the Catholic Church. A sign of what is happening was seen the day before yesterday, Palm Sunday, during a meeting in the Paul VI Hall of twelve thousand cantors and young people from the Neocatechumenal Communities with the Holy Father.

While they were waiting for the arrival of the Holy Father, Kiko Argüello, who with Carmen Hernández and Fr. Mario Pezzi, is one of the initiators of the Neocatechumenal Way, rehearsed with the young people the songs for the Paschal Triduum and the Vigil, which the Neocatechumens celebrate throughout the night and which they consider to be the pivot of the whole of baptismal spirituality. After the entrance of the Holy Father, a life-sized wooden sculpture of Christ crucified, a gift of the communities of Ecuador, was brought in procession, accompanied by seminarians of the Roman college 'Redemptoris Mater' carrying palm branches, to preside over the meeting. "Carrying Christ crucified in the world is a new dimension of love", said Kiko in the presence of the Pope. "Christ crucified is good news, not an example of oppression or masochism. The world today wants to do away with the crucifix and lives terrified of any kind of suffering. Christ has opened a way through death. We suffer precisely because we do not love in this way, giving ourselves totally to the other. Is it possible to love like this? Yes, because he gives us his nature and from heaven sends his Holy Spirit which has overcome death and gives us eternal life within us, a new life which allows us to love the other with his defects over and above death. To love like this is happiness. How can we not bring this water to the desert that is the world of today?"

Kiko then invited those who had heard the call to the priesthood or the contemplative life to stand up, and sixty five young people went to kneel in front of the Holy Father (forty young men for the seminary and twenty five young women to enter enclosed convents)...

To see this reflowering of vocations is a surprise. In the last three years more than two thousand young people from the Neocatechumenal Communities have entered various seminaries throughout the world to prepare for the priesthood. A diocesan college, Redemptoris Mater has been opened in Rome to form presbyters for the 'New Evangelisation' called for by John Paul II. These future presbyters, without forming a congregation, but belonging to their dioceses and supported by their own communities, will go with the families who have finished the period of Neocatechumenal formation and who have offered themselves in their hundreds to go and evangelise in the poorest, the most miserable and most dechristianised areas of the world...

Here follow the words of the Pope. (Cf. *L'Osservatore Romano*, 28-29th March 1988.)

With today, Palm Sunday, we have begun Holy Week and, at the same time, we have celebrated the third World Youth Day. This morning, in St Peter's Square we celebrated both. I am very happy to find myself among you, young people, to find myself singing, because this is a day of song: *Pueri hebraeorum portantes ramos olivarum...* We know this antiphon for Palm Sunday very well. It is a day for you young people; for singing: 'Hosannah! Blessed is He who comes in the name of the Lord!' It is a day characterised by the announcement of the Prophets. But we know well that inside this joyful and exultant celebration of the Palms, the Church is leading us by the hand to the Passion of Christ. This transitory joy covers and hides in itself the mystery of the Passion and of the cross that is the paschal mystery.

You have met here to discover the mystery of the cross

On this day you have met not only to sing like the young people of Jerusalem, but to discover the figure of the crucified one, of Jesus, who is on the cross, in agony. This afternoon you have prayed for many hours. You have meditated and prayed. Entering into the mystery of Palm Sunday, the mystery of the passion of Christ, of the Cross and of his Resurrection, you have thought together about the Church and the mission of the Church, because Christ died on the cross to give new life to humanity.

As the Fathers said, the Church was founded above all in the moment of his death; our salvation flowed out from his side. Symbolically a new reality opens up, a new divine mission which embraces humanity. This is how the Church is born, that, as the Second Vatican Council says, is 'in

Christ as a sacrament... of intimate union with God and of the unity of the whole human race' (LG, 1).

The paschal mystery is the foundation of the mission of the Church

Jesus prepared his Apostles for this moment. In fact, after the resurrection, with his pierced hands, feet and side, he came to his Apostles to give them the Holy Spirit and to announce this mission that was awaiting them, was awaiting this new Israel, of which they, the Apostles, are the beginning and the prefiguration.

And so the Church begins to fulfil its mission and becomes missionary. If we think seriously about the paschal mystery of Christ, we cannot separate the Church from its mystery and its mission. You are here reflecting on, thinking and praying about the mission of the Church throughout the world. This mission needs missionaries, needs Apostles. Missionaries continue the mission of the apostles. The Second Vatican Council says that by its nature the Church is missionary. Missionary means apostolic; means sent. You are living this moment of the call and the mission of the Church, which is made up of various charisms and ministries. The unique mission of the Church emerges, above all today, from the base of the lay apostolate. But priestly and religious vocations are needed for the Church and her mission. Here I have seen several young people who came forward spontaneously to say to this assembly: 'Here I am.' I thought immediately that this offering could not be made if not before God. But if it is made before men too, it is made above all in the family.

You are a family

And you are a family. If this choice can be made like this, spontaneously, under the power of the Holy Spirit, it means that you are a family. If, in fact, a young man, a young woman, can come forward in front of everyone and say in front of everyone and to Christ crucified, 'Here I am', it means that God loves you, God is calling you.[5]

May the Lord bless the work for vocations in your big family that is growing day by day

(*John Paul II: audience with young people from the Neocatechumenal Way, Palm Sunday, 27th March 1988* – cf. *Avvenire*, 29th March 1988.)

I am very aware, deeply aware of the grace of the priestly and the religious vocations. It is a grace for those who are called but, at the same time, a gift for the community, for

5. The text continues below.

117

the Church, for her mission and for her durability. If the Church, as the Second Vatican Council reminds us, is a priestly people, if all the faithful have a priesthood in common, that comes from baptism, then we see all the more the need for those who are called to the priesthood to arouse awareness of this common priesthood and to express this priestly characteristic that belongs to all the partners; and then to serve. In fact the priesthood is a very important ministry.

The vocation: to follow Christ – poor, virgin and obedient

We know this from negative and painful experience because of the lack of priestly and religious vocations. The Church cannot be herself if she does not aspire to the Kingdom of Heaven, indeed, if she does not anticipate this Kingdom of Heaven here, on earth. People, men and women, need to be able to follow the poor Christ, the virgin Christ, Christ obedient to death. These are fundamental, essential, constitutive aspects of the Church.

Vocations: proof of the authentic catholicity of the local Churches, the parishes, families

When there are priestly and religious vocations, there is proof of the authentic catholicity of the local Churches and of the parishes, and also of Christian families. At one time, and perhaps also today, families boasted of having priests and religious among their sons and daughters. The family, we know, is the domestic Church, the living and life-giving cell of the Church. I have told you what I have in my heart. I am grateful to the parents, to the families and to the communities that are able to cultivate and to bring vocations to maturity always and everywhere. I am grateful to your families and your communities that are concerned to raise up, to cultivate and to bring vocations to maturity. May our crucified and risen Lord bless this vocational work of your great family that is growing day by day. May our Lord give to everyone a deep and courageous Christian vocation: to the couples, the vocation of marriage, of the couple, of the family, of parents, of educators; to those who feel another call inside, the capacity to follow the priestly and religious vocation, welcoming this gift of the Holy Spirit that always comes from the pierced heart of Our Saviour who hangs on the cross.

New evangelisers

(John Paul II: inauguration of the 'Redemptoris Mater' Archdiocesan Seminary, Santo Domingo, 11th October 1992 – Translated from the Italian edition of *L'Osservatore Romano,* 12-13th October 1992.)

The 'Redemptoris Mater'
Seminaries:
a contribution to the
work of the new
evangelisation

It gives me particular joy to be able to inaugurate, on such an important date, in Santo Domingo, the Missionary Archdiocesan Seminary 'Redemptoris Mater', which, in recognition of the 5th Centenary of the arrival of the Good News in America, wishes to make a contribution to the great work of the new evangelisation to which I have called the universal Church.

This centre, which has accepted candidates from many countries of the American continent, from Europe and from other nations, should always be animated by a missionary spirit that may be a ferment in this archdiocese and throughout the Dominican Republic, and which will launch itself all over the world following the command of the Lord: 'Go and preach the Gospel to every creature' (Mk 16:15). This was seen also in the Second Vatican Council, in the decree on the ministry and life of priests: 'The spiritual gift which presbyters have received in their ordination is not to prepare them for a limited and restricted mission, but for an enormously vast and universal mission of salvation "to the ends of the earth" (Acts, 1:8), (*Presbyterorum Ordinis*, 10).

The presence on this island, which received the seeds of the gospel preaching and from where the saving light of Jesus Christ radiated to the rest of America, of seminarians of such varying origins is also a sign of how, on the threshold of the Third Christian Millennium, from this Archdiocesan Seminary 'Redemptoris Mater' in Santo Domingo can also spread out new evangelisers who will bring Jesus Christ, 'the Way, the Truth and the Life', to the whole world.

While I raise up fervent prayers that Mary, the Star of the Evangelisation, will lead all those who receive their priestly formation in this Seminary to her son, I give to everyone, with great affection, my Apostolic Blessing.

The necessary discovery of life as a vocation as a consequence of the deepening of the sense of Baptism

(*John Paul II: audience with 8,000 young people from the Neocatechumenal Way who were taking part in a day of preparation for the World Youth Day in Denver, Rome, Vatican City, 28th March 1993* – Translated from *L'Osservatore Romano*, 29-30th March 1993.)

When I saw this crowd – certainly a big gathering – and when I learned that all of you were getting ready to go to Denver, I thought, 'But where do these find the money they need? Or maybe they intend to go on foot or by swimming, but it's difficult to imagine they would do that...'

I know that you have been here all day in this hall. I

don't know what you've been doing here all day long, nor have I asked. But I've seen this last stage, the presentation of vocations, and looking at this it would be possible to say, 'See how Kiko makes vocations.' But, thank God, it is not Kiko who makes them; it is the Holy Spirit who makes them – maybe this is not the correct word, but once it has been used it has to be used here too. It is the Holy Spirit who makes these vocations through these different human means: through this movement – oh! not a movement but a Way. All this organisational structure is human, is visible, but it is open to the influence, to the inspiration of the Holy Spirit.

I ask myself where is the nucleus of this process that, through the Neocatechumenal Way, through different people, through different circumstances, produces, gives rise to, inspires vocations to the priesthood, and to the consecrated, the religious life. I am convinced that the *punctum saliens*, the point of departure for all this is the discovery of the richness, of the divine and sacramental depth of Baptism. Our first vocation is that of Baptism. In holy Baptism, in this sacrament *ex aqua et Spiritu Sancta*, in this rebirth in the death and Resurrection of Christ are found all the vocations, rooted there. And a profound discovery, lived from Baptism, brings with it as a possible, indeed a necessary consequence, the discovery of life as vocation.

Here can be understood the sense of the name: Neocatechumenal Way. In the first centuries of the Church there was the traditional Catechumenate and it still exists in mission countries and it is a great good for the Church: it prepares Christians, prepares vocations. You were baptised when you were babies, perhaps in the first days of your life. For the discovery of the riches of holy Baptism, the many divine and also human riches, the Catechumenate has to come afterwards. St Paul described them, especially in the *Letter to the Romans*, but today it would be possible to write a much wider, a much more detailed commentary about these riches which are proper to Baptism, which are divine and human riches together. One of these riches is precisely that Baptism is not static. It would be possible to do it once and be finished with it. It happens at one moment of one's life and then it is finished. It is registered in the parish records and is over and done with. But instead, no, it is not static, it is dynamic: it provokes, it opens up a way in the Christian life. But this way can remain undiscovered. Your Neocatechumenal Way helps to discover this baptismal way – this way that begins with Baptism – and which ought to bring each one of us to a vocation, above all to the universal Christian vocation. To be a Christian is already a stupendous vocation and then we know very well that in this Christian vocation that is for all believers, all the baptised, there are different vocations. Marriage, certainly, is sacrament and vocation. To consider it using other categories is not an adequate way to deal with it, is not the suitably Christian way of dealing with it. Marriage is a great vocation: *sacramentum magnum*, as St Paul says in the *Letter to the Ephesians*.

But there is an economy in the Church, a supernatural economy, and vocations are ordered for the good of the Church. These vocations which we have seen presented here today are necessary, indispensable, for the good of the Church. They are indispensable, and we know very well how indispensable are priests in the Church and from an other point of view how indispensable are consecrated persons, religious, contemplative and apostolic. In a certain sense all are active and in a certain sense all are contemplative. How indispensable they are for the life of this organism that is the Church.

There, I wanted briefly to make a short comment on this assembly of yours today, on this preparation of yours for the meeting in Denver. It is a good thing that you are preparing yourselves because this experience of Denver will surely be a great experience of faith, of baptismal faith, as the other World Youth days have been: Rome, Buenos Aires, then Santiago de Compostela, and lastly Czestochowa.

I hope that you will continue for a long time on the way of Christian life, of Christian vocation

I hope that you will go on for a long time on this way that you have discovered thanks to the Neocatechumenal Way, this way of Christian life, of Christian vocation that each one of us has, and then I hope that you will go on with this way of vocation to the priesthood or to the consecrated life that you have discovered thanks to this Neocatechumenal Way. And I hope that you will go to Denver, even if you are not very rich; you will find the a means. I don't now how, but you will find it.

Way also means journey; so I wish you a good journey.

The 'Redemptoris Mater' Seminary

(Homily of the Holy Father John Paul II, during the Eucharist with the Seminarians of the 'Redemptoris Mater' of Rome, on the 31st October 1993, in the 'Redemptoris Mater' chapel, Vatican City – Translated from the Italian edition of L'Osservatore Romano, with some additional material taken from a tape recording.)

Praised be Jesus Christ!

Venerable Brothers in the Episcopate and in the Priesthood, **brothers and sisters**!

'Like a mother feeding and looking after her own children, we felt so devoted to you' (1 Th 2:7): **the words of St Paul to the Thessalonians**.

Every presbyter should be able to make his own these words that we have just listened to. *The maternal image* that he applies to himself is in fact one of the most evocative there is for expressing *the beauty of the priestly vocation.* Not only does it show a rare intensity of affection and dedication but it also suggests the intimate connection that exists between the apostolic ministry and the mystery of the *new 'birth'* in Christ through the Holy Spirit (cf. John 3:5-8). **The mother who looks after her own offspring, the mother who feeds them**.

As bearer of the 'divine word of the preaching', the Apostle sees himself as *instrument of this spiritual regeneration,* **sees himself as a mother.** For the brothers and sisters he incarnates the 'maternity' of the Church. Having been called to gestate them in Christ through the Gospel (cf. 1 Co 4:15), he rightly feels himself to be **not only a father but also a mother to them**; 'father' and 'mother', ready to give not only the Gospel, but his 'whole life' for them (cf. 1 Th 2:8).

What a difference between this image of the apostolate and that which emerges in the other two readings, which are full of severe and cutting admonishments! These are directed to the priests of the Old Covenant, to the scribes and the pharisees, but point out the risks of deviation which lie in ambush in our ministry too.

'But you, you have strayed from the way; you have caused many to stumble by your teaching' (Ml 2:8).

These words of the prophet Malachi underline the great responsibility of the ministers of the altar and the Word. Their inconsistency is doubly serious because it is accompanied by scandal. Alas for those who should be the educators of God's people and instead are a stumbling block for them!

No less harsh are the words of Jesus addressed to those who are seated on the chair of Moses, not as *humble servants of the Word of God* but as *avid seekers after the applause* of men. In them, word and life are in strident contrast: they are teachers of what they do not practise, they impose burdens that they themselves do not dare to carry, they claim a title – that of 'rabbi' – that does not belong to them, because there is 'only one Teacher, the Christ' (cf. Mt 23:10).

Here the Word of God presents us with, on the one hand, the

(NOTE: The eucharist was of the 31st Sunday in the year. The sections in **bold** type are the spontaneous words of the Holy Father and were not in the original printed text; the sections in *italic* were so in the original text.)

authentic model of the priestly and apostolic vocation and, on the other, with the ways in which it can become *degenerate*. **The Word of God of this liturgy** is very apposite for this meeting with you, 'Redemptoris Mater', superiors and students, clerics, of the Roman seminary **which has taken the same name as this chapel: 'Redemptoris Mater'. It reminds us very much of the redemption, of 'Redemptor Hominis', 'Redemptoris Mater', 'Redemptoris Custos' and also 'Redemptoris Missio', all of them linked. So I greet the seminarians and the superiors of 'Redemptoris Mater' in this chapel dedicated to the Redemptoris Mater.**

I greet the Cardinal Vicar of Rome, Camillo Ruini, who in a certain sense has the prime responsibility for your Seminary since, while defining itself by its *missionary purpose*, it has taken shape as a *Seminary of the Diocese of Rome* – **which it is**. I greet your Rector, Mgr. Giulio Salimei, and your Spiritual Director, Mgr. Maximino Romero de Lema, **and I thank both of them, after many years of work in the Roman Curia and the Roman Vicariate, for having taken on these important educational responsibilities in 'Redemptoris Mater'**. I greet all of you, my very dear seminarians, I greet you individually, **seeing in you future priests, who have already made a choice**, and who have begun a journey towards the priesthood **of Christ**.

It is significant and important that you have discovered your priestly vocation while following *the Neocatechumenal Way* and that now you are doing your formation in accordance – as ought to be the case – with the directions given by the Church for all candidates for the Priesthood. The end to which you are directed is to be deeply *rooted in Christ*, accompanied by a total and heart-felt adherence to the Church. This is the irreplaceable basis of an authentic priestly formation and it is also the guarantee of God's blessing **in this way that is priestly and Neocatechumenal, Neocatechumenal and missionary, apostolic and missionary**.

And so it is with joy that I learn that *many other vocations* like yours are flowering in the path of your spirituality, **the Neocatechumenal Way, not only here in Rome but in other places, in different countries in Europe and throughout the world**. It is precisely in the deepening of the spiritual life **characteristic of this way**, that there is found, in accepting an *'evangelical radicalism'*, fertile soil for a vocation to bloom. God never stops calling, but only a profound intimacy with Christ allows us to hear his voice, to welcome it with alacrity and follow it with perseverance.

(We need to have a profound awareness of the fact that) there can be no 'generators' of faith who have not first been 'generated' in faith themselves. Paul could announce Christ because he could say in all truth: 'It is no longer I who live but Christ who lives in me' (Gal 2:20). **This is why he could announce Christ, because** he had been generated in Christ first, was one with Christ, permeated with Christ. 'It is no longer I who live, but Christ who lives in me'. So when he feels himself to be and calls himself 'father' of his communities, he is not claiming an undeserved title, as prohibited in today's Gospel, because his paternity was nothing other than a transparent manifestation of the paternity of God. **At the same time he calls himself 'mother' and indeed gave a certain precedence to the apostolic maternity which was precisely his attitude towards these communities**.

In fact the ministry of the priesthood has to be understood in its intimate connection with the mystery of Christ. All the Church is called in some way to make Christ 'visible', **present** in the history of men, but this is the task **above all of the priest**, of the presbyter, who is called to act *in persona Christi*, called to represent him as 'shepherd' and 'head' of his people, **of his flock, of his community**.

The priest has to be a person conquered, '*captured*' by Christ (cf. Ph 3:12). It is a truly 'great' ministry even if it is a greatness characterised by the humility of service: 'The greatest among you must be your servant' **as Jesus says** (cf. Mt 23:11).

In this chapel of the Redemptoris Mater I greet you once again. I feel very happy to be able to celebrate this Eucharist with you and I offer it to the Lord for your perseverance. May God help you to walk on the ways of holiness, of joy, towards all the peoples to whom his Providence will lead you.

It's good that the Cardinal Vicar has given us this free Sunday: no parish in Rome to be visited! Beside the Roman Seminary there is the 'Redemptoris Mater': it is worth having this Sunday free!

I wish for you the presence, **the support of Mary, the Most Holy Mother of the Redeemer. If you entrust yourself to her, to her maternity, you really will feel 'tranquil and quiet', like 'children in the arms of their mother' (the words of today's responsorial psalm). May Mary obtain for you the grace to be able to spend yourselves for the Kingdom of God with the ardour of the apostle Paul, in obedience and total fidelity to the Church**, to the Church who is also Mother, as all of Tradition and the second Vatican Council teach us: the Church is also Mother, in imitation of the Mother of Christ. This Church generates you, **she has generated you in faith and in this Church you are called to be presbyters, to serve to the end of your days. May this be so.**

APPENDICES

The Neocatechumenal Way: a brief synthesis[1]
(by Kiko Argüello and Carmen Hernández)

The Lord has called us to live a way of conversion, through which we are coming to discover the immense riches of our faith in a post-baptismal catechumenate. During this catechumenate, gradually, stage by stage, step by step, we are descending to the waters of eternal regeneration, so that the baptism the Church has conferred on us in the past, may by our adherence to it, become a sacrament of salvation, good news for all men. Through the Neocatechumenate, a way of Christian initiation that develops **a pastoral work of evangelisation for adults** is opened up at the centre of the parish. This evangelisation is bringing to a living faith many of our brothers and sisters who today live a Christianity of habit, and is giving to many people submerged in a secularised world the possibility of meeting Our Lord Jesus Christ through Christian communities which live their faith at an adult level: of love in the dimension of the cross and perfect unity.

How the Neocatechumenal Communities came into being

This way began in Madrid in 1962 among the slum dwellers of the shanty town 'Palomeras Altas'. Kiko Argüello and Carmen Hernández had gone there, called by the Lord to live their Christianity among the poor, really sharing the lives of those who, in their misery, bear the consequences of the sins of our society. They were then asked, by the very people with whom they were living, to proclaim to them **the good news** of our Saviour Jesus

---

1. These notes by Kiko Argüello and Carmen Hernández are taken from a brief document giving information on the Neocatechumenal Way that was prepared for Pope Paul VI in 1974, and which was also presented, with slight variations, to the Plenary Assembly of the Congregation for the Evangelisation of Peoples in 1983.

Christ. This word, at first weak and stammering, because it is difficult to preach the Gospel to people without culture or education, began to take shape in a catechetical synthesis: a powerful **kerygma** which, in the measure in which it descended upon these poor people, brought about the birth of a new reality: **koinonia**.

To our astonishment, we witnessed **a word** which, taking flesh among these poor people who welcomed it with joy, brought to birth a **community** in prayer and a surprising **liturgy** as the response of all these brothers, laden with sins, who blessed the Lord for having remembered them. So, in the space of three years, we saw appearing before our eyes a tripod on which would be based the Way that the Lord was creating: the embryo of a Catechumenate, in a Church where fraternal communion was coming into being, in which love took on a dimension which surprised everyone: the dimension of the cross where one dies for the enemy.

How they spread

This love, made visible in a small community, was **the sign** which called to faith many people whose lives were far from the Church. The result was that the parish priests of St Frontis in Zamora and of Christ the King in Madrid invited us to bring to their parishes the experience of the catechesis they had observed. To our surprise, even in these parishes where the social environment was quite different from that of the shanty town, we saw how communities on a way towards conversion were born after the announcement of the **kerygma** and two months of catechesis.

When the Archbishop of Madrid at that time, the Most Rev. Mgr Casimiro Morcillo, came into contact with this reality, he supported it enthusiastically, and he himself sent us to the parishes who wished to begin the experience, while urging us to act in union with the parish priest. This experience spread rapidly in Madrid and other Spanish dioceses.

In 1968, we were invited to come to Rome, bearing a letter from the Archbishop of Madrid for Cardinal Dell'Acqua, then Vicar of Rome, and we began the same catechesis in the parish of Canadian Martyrs. It then spread throughout the diocese, through the preaching of catechists elected by the first communities, and in many other countries, in all the continents, including the missionary countries.

Itinerant catechists

Very soon requests from parish priests in other dioceses gave rise to the charism of itinerant catechists. They leave their own communities for a certain time, and make themselves available to take the Neocatechumenate to the dioceses who ask for it.

Many teams of itinerant catechists, after an experience of evangelisation in their own country, have been called by the Lord to open the way in other nations, from whom numerous requests have come – from bishops and parish priests – particularly since 1972 onward.

One of the greatest experiences we have today, and one for which we bless the Lord, is to see how God allows us to announce the Gospel in so many parts of the world. And not only do we proclaim the **kerygma**, but a community-based way for the gestation of faith appears, through which, with time, the parish can pass from pastoral work concentrated on the sacraments to one of evangelisation.

A concrete way of evangelising those who are far-away

The Neocatechumenal Way is lived out within the existing structure of the parish, and in communion with the bishop, in small communities each composed of people who are different in age, social status, outlook and culture. It is not a group formed spontaneously, neither is it an association, nor a spiritual movement, nor an elite within the parish. Rather, it is a group of people who wish to rediscover and to live Christian life to the full; to live the essential consequences of their Baptism, by means of a **Neocatechumenate** divided into different stages, like that of the early Church, but adapted to their condition as baptised persons. As a consequence, these communities have the mission of being, at the centre of the parish, the sign and sacrament of the missionary Church (*Synod of Bishops*); of opening a concrete way of evangelising the 'far- away', by giving – in the measure to which faith has been developed – the signs that call pagans to conversion; that is **love** in the dimension of the cross, and **unity**. 'Just as I have loved you, you must also love one another. By this love you have for one another, everyone will know that you are my disciples' (John 12:34-35). 'May they all be one. Father, may they all be one in us, as you are in me and I am in you, so that the world may believe it was you who sent me' (John 17:21).

Bringing the Council to the parishes

In the light of the Second Vatican Ecumenical Council, the Neocatechumenal Communities seemed to us a concrete way of rebuilding the Church in the form of small communities which are the **visible body of the risen Christ** in the world. They do not impose themselves; they consider it a duty not to destroy anything, but to respect everything. They present themselves as the fruit of a Church in renewal, one which tells its Fathers that they have been fruitful, for the communities have been born of them.

Charisms and ministries

Where the experience develops, one catches a glimpse of a new structure for the local Church, formed of small Christian communities like an organic body which, in the measure in which faith blossoms within her, brings charisms to maturity and requires ministries to help, to serve and to make such a renewal possible, since they are the means willed by God to make his Church grow constantly (Eph 4:11; 1 Cor 12). So we are seeing the charisms which make the complete Christ present; Christ the Apostle, the Prophet, the Deacon, the Pastor, the Teacher, faithful to the Father, united with his Church, compassionate towards all who suffer, etc. And these charisms appear in every community: in the presbyter, in the responsibles (for whom we have requested the diaconate), in the itinerant and local catechists, in the virgins, widows, married couples, etc.

THE NEOCATECHUMENAL PROCESS

The Spirit of the Way

The primary objective aimed at in this Neocatechumenate or initiation to faith is the formation of the community. The latter, at first, is very imperfect, for it is always conditioned by the adherence of the individual to the Word. Then, little by little, our own defects come to our aid, obliging us to constantly rethink our faith. Our inability to love others, that is, to accept in them what destroys us, namely their faults, raises a great question mark for us. To love begins to appear like the destruction of our self, that is, of what is our security. To love means to die, and our tragedy is that we do not want to die. To love the other when he is different from me will always mean a leap in the dark, it will mean to overcome death.

The second chapter of the letter to the Hebrews (Heb 2:14f), says that all his life man is enslaved to evil and the devil because of his fear of death: for this reason Jesus Christ has come 'to destroy through death the lord of death, the devil, and to set free all those who had been held in slavery all their lives by the fear of death' (Hebrews 2:14f).

If to love means really to transcend ourselves totally in the **other**, that is, to die to our self (and all of us are subjected to the devil during our lives because we are afraid of death), it is clear that if death has not been overcome in us by the resurrection of Jesus Christ, we cannot love. What then will the sign be that we have risen with Christ? **A love over and above death, love in the dimension of the cross, love for the enemy**, 'as I have loved you' (Jn 13:34-35). 'By this love everyone will know that you are my disciples.' This is why it is necessary to be born from God, to receive through the Holy spirit the new life of Christ risen from the dead. 'We know that we have passed out of death into life, and of this we can be sure because we love the brothers' (1 John 3:14).

Where are these communities born?

Where are they born, these communities which make the Risen Christ present by radiating the love they have gratuitously received? The answer is: in the **parish,** which seems the most suitable place for the local Church to appear as the 'sacrament of salvation', without creating a parallel Church, without destroying anything, gradually taking on the reality of the Church of today and the period of transition through which she is going.

The mission of the parish

Today, most traditional Christians live their faith at a childish level as is clearly shown by the divorce between religion and life in them. Hence the absolute necessity for a serious process of conversion which takes place in our everyday experience. It is a time, guided by the Word of God and by celebrations of Penance and the Eucharist, and lived within the concrete framework of a community, to experience Christ the Saviour, to experience the Kingdom of God which is reaching out to us, and to experience the joy of peace.

To arrive at this, it is necessary to give signs of faith in the surrounding situation, signs which make Christ present and credible, and signs which clearly show the man in the street that Christ loves him to the point of being ready to free him from his alienation, from his suffering, from death.

'Just as I have loved you, you must also love one another. By this love you have for one another, everyone will know that you are my disciples.' 'Father, may they be one in us, as you are in me and I am in you, so that the world (the man in the street) may believe it was you who sent me.'

The signs of faith call the parish to conversion. Through the love and unity of these communities the whole parish is called to conversion so that it can be seen that where these communities have been formed, the parish has been revolutionised in a positive way. The signs they create around them raise questions marks and as a result call many people who were far from the Church to enter similar communities in the parish. In this way, a new parochial structure has begun to appear; without destroying the existing one, it makes all brothers aware of the absolute need today for a deepening of the faith.

It is the return to the community, to the **people of God** of the early Church: communities in which the signs of love in the dimension of the Cross and of perfect unity act as yeast, light, and salt, on the surrounding environment. Once again, the cry, 'See how they love one another' arises among men, calling them to conversion.

How the Way begins

When a parish priest wishes to start this Catechumenal Way in his parish, he contacts parishes in which Neocatechumenal Communities already exist. Once he is aware of what the Way is about, and if he agrees to be involved in it himself, he asks for catechists to be sent to him. They undertake to begin the Neocatechumenate, and to guide it in communion with him. The catechists also speak to all the priests in the parish, presenting to them the necessity of undertaking a pastoral work of evangelisation in the parish, through a post-baptismal catechumenate. Then they meet the various parish groups. Finally, they issue an invitation to all the faithful during Sunday Mass. The team of catechists is made up of a priest who guarantees the orthodoxy and the ecclesiality of the announcement, a couple, and a young man, who make up a small community of evangelisation.

FIRST STAGE: THE KERYGMA

The first stage is the **kerygma**, the proclamation of salvation, which is developed by means of a direct and existential dialogue, which looks at the impact of Christianity on the lives of the people. The catecheses are based on a tripod upon which the whole catechumenate will be based: **Word-Liturgy-Community**.

The pre-catechumenate

Once the community has been formed, the second stage is started; the pre-catechumenate. This is a period of **kenosis** in which each of the brothers tests his faith by walking together with the others, also imperfect and sinners, in the newness of a concrete community which acts as a mirror, to show each one clearly his own reality, thus calling them to conversion.

In this labour, the community needs a word to enlighten it about its reality and to help it. Thus it celebrates the **Word of God** once a week, on appropriate themes – water, lamb, bride etc. – as an initiation into the language of the bible. The Sunday

Eucharist is celebrated on Saturday evenings.[2] Once a month the sacrament of **Penance** is celebrated. On one Sunday every month there is a retreat to give everyone the opportunity to talk freely about their own experience of the Word, to say how much it has influenced their lives: at work, in the family, in sexual matters, in social relationships, in connection with money, etc.

After about two years, the catechists who watched over the beginning of the community return, and in a three day retreat, prepare it for the first scrutiny for the passage to the catechumenate. In this scrutiny, in the presence of the bishop, the first part of their Baptism is put before the people, so that they can say 'Amen' and so that the grace that this sacrament conferred on them may grow and work. Thus the door of the catechumenate is opened to them.

SECOND STAGE:
THE POST-BAPTISMAL CATECHUMENATE

The catechumenate consists of two periods. During the first one, the community perseveres with the Word, the Eucharist, and brotherly communion, experiencing the power of Christ, who leads the Neocatechumens to put God at the centre of their lives, gradually stripping themselves, but without effort, of all idols (money, career, affections), while they keep watch, like the virgins waiting for the bridegroom. After about another year, the catechists return to prepare the scrutiny for the final entry into the catechumenate, so that if the first scrutiny could be compared to a door opening, at the second scrutiny the door closes. The catechumens are now initiated by the catechists into deep and daily individual prayer, with the presentation of the psalms to them. Then, through the *Traditio* and *Redditio Symboli,* they

---

2.   The pastoral praxis in the Neocatechumenal Way of celebrating the Eucharist on Saturday evening is linked to modern liturgical reform. This was begun by the Holy Father Pope Pius XII, with the restoration of the Paschal Vigil to the night of Holy Saturday, which over the centuries had come to be anticipated on Holy Saturday morning. (Apostolic Constitution *Christus Dominus*, in AAS, 45, 1953, 23- 24.) The Second Vatican Council ratified the restoration and, consistent with it, offered the possibility of celebrating the Eucharist after Vespers of Saturday, resuming the way of calculating time in the ancient Hebrew and Christian tradition. (*Eucharisticum Mysterium,* n. 28; *General Norms on the liturgical year and the calendar,* n. 3; *Code of Canon Law*, n. 1248.) This restoration, welcomed from the beginning by the Neocatechumenate, has allowed people to experience the pedagogical richness which comes from linking the Eucharist to the Paschal Vigil and also the mystagogical richness of the Eucharist which on the one hand overflows from the sacrament of initiation and on the other, as a part of a post-baptismal Catechumenate, is experienced as food, source and culmination of the whole Christian life. This is why it is so essential in the Neocatechumenate. Finally, from a more practical point of view, it allows the parish priest to be at the centre and to harmonize all the catechetical process and the liturgical life of the parish with their various components. A fact not to be ignored, and one emphasised by many pastors, is that the young people of the Communities readily give up their dances and discotheques on Saturday nights to celebrate the Eucharist in community.

discover how the Baptism that was once given to them by the Church makes them people who are sent, witnessing to their faith where they work, in their families, and above all by working in the parish in an apostolate made explicit in the announcement of the Gospel, two by two, in the houses of their neighbourhood, and in the work of parish catechesis, etc.

At this stage of the Way, the members of the community become responsible for transmitting their faith to their children. So three kinds of meetings take place: one in the family with the participation of the children, another meeting is in the community, and finally there are meetings of all the parish communities for the great feasts, like the Passover Vigil.

We have discovered that the greatest joy and the centre of our life is in the celebration of Easter, in a great vigil which lasts until the rising of the morning star.

After this, the discovery of how baptism makes us children of God takes place through the rediscovery and the study of the Our Father in the context of deep and wonderful prayer in which we are taught to cry '**Abba, Father**!'

THIRD STAGE: ELECTION AND THE RENEWAL OF THE BAPTISMAL PROMISES

The period of the post-baptismal catechumenate leads the Neocatechumens to simplicity, to make themselves small, to abandon themselves to the will of the Father. This will enable them – always guided by the catechists in close union with the parish priest – to pass, by means of this abandonment, to a spirituality of praise and thanksgiving. They are then ready to start on the last stage of the way: election and the renewal of the baptismal promises. So they have passed through the three fundamental stages of Christian life: humility (precatechumenate), simplicity (post-baptismal catechumenate) and praise (election and the renewal of baptismal promises).

THE FAMILY OF NAZARETH: IMAGE OF THE NEOCATECHUMENAL COMMUNITIES

Nicodemus asks Jesus, 'How can a man be born when he is old? Can he enter a second time into his mother's womb and be born?' (John 3:4).

This sentence illustrates the spirit of the Neocatechumenal Communities: to return to the womb of the church, to go back to our Mother, the Virgin, so that she may regenerate in us the seed that we carry within us of baptism, and make it to grow. We call this time of gestation and growth, the Neocatechumenate. Mary, the image of the Church and of every Christian, receives the announcement of a joyous good news: the Messiah will be born in you. After she has accepted these words the Holy Spirit covers her with his shadow and begins the gestation of the new creature: Christ Jesus, who will gradually be formed until the day of his birth in Bethlehem. Annunciation, gestation, birth and hidden life in the little community of Nazareth where the child will grow until he reaches the age to undertake the mission that his Father has entrusted to him: these are the stages through which we ourselves wish to pass, convinced that, through them, the Church can be renewed, in order to give an answer to the new times and serve the modern world.

Christ, who has been constituted by God life-giving spirit, the first-born of a new creation, makes his work of salvation accessible to the world in the **Koinonia**, in the **Agape** of a people resurrected by him in a Church, a community of men who love one another, because of the Spirit poured over them, that is, **the Holy Spirit**.

The Neocatechumenate presents itself as a period of gestation, in the womb of the Church. In these people who, like Mary, say their 'Amen' to the annunciation of the Saviour, the Word begins to generate a new creation, the work of the Holy Spirit.

The Church is presented as a Mother who begets, gives birth, and brings up her children until they reach the stature of the new man of whom St Paul says, 'It is no longer I who live, it is Christ who lives in me' (Gal 2:20).

And this community, in which Christ makes himself visible, lives in **humility**, **simplicity and praise**, like the Holy Family of Nazareth, aware that it has a task to carry out: to give Christ time to grow in it in order to carry out the mission entrusted to him by God, the mission of the Servant of Yahweh.

Appendix II

Texts of the Congregation for Divine Worship on the Neocatechumenal Way

A COMMENT BY THE SACRED CONGREGATION FOR DIVINE WORSHIP

The following evaluation of the Neocatechumenate, given by the Sacred Congregation for Divine Worship, appeared in Latin in the Congregation's official journal Notitiae *(nn. 95-96, July-August 1974, page 229), after several meetings with those responsible in the Congregation on the subject of the rites of the Neocatechumenal Way. This comment followed the address of Pope Paul VI at the General Audience on 24th April 1974 (reported on page 228 of the same issue) and the address of the same Pope Paul VI to the parish priests and responsibles of the Neocatechumenal Communities in his audience of 8th May, 1974.*

Omnes reformationes in Ecclesia novos gignerunt inceptus novasque promoverunt instita, quae optata reformationis ad rem deduxerunt.

Ita evenit post Concilium Tridentinum; nec alter nunc fieri poterat. Instauratio liturgica profunde incidit in vitam Ecclesiae. Spiritualitas liturgica novos germinare flores sanctitatis et gratiae necesse est, nec non instensioris apostolatus catholici et actionis pastoralis.

Praeclarum exemplar huius renovationis invenitur in 'Communitatibus neo-catechumenabilus', quae ortum habuerunt Matriti, anno 1962, opera quotumdam iuvenum laicorum, Exc.mo Pastore Matritensi, Casimiro Morcillo, permittente, animante et benecidente, 'Communitates' eo tendunt ut in paroeciis signum existent Ecclesiae missionariae, viamque conantur aperire evangelizationi eorum, qui vitam christianam paene dereliquerunt.

Ad hunc finem Sodales quaerunt vitam liturgicam inensius

vivere, incipiendo a nova catechisi et praeparatione 'catechu-
menali', nempe percurrendo, spirituali itinere, omnes illas phases
quae in primaeva Ecclesia catechumeni percurebant antequam
sacramentum baptisti acciperent. Cum hic agatur non de
baptizandis, sed de baptizatis, catechesis eadem est, sed ritus
liturgici aptanatur situationi christianorum baptizatorum iuxta
suggestiones iam datas a Congregatione pro Culto Divino [1]

'Communitates' in paroeciis eriguntur, sub moderamine
parochi. Sodales semel vel bis in hebdomada coadunantur ad
audiendum verbum Dei, ad colloquia spirituali agenda, ad
Eucharistiam partecipandam.

This is our translation:

All the reforms in the Church have given rise to new principles, and have promoted new norms to enable the purposes of the
reform to be put into practice.

This was so after the Council of Trent; and it could not be
otherwise in our own day. The renewal of the liturgy penetrates
deeply into the life of the Church. Liturgical spirituality must, of
necessity, germinate new flowers of sanctity and grace, not to
mention a more intense Christian apostolate and spiritual action.

An excellent example of this renewal is to be found in the
'Neocatechumenal Communities' which arose in Madrid in 1962,
through the initiative of some young lay people, with the permission, the encouragement and the blessing of the most excellent
Pastor of Madrid, Casimiro Morcillo. The communities aim at
making visible in the parishes the sign of the missionary Church,
and they strive to open the road to evangelisation for those who
have almost abandoned the Christian way of life.

To this end, the members of the 'Communities' seek to live
the Christian liturgical life more intensely, starting with a new
catechesis and the 'catechumenal' preparation, passing through,
with the help of a spiritual way, all those stages which the
catechumens in the primitive Church went through before receiving the sacrament of Baptism. Here, it is not a matter of people to
be baptised, but of people who are baptised. The catechesis is the
same, but the liturgical rites are adapted to the conditions of
baptised Christians, according to the directive already given by
the Congregation for Divine Worship.[1]

The 'Communities' in the parishes are set up under the direction of the parish priest. The members meet, once or twice a
week, to listen to the divine word, for spiritual dialogue, and to
participate in the Eucharist.

---

1. Cf. *Rite of Christian Initiation of Adults*, chapter IV; and: *Reflections on Chapter IV of 'Ordo init. christ. adultorum'*: Notitiae, 9, 1973, pp. 274-282.

NOTE BY THE CONGREGATION FOR DIVINE WORSHIP ON THE CELEBRATION IN GROUPS OF THE NEOCATECHUMENAL WAY[2]

The Congregation for Divine Worship and for the Discipline of the Sacraments has often received requests, also on the part of bishops, concerning the celebration of the Eucharist in groups of the 'Neocatechumenal Way'. Concerning this, and without prejudice to further interventions, this Department declares the following:

1. The celebration of groups particularly gathered for their own specific formation are foreseen in the Instructions, *Eucharisticum Mysterium* of 25 May 1967, nn. 27 and 30 (*AAS* 59, 1967, 556-557) and *Actio Pastoralis* of 25 May 1969 (*AAS* 61, 1969, 806-811).

2. The Congregation consents that among the adaptations foreseen by the Instruction *Actio Pastoralis* nn. 6-11, the groups of the above-mentioned 'Way' may receive communion under two species, always with unleavened bread, and transfer *ad experimentum* the Rite of Peace to after the Prayer of the Faithful.

3. The Ordinary of the place must be informed habitually or *ad Casum* of the place and time in which such celebrations will take place; they may not be held without his authorisation.

On the occasion of this declaration, this Congregation repeats what has been said in the Instructions cited above, and especially the following recommendations:

"Pastors of souls are greatly exhorted to desire to consider and deepen the spiritual and formative values of those celebrations. They achieve their scope only if they lead the participants to a greater awareness of the Christian mystery, to an increase of the divine worship, to insertion into the structure of the ecclesial community, and to the fruitful exercise of the apostolate and of charity towards the brothers and sisters" (*Action Pastoralis*).

Given at the offices of the Congregation for Divine Worship and for the Discipline of the Sacraments, 19th December 1988.

EDUARDO Cardinal MARTINEZ SOMALO
Prefect

VIRGILO NOÉ
Titular Archbishop of Voncaria
Secretary

2. Cf. *L'Osservatore Romano*, English edition, 9th January 1989.

The 'Redemptoris Mater' Seminaries

WHAT ARE THE 'REDEMPTORIS MATER' SEMINARIES?

They are one of the most important fruits of the conciliar renewal; a complete new reality, desired by the Second Vatican Council which in *Presbyterorum Ordinis* n. 10 said, *"The presbyters should remember that concern for all the Churches falls on them... and where it is necessary (because of a lack of clergy) not only a functional distribution of Presbyters should be facilitated, but also the implementation of special initiatives that will favour particular regions or nations or the whole world. To this end, the creation of International Seminaries for the good of the whole Church according to norms to be established and respecting the rights of the local Ordinary would be useful"* (PO 10).

In 1991, the Intercongregational Commission set up by Pope John Paul II to deal with the serious scarcity of priests in many parts of the world recognised that:

*"This idea of the Council has been applied in the 'Redemptoris Mater' seminaries which prepare presbyters for the new evangelisation according to the programme of the Neocatechumenal Way... this would realise a new form of ministry: **the diocesan missionary"** (L'Osservatore Romano*, Italian edition, 15.3.91).

As stated in the Statutes and Rule of Life, the 'Redemptoris Mater' Seminaries are not seminaries of the Neocatechumenal Way, but truly diocesan seminaries which depend on the bishop. The students in these colleges receive the same theological formation as the other seminarians of the diocese. They do a year of pastoral work in the parishes as deacons and two years in the diocese as presbyters before the Bishop can send them in mission. But if the Bishop has urgent need of them in his diocese, he can place them where he wishes, given that they are ordained without condition.

A characteristic of these Redemptoris Mater Seminaries is that they are international: they are **for the whole world** and at the service of the Church.

Experience has shown that the combining of a way of initiation to the Christian life – the Neocatechumenal Way – with the formation of the presbyter is a great help for the psychological, affective and human development of the candidates. (Before being presbyters they are Christians, and in the way of faith they learn prayer, obedience, the sense of the Cross, to be in communion, etc.) Above all, it is a help in uniting the mission with the parish, since the Neocatechumenal Way is a time of formation that finishes in the parish with living, adult, missionary communities united to the parish priest and the bishop.

These are the 'Redemptoris Mater' seminaries so far erected throughout the world:

'REDEMPTORIS MATER' SEMINARIES

EUROPE:	AMERICAN CONTINENT:
Rome (Italy)	Newark (USA)
Macerata (Italy)	Santo Domingo (Dominican Republic)
Madrid (Spain)	Medellin (Columbia)
Warsaw (Poland)	Brasilia (Brazil)
Berlin (Germany)	Calloa (Peru)
Pola (Croatia)	Guadalajara (Mexico).
Lugano (Switzerland)	San Salvador (El Salvador)
Strasbourg (France)	
Vienna (Austria)	
ASIA:	AUSTRALIA:
Bangalore (India)	Perth
Takamatsu (Japan)	
Kaoshiung (Taiwan)	

There is a total of more than 1000 seminarians in the various seminaries, and in the National Vocational Centres about 1500 young men are preparing to enter the seminary.

In Rome, where the first 'Redemptoris Mater' Seminary began in 1987, about 100 presbyters have already been ordained, and are now working in the parishes, or are in mission in other dioceses throughout the world where the bishops have requested their services from the Cardinal Vicar.

DECREE OF ERECTION OF THE 'REDEMPTORIS MATER' SEMINARY, ROME

The Church of Rome, founded by the holy Apostles Peter and Paul and irrigated with their blood, ever faithful to the universal mission of its Bishop, the Pope, in the service of Truth and Charity, for the announcement of the Gospel of salvation to the whole world, in communion with the local sister Churches, has listened with veneration to the call the Holy Father made to the National Episcopal Conferences of Europe, in the letter signed on 2nd January 1986, for a new evangelisation of the European countries where Christianity has long been established.

With joy she has seen arise within her generous impulses for the courageous witness of faith on the part of priests, religious and lay Christians.

Of particular significance among these is the offer that has come from the Neocatechumenal Way to found a Centre of formation to the priesthood for those brothers who make themselves available for the specific task of taking the Gospel to countries which are distancing themselves from their ancient Christian roots.

After lengthy reflection, prayer and evaluation of the proposal in the light of the Spirit of God, believing that I have correctly interpreted the pastoral concern of the Supreme Pontiff, and having listened to the Episcopal Council of Rome, with the present decree establish the 'Diocesan College for the formation to the presbyterate for the new evangelisation' under the patronage of the Most Holy Virgin 'Redemptoris Mater'.

It will be governed under the norm of a precise 'statute' and according to a 'Rule of Life', attached to the present Decree, *ad experimentum* for three years.[1]

Given at Rome, from the Lateran Palace, on the 14th February 1988, Feast of Ss. Cyril and Methodius.

UGO Cardinal POLETTI
Vic. Gen.

Prot. n. 218/88

---

1. With a further decree (Prot. n. 913/90), dated 1st October 1990, Cardinal Poletti confirmed 'definitively, the Statute and Rule of Life' of the 'Redemptoris Mater' College, Rome. Of particular interest is the judgement expressed to Cardinal Poletti by the 'Sacred Congregation for Catholic Institutions' after a careful examination of the Statute and Rule of Life of the Diocesan College 'Redemptoris Mater' (30th January 1988, prot. 1414/87). Among other things, this says, "It is a diocesan College with the aim of being missionary for the good of the universal Church. It is a reply to the perspective emphasised by the Second Vatican Council (LG 17; ChD 6; AdG 38; OT 20) and afterwards given precision in the *Motu Proprio* 'Ecclesiae Sanctae' and in the 'Directive Norms' quoted above. According to the latter document, the local Churches must increasingly take account of their common responsibility, and, sensitive to cries for help, show themselves ready to help those who are in need (n. 16). It is for this reason that the diocese of Rome has taken on the task of 'encouraging men in vocations for the missions and also of directing the attention of candidates to the priesthood to the universal dimension of their mission and therefore to their availability to serve outside the diocese' (*ibid.* n. 14). In this way, the recommendation of the decree *Optatum Totis* can also be satisfied, namely that future priests should be 'penetrated by that truly Catholic spirit which accustoms them to look beyond the confines of their own diocese, nation or rite, and to go to meet the needs of the whole Church, ready in their souls to preach the Gospel anywhere' (n. 20). ... This initiative therefore is putting into practice the Second Vatican Council's missionary and evangelising thrust. Thanks to it, the diocese of Rome, *universo caritatis coetui praesidens*, is taking an important step forward in this matter, one that will not fail to stimulate and encourage other local churches."

Letter of the Holy Father John Paul II to the European Bishops meeting in Vienna

(14-17 April 1993)

On the invitation of Kiko Argüello and Carmen Hernández – the initiators of the Neocatechumenal Way – joined by Cardinals Angel Suquia of Madrid and Josef Glemp of Warsaw, more than 120 bishops from all over Europe met in Vienna from 14th to 17th April 1993 to exchange experiences on the Neocatechumenal Way as a instrument for the new evangelisation. Also taking part in the meeting were Cardinal Groer of Vienna, who inaugurated the proceedings, and Cardinal Sterzinsky of Berlin and Cardinal Lopez Rodriguez of Santo Domingo, president of CELAM (the Conference of Latin American Bishops). It was in Santo Domingo in 1992 that the first meeting of Latin American Bishops organised by the Neocatechumenal Way was held, a meeting in which more than 150 bishops took part.

The happy outcome of that meeting – at the end of which many of those present expressed their gratitude for having been able to know in more depth the marvels that God is working through the Neocatechumenal Way (thousands of vocations, the reconstruction of the family, many young people flocking to the communities) – contributed to the decision to offer the same possibility to the European Bishops.

About half of the Bishops – almost as though to underline how strongly the need for evangelisation is felt in these parts – came from countries of eastern Europe: Slovakia, the Czech Republic, Croatia, Serbia, Macedonia, Slovenia, Rumania, Hungary, Byelorussia, Khazakstan, Lithuania, Russia, Poland and the Ukraine. The others came from Italy, Spain, Germany, Austria, England, France, Holland, Portugal, Sweden, Switzerland and Turkey.

The Holy Father wished to be present at the meeting through a special letter brought to the participants by Mgr. Paul Josef

Cordes, vice-president of the Pontifical Institute for the Laity. For the Holy Father, the Neocatechumenal Way is one of the 'valid instruments' that was awakened by the Holy Spirit, through the Second Vatican Council, to reply to the questions of contemporary man. 'The Neocatechumenal Way,' writes John Paul II, 'in which itinerants and missionary families mature, can reply to the challenges of secularism, the diffusion of the sects and the lack of vocations.' Indeed, it forms 'living cells of the Church', renews the 'vitality of the parishes by means of mature Christians', 'appears particularly adapted to contribute in dechristianised zones to the necessary *reimplantatio Ecclesiae*, and in the various 'Redemptoris Mater' diocesan seminaries prepares presbyters ready to accompany and support the work of the new evangelisation with their ordained ministry.

Here follows the complete text of the Pope's letter.

Venerable Brothers in the Episcopate,
Dearest Brothers and Sisters!

It is a cause of great consolation for me, just a few years since my appeal for a new evangelisation of Europe, to know that you are gathered in Vienna to reflect together upon the fruits of the missionary activity which the priests, itinerants and families of the Neocatechumenal Way are carrying out with a generous impulse and great zeal for the Gospel.

On the occasion of the opening of the work of the Special Assembly for Europe, on June 5th 1990, I noted with regret that in our continent many people are used to looking upon reality "as if God did not exist". Within such a perspective, I added, man "becomes the source of the moral law, and only those laws which man gives to himself constitute the measure of his conscience and of his behaviour" (*Insegnamenti*, vol. XIII, 1, 1990, pp. 1517f). On the other hand, it cannot be denied that the Holy Spirit, by means of the Vatican Council, has raised up valid instruments with which to respond to the questions of contemporary man, and among these is also the Neocatechumenal Way. After various years, having regard to the results which have been achieved, I decided to encourage this experience in writing, in view of the new evangelisation, wishing that this experience be helped and valued by my brothers in the episcopate (cf. letter of the 30th August, 1990).

Many of you are direct witnesses of such results and also protagonists through the help you have given to spreading this new ecclesial reality; therefore your reflection today is particularly important, as was that of the bishops of the American continent during the meeting last year in Santo Domingo.

The Neocatechumenal Way, in which the itinerants and the family missionaries mature, is able to respond to the challenge of secularism, the diffusion of sects and the shortage of vocations. The reflection upon the Word of God and the participation in the Eucharist make possible a gradual initiation into the sacred mysteries, to form living cells of the Church and renew the vitality of the parish by means of mature Christians capable of bearing witness to the truth through a radically lived faith.

This Way appears particularly qualified to contribute in dechristianised areas to the necessary *reimplantatio ecclesiae*, leading man in his moral behaviour towards obedience to revealed truth and even reconstructing the very fabric of society, which has decayed due to a lack of knowledge of God and His love. Already, in some regions, nuclei of missionary families are being formed which can be the light of Christ and an example of life.

But such a mission would not be possible without presbyters prepared to accompany and sustain with their ordained ministry this work of the new evangelisation I am grateful to the Lord who has willed to raise up numerous vocations and therefore the setting up of the diocesan and missionary seminaries in various countries of Europe, called by the sweet name of the Virgin Mary, 'Redemptoris Mater'.

I also place your meeting under her maternal protection and her powerful inspiration, that it may give you further impetus and courage in your apostolic commitment towards contemporary man, who needs the guidance of pastors and of witnesses sent by them, in order to know God, to invoke His name and to receive salvation from Him.

May the light of the Risen Lord, which we have solemnly celebrated in the Paschal Vigil, continue to shine within you, sustaining you in your mission in the service of the Church and of the whole of humanity.

From the Vatican, 12th April 1993

JOHN PAUL II

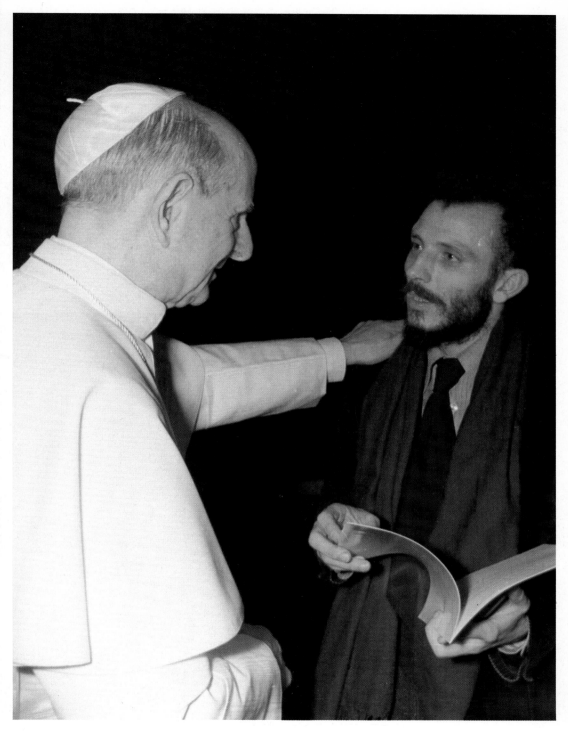

12th January 1977: *His Holiness Paul VI with Kiko Argüello.* (Photo Felici)

12th January 1977: *Two more moments from the meeting with Paul VI.* Right: *Kiko Argüello and Carmen Hernández, initiators of the Neocatechumenal Way, presenting the Pope with the picture of the "Servant of Yahweh" painted by Kiko.* Below: *Paul VI blesses Carmen, imposing his hands.* (Photo Felici)

2nd November 1980: His Holiness John Paul II in conversation with Carmen Hernández and Fr. Mario Pezzi during a visit to the parish of Canadian Martyrs (right) *and with Kiko Argüello* (below). (Photo Felici)

Top left: **2nd November 1980**: *The visit of John Paul II to the parish of the Canadian Martyrs.* (Photo Felici) Above: **7th January 1982**: *a private audience with the itinerant catechists of the Neocatechumenal way.* (Photo A. Mari) Below: **4th December 1983**: *The Pope's visit to the parish of St Frances Cabrini. During his years as Pontiff, John Paul II has already visited more than 30 parishes in Rome where there are Neocatechumenal Communities. (The Way is present in over 80 of the 320 parishes of Rome.)* (Photo R. Caponigro)

Left: ***31st March 1985***: *The meeting of John Paul II with more than 1200 young people of the Neocatechumenal Way on their way towards the priesthood, in the Sistine Chapel.* (Photo A. Mari)
Below: ***28th December 1986***: *The Eucharist celebrated with the Pope at Castel Gandolfo, attended by more than 400 itinerant catechists of the Neocatechumenal Way. At the end of the meeting John Paul II presented them with the missionary cross.* (Photo A. Mari) Next page: ***30th December 1988***: *The Feast of the Holy Family: The Eucharist with the Pope in the "Tent" at Porto San Giorgio (Ascoli Piceno) and the sending out on mission of the Families of the Neocatechumenal Way for the New Evangelization.* (Photo Plast Proget Adriatica)

30th December 1988: *The Feast of the Holy Family.* Left: *a moment in the Eucharistic Celebration under the "Tent".* Right: *The Pope gives a missionary cross to one of the 72 families sent out in mission.* (Photo Plast Proget Adriatica)

8th May 1991: *His Holiness John Paul II in conversation with Carmen Hernández*

Some fruits of the Neocatechumenal Way

SOME STATISTICS ON THE NEOCATECHUMENAL WAY IN THE DIOCESE OF ROME

When in 1974 Pope Paul VI gave an audience for the first time to a group of priests and lay people from the Neocatechumenal Communities he said, "Living and promoting this awakening is what you call a form of 'post-Baptismal programme' which in today's Christian communities can renew those effects of maturity and deepening which in the primitive Church were achieved in the period of preparation before Baptism".

Nearly twenty years after this first meeting these 'effects of maturity and deepening' are beginning to be seen in those parishes and dioceses where the Neocatechumenal Way has been consolidated as a style of pastoral work, without either imposing itself as the only one or attacking any of the other charisms and organisms which make up the plurality of the parish.

As an example of this we present, with a series of diagrams, some data on the Neocatechumenal Way in the diocese of Rome. The first itinerant team (Kiko Argüello, Carmen Hernández and Fr Francesco Cuppini) gave catecheses in the parishes of the Holy Canadian Martyrs (1968) and of St Frances Cabrini, St Luigi Gonzaga and the Nativity (1969). From these first four parishes began all the development of the Way in Italy and in various other parts of the world.

In May 1992 the Neocatechumenal Communities were present in the diocese of Rome as follows:

Parishes	82
Communities	349
Members	11,846

1.

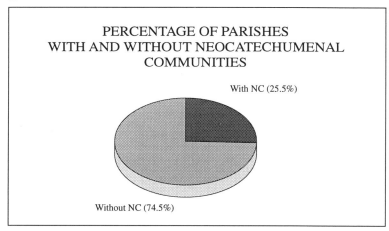

The Neocatechumenal Way is present in a quarter of the parishes of the diocese of Rome (25.5%) and in all five of its pastoral areas (see fig. 2), with a noticeably larger presence in the North and East sectors, both as regards the number of parishes (19 and 34 respectively) and of communities (115 and 131).

2.

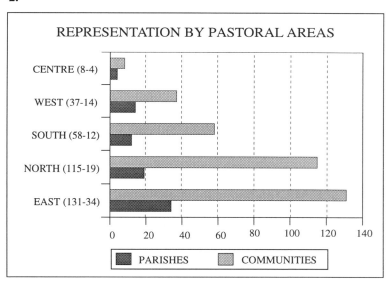

3.

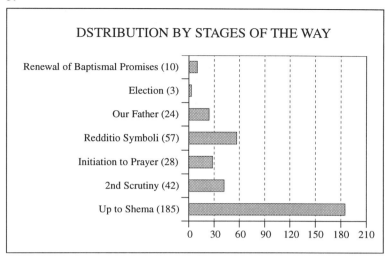

Fig. 3 shows the distribution of the communities in Rome according to the main stages of the Way; 185 of them in the initial phase, which lasts three or four years (until the stage called the 'Shema' – a Hebrew word that means 'Listen', cf. Dt 6:4ff.) This shows how after twenty years the Way is in a notable phase of expansion.

4.

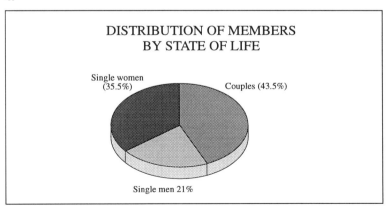

The Neocatechumenal Communities solve some of the most serious problems of the pastoral situation of today: families (fig. 4 shows that 43.5% of the members of the communities are couples, a total of 2585 couples in the 349 Roman communities); youth (fig. 5); adults (fig. 6); the transmission of faith to children (fig. 7).

5.

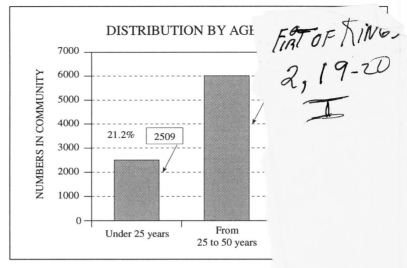

Fig. 5 shows something very important from a pastoral view-point: in the Neocatechumenal Communities more than 50% of the members are between 25 and 50 years old, the age group most absent currently in the Italian church, according to official statistics. Because of this situation, some years ago the diocese of Rome had as its pastoral programme for the year a bid to bring this age group into the life of the church. More than one fifth of the members of the communities (21.1%) are young people below the age of 25 and 27.9% are above the age of 50.

This fact, taken with the percentage of couples in the Way (43.5%) – many of whom are young – confirms that in the Neocatechumenal Communities there is a vast number of people of the age group most significant for family life and for a Christian presence in society.

6.

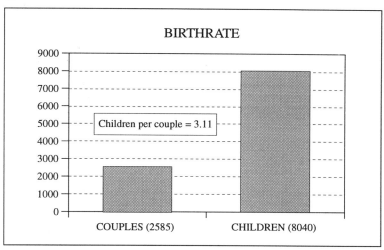

The average number of children per couple in the Neocat-echumenal Communities (3.11%) is noticeably higher than the national average. The openness to life in obedience to the will of God of the couples who follow the Neocatechumenal Way is the first source of the many vocations that the Way is producing in some parishes.

7.

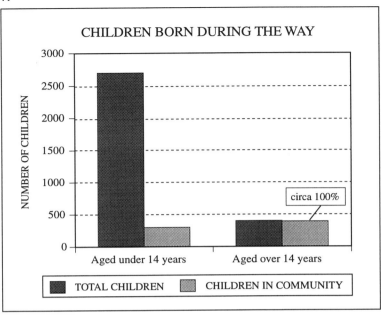

Almost 100% of the children – age 14 and upwards – of couples who are in the Way are themselves in a community (fig. 7). This datum, one of the most important of this research, might be surprising, given the situation of today's youth. But it shows that through the Way these families have received the capability of transmitting the faith to their own children. We must add that this is possible due to: (1) the force that comes from celebrating the liturgy in small communities where the children who have made their first Communion always go with their parents to the Eucharist, in which they participate very actively; (2) the celebration of the Eucharist on Saturday night that allows the families, during all the time of the Way, to dedicate Sunday morning to a domestic liturgy in which the parents, and the grandparents, transmit the faith to their children. When they are 13 these children are invited to attend a catechesis for adults and to be in their own community which helps them during puberty and adolescence. (The Neocatechumenal Way took 50,000 young people from Europe alone to the 6th World Youth Day in Czestochowa in 1991.)

8.

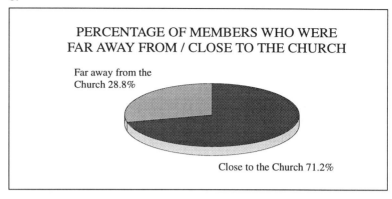

PERCENTAGE OF MEMBERS WHO WERE
FAR AWAY FROM / CLOSE TO THE CHURCH

Far away from the
Church 28.8%

Close to the Church 71.2%

Almost 30% of the membership of the communities is made up of people who were far away from the Church. Starting with those who are near, the pastoral action of the Neocatechumenal Way aims to reach those who are far away. In this way it helps the parish to be a centre of evangelisation. This begins from the rediscovery of Baptism and, through a gradual reconstruction of the person that is both psychological and Christian, brings the members to live all the richness of the Christian vocation.

9.

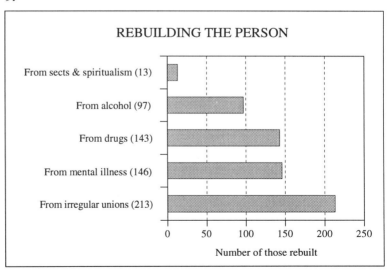

REBUILDING THE PERSON

From sects & spiritualism (13)

From alcohol (97)

From drugs (143)

From mental illness (146)

From irregular unions (213)

Number of those rebuilt

Fig. 9 shows some situations of particular social interest from which some of the members of the communities come (7%). A significant number have been helped to give up drugs and a significant number of irregular unions have been regularised.

151

10.

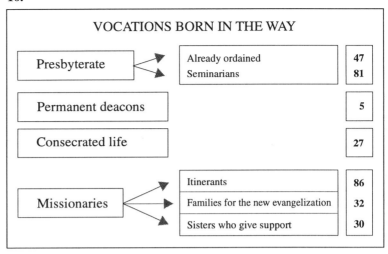

Particularly interesting is the large number of vocations that the Way is producing in the various parishes of the diocese of Rome (fig. 10): for the diocese itself (presbyters and deacons), for the various forms of consecrated life, especially the contemplative life, and for work throughout the whole world (itinerants, families in mission, women who help and support these families).

11.

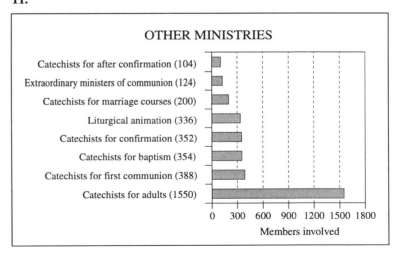

At a certain point of their journey towards maturity in faith the members are invited by their catechists to help with other realities of the parishes (catechesis, liturgical animation etc.). As fig. 11 shows, today almost 3500 members are doing this service in the parishes of Rome.

12.

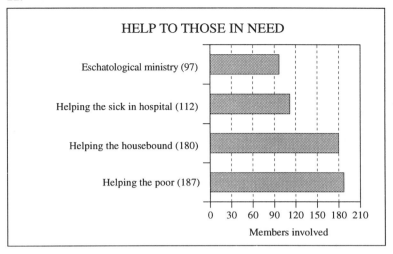

HELP TO THOSE IN NEED

Eschatological ministry (97)
Helping the sick in hospital (112)
Helping the housebound (180)
Helping the poor (187)

0 30 60 90 120 150 180 210

Members involved

Another 576 members are helping with particular forms of service in their parish (the eschatological ministry, work for the poor, the sick, etc.). By the 'eschatological ministry' is meant the moral and religious support offered to families or individuals who have lost someone close to them.

13.

ACTIVITIES OF SUPPORT IN SACRAMENTAL PASTORAL WORK FOR OTHER PARISHES

St Gerard Majella	40
St Rita at Tor Bella Monaca	20
St Hilary	10
St Alexander	10
St Remigius	4
Riano Flaminio	10

Some parish priests, especially from the outskirts of Rome, who are overloaded with pastoral work (preparation for Baptisms, First Communion, Confirmation, etc.) knowing that the Way gives a preparation in faith to adults, have asked for help from parishes that have many Neocatechumenal Communities. Fig.13 shows the parishes that have asked for this help and the number of members of the community who are involved in this work.

14.

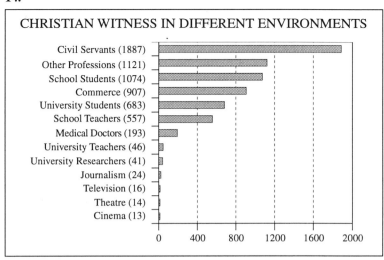

CHRISTIAN WITNESS IN DIFFERENT ENVIRONMENTS

Civil Servants (1887)
Other Professions (1121)
School Students (1074)
Commerce (907)
University Students (683)
School Teachers (557)
Medical Doctors (193)
University Teachers (46)
University Researchers (41)
Journalism (24)
Television (16)
Theatre (14)
Cinema (13)

0   400   800   1200   1600   2000

The last diagram shows some of the work environments where members of the communities in Rome (exactly 6576 or 55.1% of the total) are called to bear witness to their Christian vocation in their profession, in their everyday work.

ITINERANTS	
Areas in Italy, Europe and the rest of the world where itinerant catechists of the diocese of Rome are working	
ITALY	EUROPE
Veneto Lombardia Umbria Marche Abruzzi Liguria Puglia Basilicata	England Germany Belgium Holland Poland Rumania Hungary Turkey Russia Malta
AMERICAS	AFRICA
USA Mexico Panama Colombia Venezuela Equador Argentina	Egypt Ivory Coast Zaire Uganda Nigeria
ASIA	AUSTRALIA & PACIFIC
Korea Japan Philippines India	Australia

FAMILIES IN MISSION

List of countries where some families of the Neocatechumenal Way from Rome are currently in mission

EUROPE		ASIA	
Norway	1	China	1
France	2	Japan	2
Germany	9		
Austria	1	**AFRICA**	
Holland	3		
Russia	1	Ivory Coast	2
Serbia	1		
AMERICAS		**AUSTRALIA & PACIFIC**	
USA	4	Australia	4
San Salvador	1		

THE PARISH AND THE NEOCATECHUMENAL WAY AS THEY APPEAR IN A STATISTICAL SURVEY OF THE SPANISH EPISCOPAL CONFERENCE

One often reads about the Neocatechumenal Way, or hears from various Pastoral Councils, or among 'insiders', when this experience of evangelisation is discussed, a series of assertions more or less accepted by everyone: the Way thinks that it is the only ecclesial reality; the parishes which have this pastoral experience neglect the others; Neocatechumenal groups are closed in on themselves without any contact with the rest of the parish, or with outside social situations, etc.

A preliminary organic research, even if it is not specific, about the relation between the parish and the Neocatechumenal Way, has been made using material from a wider survey by the Spanish Episcopal Conference and its findings are extremely significant. The Neocatechumenal Way in Spain has the same presence, at least numerically, and the same penetration of the parish and diocesan fabric, as it has in Italy, with about three thousand communities in each country.

In a questionnaire to prepare for the National Congress of 1988 on the theme 'The Evangelising Parish' one of the questions asked by the commission of the Spanish Episcopal Conference was whether Neocatechumenal Communities existed in the parish. Some years after this, Fr Francisco Azcona San Martin, director of the Statistical and Sociological Office of the Conference, worked on a study comparing the answers of the parishes which have the Way with those which do not.

The data – certainly relative, as the author himself suggests in the conclusion of his work, because they do not go directly and deeply into the reality of the Neocatechumenate, nor consider the length of time the Way has been in the parish, nor its penetration of the parish, nor directly the structure of the Neocatechumenal Communities – are nevertheless very useful for looking at the relationship between parish and the Neocatechumenal Way.

The information gathered by the survey offers a statistical first point of reference that, if confirmed by other and more specific research, will not only give the lie to the gratuitous and generalised statements about the Neocatechumenal Way that were mentioned above, but will be able to throw new light on this 'specific charism', on its real relationship with the parish, on its being a 'gift of God' for the reconstruction of the Church today, bringing with it the renewal of the Second Vatican Council to the parish.

Here follows, with the kind permission of the author, almost the whole of Fr San Martin's study.[1]

1. Fr F. Azcona San Martin, a priest of the diocese of Pamplona, studied sociology at the Gregorian and Angelicum Universities in Rome (1960-64). For twelve years he taught research techniques at the School of Social Work, 'St Vincent de Paul', in

The Neocatechumenal Communities:
an experience of new evangelisation through the parish
(*by Fr Azcona San Martin*)

On the basis of a working hypothesis[2] I went to brush the dust off the data of a survey, carried out throughout the whole of Spain, in preparation for the Congress 'The Evangelising Parish', which was held in Madrid in 1988 as part of the Pastoral Plan of the Spanish Episcopal Conference. The general data, even though not complete, were published in the book *The Evangelising Parish*.

One of the 102 questions – no. 19 – asked: 'Are there Neocatechumenal Communities in the parish?' I wanted to compare this question with all the others to see if there were significant differences, according to whether the replies were affirmative or negative.

Technical details of the survey

– The questionnaire was compiled by the Spanish Episcopal Commission for Pastoral Work.

– The questionnaire was completed either by the parish council, by the parish priest, or by an assistant priest. The questionnaire focused on the parish.

– The data was collected in May and June 1988.

– The selection of a representative cross-section of parishes was made by:

1. Ensuring that the geographical spread reflected the proportional concentrations in the regional areas: North, East, South, Centre. Data was collected from parishes in every diocese in Spain.

2. Taking into account the number of inhabitants in the parishes. (More than half of the 22,000 parishes in Spain have less than 500 faithful: the representative nature of these is in proportion to the number of inhabitants.)

Pamplona and was director of the Statistical Office of his diocese. For several years he worked in Venezuela, following which he was made Vicar General of the diocese of Pamplona and its General Secretary. Today he directs the Office of Statistics and Sociology of the Spanish Episcopal Conference. The editor of the Italian edition of this book translated his work into Italian from which this English translation has been made.

2. The author bases his research on the following **working hypothesis**: 'If a determining feature of the Neocatechumenal Way is evangelisation beginning from the parish, if the Church officially recognises this Neocatechumenal form of Christian initiation as an itinerary of faith that is valid for the society and man of today (cf. the *Letter of John Paul II to Monsignor Cordes* of 30/8/1990), if it offers to the dioceses this concrete instrument of evangelisation: is this recognition and support due only to sympathy or like-mindedness, or is there something more real that can be proved statistically? **My hypothesis is that this situation must necessarily be observable in the research and statistics that look at current experiences in the Church and in the parishes.'**

3. Taking into account the types of population in the parishes which were surveyed: rural, semi-rural, inner city, suburban.

– The data used was collated from 1831 questionnaires from 1831 parishes.

– Margin of error: we are reasonably certain (95.5%) that with the results obtained there is only a 2% margin of error (using Tagliacarne's method).

– The statistics were collected by the Office of Statistics and Sociology of the Episcopal Conference.

Sociological profile of the Spanish Parishes in which the Neocatechumenal Way is present

Although there are Neocatechumenal Communities in every kind of parish, these are the most noticeable characteristics:

– They are present mostly in parishes in urban centres with more than 20,000 inhabitants: as much in the inner cities (29.7%) as in the suburbs (28.7%), and in semi-rural parishes with between 1,000 and 20,000 inhabitants (36.4%). They are less present in parishes in rural areas with less than 1,000 inhabitants (4.6%).

– They are present in parishes with 1,000-10,000 inhabitants (76.4%) and above all in parishes with 5-10,000 inhabitants (44.1%).

– The parishes in which the Neocatechumenal communities are to be found are mostly made up of people who work in the services sector (32.8%) and in the industrial sector (27.2%).

– The economic level of the parishes is usually medium to low (71.8%).

– The political tendency in the areas where parishes have Neocatechumenal communities is towards the left (50.3%).

VOTING PATTERNS	Parishes with Neocatechumenal communities (%)	
	Yes	No
Right	12.8	21.3
Centre	29.7	29.5
Left	50.3	43.9
No opinion / No reply	7.2	5.3
Total	100.00	100.00

– They are to be found mostly in parishes which consider themselves 'in the process of change' (53.8%) or 'renewed according to the Council' (30.8%).

Voting patterns	Parishes with Neocatechumenal communities (%)	
	Yes	No
Very traditional	2.6	2.2
Traditional	11.3	22.9
In the process of change	53.8	45.3
Renewed according to the Council	30.8	26.4
Greatly renewed or postconciliar	0.5	2.8
No opinion / No reply	1.0	0.4
Total	100.0	100.0

– Neocatechumenal communities are to be found within a general parish structure in which there are other groups and communities (67.2%).

15.

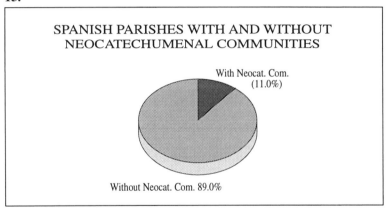

SPANISH PARISHES WITH AND WITHOUT
NEOCATECHUMENAL COMMUNITIES

With Neocat. Com.
(11.0%)

Without Neocat. Com. 89.0%

This chart indicates that 11% of parishes surveyed have Neocatechumenal communities. In fact the percentage of all the parishes in Spain which have Neocatechumenal communities is slightly less, but it may be said that 11% of the population of Spain is served, as it were, by parishes which have these communities. To explain: of the 22,400 parishes in Spain, a quarter have less than 100 inhabitants; a quarter have between 100 and 500; 13% have between 500 and 1,000; 17% between 1,000 and 5,000; 12% have between 5,000 and 10,000; and 8% of parishes have more than 10,000 inhabitants. These 8% have a larger population than the smaller ones and are therefore more representative.

The precise results of the survey are as follows: parishes with Neocatechumenal communities, 10.6%; without, 85.7%; no opinion/no reply, 3.7%. This last response 'no opinion/no reply' is due to one of the following factors: the communities are in the process of being formed; they are a small and uncertain reality in the parish; or, more simply, because those interviewed did not reply.

16.

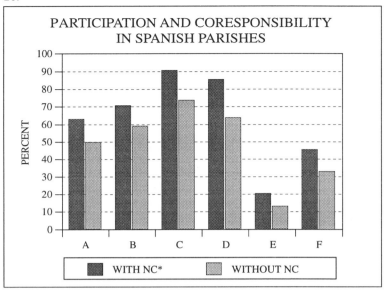

Types of Participation	With NC %	Without NC %	Difference %
A: Parish Council	63.1	49.6	13.5
B: Council for financial affairs or financial commission	70.8	59.0	11.8
C: Pastoral programme or other types of programming	90.8	73.5	17.3
D: 'Caritas'	85.6	63.6	22.0
E: Lay ministries	20.5	12.9	7.6
F: Extraordinary ministers of the Eucharist	45.6	33.1	12.5

The bar chart reveals the following: 63.1% of Spanish parishes with Neocatechumenal communities have Parish Councils, as do 49.6% of parishes without Neocatechumenal communities. In parishes with Neocatechumenal communities the types of participation listed above are about 14.1% higher on average.

'Evangelization requires that we pass from clericalism and passivity among the laity to a missionary co-responsibility on the part of the entire People of God' (Congress on 'The Evangelizing Parish', Part 3, III, 1).

* NC = Neocatechumenal communities.

17.

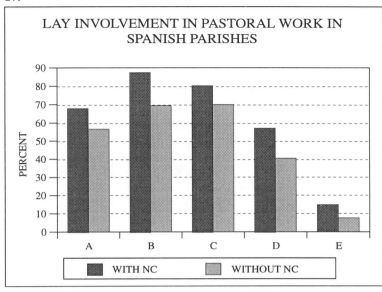

LAY INVOLVEMENT IN PASTORAL WORK IN SPANISH PARISHES

Aspects of Lay Participation in Spanish Parishes	With NC %	Without NC %	Difference %
A: Parish assistance to those seeking help and guidance	68.2	56.6	11.6
B: Lay responsibility in the principal areas of pastoral work: catechesis, liturgy, 'caritas', administration, youth pastoral, etc.	87.7	69.9	18.3
C: Lay people who assist the priest in preparing and directing the participation in the principal liturgical celebrations	80.5	70.0	10.5
D: Lay people and priests who normally visit the infirm	57.4	40.4	17.0
E: Help to priests to prepare the homily	14.9	7.6	7.3

The participation and active involvement of lay people in the pastoral activities listed above is greater in the parishes in which the Neocatechumenal communities are present. The average difference is 12.9%.

'Our parishes must increase the level of participation of the laity, seeking to involve lay people in missionary activities and in the evangelizing presence in the world, and welcoming in an effective way the experience of lay people into the heart of parish life' (Congress on 'The Evangelizing Parish', chapter 23).

18.

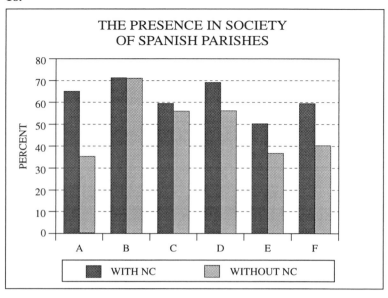

THE PRESENCE IN SOCIETY
OF SPANISH PARISHES

Aspects which indicate an active presence of Spanish parishes in society	With NC %	Without NC %	Difference %
A: In catechesis for adults emphasis is placed upon the missionary dimension, involvement, evangelizing presence in society	65.1	35.1	30.0
B: Openness to the problems and concerns of the neighbourhood or town	71.3	71.1	0.2
C: In the preparation of pastoral workers and of the liturgies the problems of the neighbourhood or town taken into account	59.5	56.0	3.5
D: The parish organises and collaborates in social activities and programmes for the unemployed, drug abusers, aged and infirm	69.2	56.2	13.0
E: There are organised groups attending to the pastoral of the infirm	50.3	36.8	13.5
F: More than a third of the economic resources of the parish are devoted to the needs of the poor	59.5	40.3	19.2

The average difference is 13.2%.

'The new evangelization requires that our parishes show clear signs, in their life and activity, of fraternity with the poor and the outcasts of our time' (Congress on 'The Evangelizing Parish', chapter 27).

19.

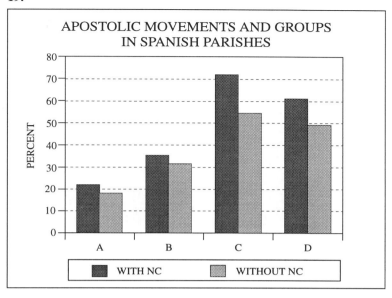

Associations in Spanish Parishes	With NC %	Without NC %	Difference %
A: Movements of Catholic Action	22.1	18.2	3.9
B: Groups of matrimonial preparation	35.4	31.6	3.8
C: Other apostolates	71.8	54.5	17.3
D: Confraternities	61.0	49.2	11.8

It does not seem possible to prove the hypothesis of those who say that in the parishes with Neocatechumenal communities all other movements disappear and that the priests neglect these other movements.

There are more movements represented in the parishes where there are Neocatechumenal communities than in those where there are not; the average difference for the whole being 9.2%.

The Neocatechumenal Way is not a movement, an apostolic group or an association. In my view it presupposes an option on the part of the parish to take on a catechumenate for adults which is like a womb for the gestation of faith directed towards the renewal of baptism and the Christian life. In this way, all the charisms of the Church can exist in the parish and can be reinvigorated.

'Evangelization has its origin in the personal experience of the salvation of Jesus Christ, lived out in a community of believers' (Congress on 'The Evangelizing Parish', Part 3, I, 1).

20.

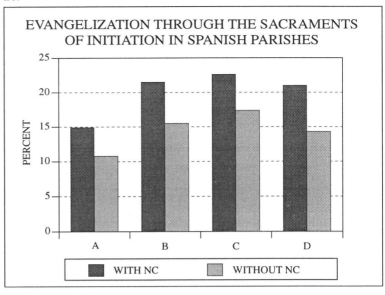

EVANGELIZATION THROUGH THE SACRAMENTS OF INITIATION IN SPANISH PARISHES

The sacraments of initiation and evangelisation in Spanish parishes in which the following are often made use of	With NC %	Without NC %	Difference %
A: The request for Baptism; in order to help the faith of parents who do not practise regularly or are far away from the Church	14.9	10.8	4.1
B: The celebration of Baptism; in order to evangelize the adults present	21.5	15.5	6.0
C: Confirmation. Quite a few young people become actively involved after receiving this sacrament	22.6	17.4	5.2
D: First Communion; to evangelize the parents	21.0	14.3	6.7

All parishes administer these sacraments. What concerns us here is to establish whether when they are administered special attention is paid to those who do not normally go to Church. The percentages are generally quite low, but the average difference of 5.5%, even if low, is not insignificant.

'Evangelization requires that parishes transform themselves from centres of religious services into a living community of believers' (Congress on 'The Evangelizing Parish', Part 3, II, 1).

21.

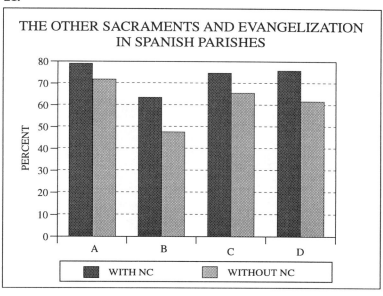

THE OTHER SACRAMENTS AND EVANGELIZATION IN SPANISH PARISHES

Administration of the other sacraments in parishes with and without Neocatechumenal Communities (% responses 'a lot' and 'a little')	With NC %	Without NC %	Difference %
A: The parishes instil in the faithful the sense of sin, the need for conversion and the joy of reconsiliation	79.0	71.9	7.1
B: Matrimonial preparation is above all a means of initiation in the faith for those who need it	63.6	47.8	15.8
C: Importance is given to the celebration of matrimony as an act of evangelization for the spouses and all those present	74.8	65.7	9.1
D: We find that some or many couples who were far from the faith, continue to try to deepen it after celebrating the sacrament	75.9	61.9	14.0

The belief that these Neocatechumenal communities are closed upon themselves and are not open to the parish would appear to be unsustainable. The average difference in these statistics is 11.5%. In the communities the catechumenate serves to strengthen faith; its aim is to help the members rediscover their Baptism and to help others do the same.

'The renewal of the parish in the service of faith, in a society which is on the road to de-Christianization...' (Congress on 'The Evangelizing Parish', chapter 25).

22.

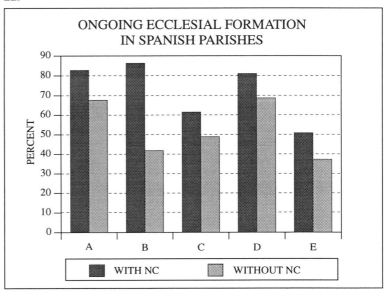

ONGOING ECCLESIAL FORMATION IN SPANISH PARISHES

Spanish parishes offer	With NC %	Without NC %	Difference %
A: Systematic catechesis for adolescents and young people	82.6	67.6	14.9
B: Systematic catechesis for adults	86.2	41.9	44.3
C: Ongoing formation for young people and adults	61.5	48.9	12.6
D: Training for pastoral workers to improve their service to the community	81.0	68.7	12.3
E: Prayer groups	50.8	37.3	15.5

The Neocatechumenal Way, which is a lengthy and structured process, leading to the renewal of one's Baptism, can be considered a means of ongoing and systematic formation. Parishes with Neocatechumenal communities reach a higher level than the parishes without, showing an average difference of +19.9%.

'Our catecheses tend to place too great an emphasis on "preparation for the sacraments". The true education in the faith is a process of Christian initiation which is celebrated in the sacraments, but which remains uncompleted until Christians who are adult and committed have been formed' (Congress on 'The Evangelising Parish', chapter 6).

23.

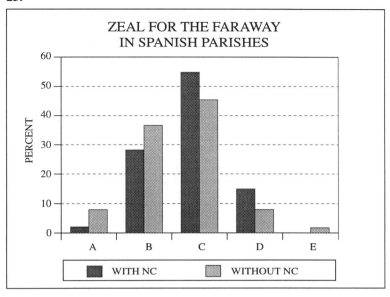

How much importance is given in the parishes to the objective of reaching the faraway	With NC %	Without NC %	Difference %
A: None	2.1	8.0	
B: A little	28.2	36.7	
C: Quite a lot	54.9	45.4	9.5
D: A lot	14.9	8.0	6.9
E: No opinion / No reply	0.0	1.8	

The replies of the parishes with Neocatechumenal communities differ from those which do not have them. The former illustrate a concern which is 16.4 percentage points greater than the latter (quite a lot and a lot) to reach the faraway.

'The parable of the lost sheep impels us to change our attitude and behaviour towards the faraway; it is precisely this which the congress is seeking to promote... the Church's calling and her deepest identity are to be found in evangelization' (Congress on 'The Evangelising Parish', chapter 3, 24).

24.

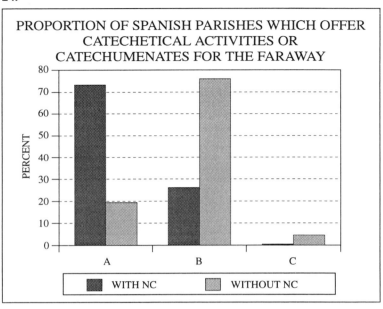

PROPORTION OF SPANISH PARISHES WHICH OFFER CATECHETICAL ACTIVITIES OR CATECHUMENATES FOR THE FARAWAY

Does the parish carry out missionary catechesis or systematic catecheses of catechumenal type which are aimed primarily at the faraway?	With NC %	Without NC %	Difference %
A: Yes	73.3	19.4	53.9
B: No	26.2	76.1	
C: No opinion / No reply	0.5	4.5	

The zeal for the faraway from the Lord is put into practice by giving them something stable and effective for renewing their faith. The difference of 53.9% within the parishes is certainly very substantial.

"We have been sent by God to evangelize our world. This apostolic vocation is a gift from God which we ought to receive with joy; it frees us from nostalgia for the past and from the desire to restore the enclosed fortress-like parish which cannot respond to this missionary vocation" (Congress on 'The Evangelizing Parish', chapter 24).

168

25.

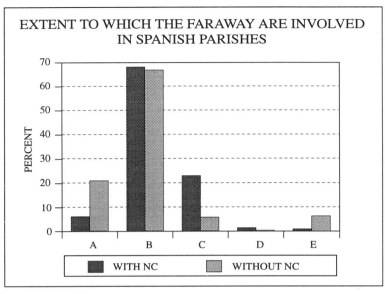

EXTENT TO WHICH THE FARAWAY ARE INVOLVED IN SPANISH PARISHES

To what extent are the faraway involved in the activities of the parish and the church?	With NC %	Without NC %	Difference %
A: Not at all	6.2	20.9	
B: Little	68.2	66.7	
C: Quite a lot	23.1	5.7	17.4
D: A lot	1.5	0.4	1.1
E: No opinion / No reply	1.0	6.4	

This demonstrates the general difficulty encountered in involving those who are far away in the life of the parish. In spite of this, there is a difference of 18.5% (combining the 'quite a lot' and the 'a lot') in favour of parishes which have Neocatechumenal Communities. On average, in those parishes with Communities four times as many of the far away from the Lord are involved in parish life as in parishes without Neocatechumenal Communities. This follows from all that has been reported so far.

"The evangelisation demands from our parishes a profound renewal in order for the saving and liberating power of Jesus Christ to shine on those men and women who have either not received the Gospel or who have received it in an insufficient way, or else have abandoned it in the midst of a society in which the vital structures (family, culture, economy, work, politics) show a a serious divergence from the Christian concept of life" (Congress on the Evangelizing Parish', chapter 17).

26.

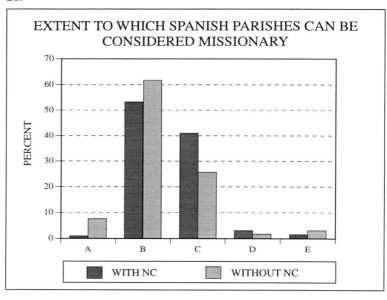

EXTENT TO WHICH SPANISH PARISHES CAN BE CONSIDERED MISSIONARY

Classification of Spanish parishes from the point of view of their concern for evangelization	With NC %	Without NC %	Difference %
A: Non-missionary	1.0	7.6	
B: Of limited missionary character	53.3	61.8	
C: Quite missionary	41.0	25.7	15.3
D: Very missionary	3.1	1.8	1.3
E: No opinions / No reply	1.6	3.1	

The categories 'quite missionary' and 'very missionary' show a global difference of 16.6%.

"The most important challenge for parishes today is the passage from pastoral action for the conservation of Christianity to pastoral action for mission" (Congress on 'The Evangelizing Parish', chapter 17).

27.

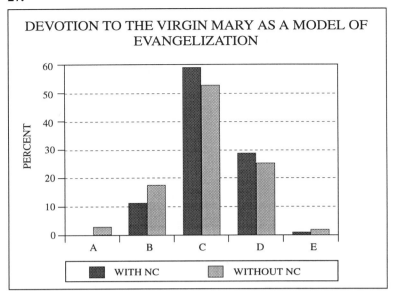

DEVOTION TO THE VIRGIN MARY AS A MODEL OF EVANGELIZATION

Do the parishes stimulate devotion to the Virgin Mary, the model and exceptional instrument of evangelization	With NC %	Without NC %	Difference %
A: No	0	2.7	
B: A little	11.3	17.5	
C: Quite a lot	59.0	52.8	6.2
D: A lot	28.7	25.1	3.6
E: No opinion / No reply	1.0	1.9	

The Virgin has a profound importance in the work of Evangelization.

In his speeches, the Pope often reminds us: "The help of the Most Blessed Mary is necessary for the discovery of the roots of your faith and the renewal of your baptismal promises".

Conclusions

The differences outlined above are not solely due to the fact that parishes have (or do not have) Neocatechumenal communities. A more detailed analysis would require the isolation of other factors, for example, the number of years which the communities have been in the parish and the extent of their integration.

However, it is beyond dispute that Spanish parishes with Neocatechumenal communities when compared with those that do not have them demonstrate the following characteristics:

– aspects of parish organization which express a greater openness, lay participation and co-responsibility;
– a greater involvement of lay people in pastoral work;
– a greater ecclesial presence in society and in the local area;
– an increased participation in apostolic movements, associations and groups;
– a greater commitment to evangelization through the administration of the sacraments;
– the availability of more focused methods for the ongoing ecclesial formation of the faithful;
– a more emphatic concern for the faraway;
– more catechetical or catechumenal activity for the faraway;
– a greater number of faraway people involved in parish activities;
– a greater number of objective elements which permit the parish to be described as more missionary.

A comparison of the results of the 40 indices analysed shows an average difference of more than 17.5%.

Another important characteristic, not analysed in this survey, is that parents almost invariably follow their children into the community when the children persevere in the Neocatechumenal Way. If the parents enter first and persevere, then in time their children join them. This has been shown to happen in almost 100% of cases.

The majority of those who become members of the new communities in parishes where this kind of pastoral is well established come as a result of personal contact in the family, at work or in the local neighbourhood. When the faith is lived with intensity and joy it is attractive and contagious.

The Church, as a social and visible body, needs to make use of those instruments which show themselves to be most useful for fulfilling her mission. Particularly in these crucial times she cannot waste her energies in things that are barren for the faith. Present culture and society, mankind, need the children of God to show themselves with strength.

FR FRANCISCO AZCONA SAN MARTIN
Director of the Office of Statistics and Sociology
of the Spanish Episcopal Conference

Complete texts of Paul VI and John Paul II

In this Appendix VI we offer the reader, in their entirety and in chronological order, some of the speeches of Paul VI and John Paul II, extracts from which, for thematic reasons, have been divided across different chapters or have not been reported in their entirety. We have not, however, included reports of those speeches which, although they have been divided, have in fact been included in their entirety in one chapter.

After Baptism

(*Paul VI: general audience, 12th January, 1977* – Text translated from the original recording by Vatican Radio.)

You are all welcome *in nomine Domini*.

Despite the fact that the season, we are in the heart of winter, is not favourable to pilgrimages, excursions, visits and reunions, we are happy to welcome you to our hall which is honoured and filled by the presence of visitors we shall now name.

You know that we greet you all truly with the awareness that you are spokesmen, transmitters of a blessing which transcends us, that is, of being representatives, ministers of a grace of the Lord which we want to communicate to all, and to communicate precisely with a sense of that union, that charity, that fusion of spirit, that unity which distinguishes us for our faith and for the good fortune that we all have of belonging to the mystical Body of Christ. To you all, we give our blessed welcome. We will accompany this with our prayers and spiritual remembrance, this moment when you, by visiting us, procure for us the true happiness of being together and of being with Christ.

Greetings: We have great pleasure and we are very moved to

have a special group of Bishops whom we welcome – so as not to prolong this preface too much – to our general audience and then separately in the adjoining room... So that you know where these Bishops come from and the importance of this other group of our brothers in the episcopate, whom we have the honour of having with us today, we shall read, as has been suggested to us, where they come from.

We have two Bishops from Mexico, a Bishop from El Salvador, from Guatemala, Honduras, the Dominican Republic; then two Bishops from Brazil, Ecuador, Peru, Uruguay, the Philippines; we have a Bishop from England; one from Spain and one from Portugal, and some others from Italy – the Archbishop of Rossano, the Bishops of Sarzana and Brugnato, of Macerata and Tolentino, of Fabriano, Rieti, Teramo, Crotone, and finally from Piazza Armerina. It is an audience with a truly catholic, not to say ecumenical nature, but catholic means more because it is a perfection which is already complete and already consummate, and so we welcome all these brethren, we try to read into their heart the reason for their coming and to respond to them with all our sympathy, and our encouragement for this very significant action of their ministry.

They accompany the large group whom we shall nominate shortly, and for whom we have reserved the little allocution which we usually hold at general Audiences. I repeat that these Bishops are all welcomed by us and I would say embraced. We are all the more united by their presence in paying homage to our Holy Church, in honouring Jesus Christ, in being anxious about the apostolate, of gaining souls in the world today, and in the common hope which continues in time and transcends time, for the final eschatology of the visible and full meeting with Our Lord Jesus Christ. To them our reverent thankfulness for their participation in this audience, our help and our blessing which should reach also, dearest brothers in the Episcopate, to your respective Dioceses, and you can be assured that our prayers, wishes, and the common hope in Christ goes with our wishes.

So now we welcome first of all the large group that forms the main part of this audience. Later, we will say something about it. It is made up of the parish priests and lay missionaries of Neocatechumenal communities. They come from different countries and, as you can see, make up a very varied community – priests, religious, lay people, and so on. To all of you, we extend a warm welcome. Later, we shall say a few words for this occasion and for the sake of the goal which unites them in this meeting and makes them profess their faith in the Church and, finally, we shall give our special blessing. We repeat, Neocatechumenal communities from various countries.

...We welcome them, this main group, giving them that small gift, shall we say, which we usually give in our general audience, that is, a word, a word upon which to meditate and reflect, and which is, if nothing else, proof of our affection for those who are listening to it.

The presence at this audience of a group noticeable because of its numbers – most of you here are part of this group – and because of the rank of the participants – your leaders, and above all the group of bishops whom you have brought with you – this group of the members of the Neocatechumenal Communities offers us, by its presence, the opportunity to draw two events of the Catholic Church to the attention of our visitors and to those listening. The first is the Synod of Bishops three years ago, in 1974, on the subject "Evangelisation in our times": the way in which the Gospel is spread today. This was the theme of the 1974 Synod which provided the subject matter of our subsequent apostolic exhortation, *Evangelii Nuntiandi* of the 8th December 1975. If we had the foolish ambition of advertising our documents, we should almost like to recommend it to you because it is so full, it is a such a tribute to all that the Bishops said in the Synod. I have tried to interpret, to gather together, all their ideas, to organise them and to make them accessible in the simplest possible language, but also, most importantly, the clearest possible, so making us bold to recommend it to you, especially to you who want to be **Neocatechumens**, that is, to give instruction and evangelise the great crowds of people you succeed in reaching. I think it would be good for you and for your students, your disciples.

The second event is still in the future, and will take place this year, beginning on September 30th: another Synod of Bishops. We will have about two hundred bishops here from all over the world, nominated by their respective episcopal conferences. What will the theme be? The theme will once again deal with evangelisation, but from another aspect, that is catechesis: how religion is taught, especially to children, to boys and girls, to young people and to adults too, at this stage of our civilisation, and how to become teachers. It is the bishops who wanted this theme, and we shall take it up again and develop it. **This shows how up-to-date you catechumens are**.

This shows an awareness that the fundamental mission of the Church is to spread the message of the Gospel, according to the last command given by Jesus at the end of his visible presence on earth – what were his words? "Go and preach!" *"Go and make disciples of all nations."* This awareness is keenly alive and at work in the Church today. How often it is said, when looking at past history that has characterised the different periods of the history of the Church, "But what were they doing?" Either there was war between certain states, or there were dogmatic problems and so on, which were of little interest to public opinion or the pastoral apostolate. The Church has been meditating again on her proper function and pastoral duties, and her first pastoral duty is to announce the Gospel and to go out to the world and say,

"Look, I am bringing you the message, the message which the angels brought to the earth, 'Glory to God and peace on earth', and then the message of Christ to announce the Gospel, that is, the good news taught to us by Jesus Christ."

This awareness of the fundamental mission of the Church to spread the Gospel message is alive and working in the Church today, and – this is beautiful – it is the task of all ministers, that is, Bishops, priests, religious men and women, and the faithful! The faithful themselves become the voice which must propagate this message; the message of the evangelical announcement which today more than ever is worth being announced for two reasons which seem contradictory. One, we must announce it because the world is deaf, and so you have to raise your voice, to find a way so that it can be understood, and so you must insist, all must be called to a new school etc. The difficulty becomes something that provokes us, it becomes the incentive to become teachers of our catechism, that is to say of the truth of the Gospel to be announced.

And there is a second reason which is exactly the opposite of the first. He who knows how to see, to read, into the heart of the masses, the heart of the world, sees that deep down there is discontent, there is restlessness, there is need of a true word, a good word, **a word which tells the meaning of life**! For the world of today no longer knows what it is, it no longer has the strength to define itself. Our world lives like a short-sighted person, or a blind man in the midst of darkness. We have the lantern, we have the lamp, **we have the Word of the Gospel, which becomes the light of the world**. The Lord told his apostles, "you are the light of the world". Well, if we are the light of the world, we must go towards these people who are lost, who are so angry, so cruel, who have become so disorientated, so without principles, without lines of conduct which are good and human; we must go towards them and say: "Look, this is the path, here is the way". And I repeat, the Church speaks for these two reasons, one being the difficulty and the other the opportunity of announcing the Gospel.

We are therefore in a marked apostolic, missionary, and didactic phase of the Church's life. We must all take part in it.

The building up of the Mystical Body of Christ on earth, in other words, our present Church, is the duty, as the Council (*Lumen Gentium* 33) says, not only of priests, bishops, etc, but of every believer. Each one must be a witness; he must be able to transmit, to transfer, at least by his example, the message of which he is the guardian. **A mute Christian does not exist**. A sterile Christian does not exist, a Christian living only for himself does not exist. He must live for the community, for the Mystical Body which is called the Church.

In this vision, it is clear and desirable that efforts should be multiplied to put this immense and urgent programme into practice: to evangelise, to catechise. There are many initiatives parallel, and somewhat similar, to yours. And there is a flourishing of works and means to give the proclamation of the Gospel a better diffusion and interpretation we might say.

We have observed how this multiform phenomenon of the Holy Church is not simply concerned with the scholastic and the didactic aspect of its activities. It is not simply the instruction of pupils by school teachers. Rather it is something wider, more pedagogical and vital, concerned with the style of life, in which the teaching of religious truth is parallel to scholastic teaching and, indeed, united to the profession of life, of which teaching is the norm and principle.

In the second place we note how this task does not place a heavy and difficult burden on those who carry it out or on those whom it helps, even though it is difficult in reality. For what is one of the greatest difficulties which priests encounter? Well, it is that no one comes. "How boring listening to preaching, listening to the lesson, learning the catechism, it tires me and I like going out, going to the cinema, playing, etc." Somehow this Church which teaches becomes so boring – but it is not so! We say it to ourselves and we say it to our people. Anyone who understands the secret of the truth which our words contain becomes as if struck by this light, by this truth and is so transformed into apostle, priest, announcer, as much as the disciple who listens: "Oh! I didn't think it was so beautiful, ah, but it's true, but just look..." I repeat, a horizon of light and beauty that is almost unexpected opens up. The fulfilment of this difficult task becomes an honour, a fortune, it becomes a vocation that enobles and exalts.

I would like to ask, if there are missionaries amongst you, why are you missionaries? It is because you are exalted by the sense of the Gospel, by what it means to announce the Truth, to announce the secret of life, God's plans, the hopes which do not die! But it becomes so beautiful that you cannot escape from it. And so we, too, become called to be apostles and announcers of this truth!

Carrying out this duty of announcing is no longer boring, just as the task of listening is no longer tiresome,. It contains in itself the replenishment of tiredness which it entails and makes its witnesses happy, it makes them secure, it makes them participants in the expectation of the goods of the Kingdom of God which they announce. In our place here at the centre of the Church, it is our duty to welcome many who come from far away, from the missions. And we welcome these people with great pleasure, and we let them speak so that we may hear their witness. Some have enormous difficulties, one does not know how they can live, what they live on, how they overcome illness, hostility, dangers, and so on, and yet – I tell you this because you, too, are happy – when they talk and define themselves, they express a happiness which has no equal with the happinesses of this world. And if we dare say, "But do you want to you stay here or to go back?" "Go back, go back!" they say. And they go in the midst of enormous difficulties because they are caught by the joy of the Gospel.

Therefore then, we say that they who with simple and generous hearts put themselves at the service of the Gospel, undergo, certainly through a secret but sure charism of the Holy Spirit, a psychological and moral metamorphosis, which transforms the difficulties into stimuli. I repeat what I was saying before, why do the missionaries return? Because there is so much to do, because there are those poor people to be consoled, because there is danger, "I have to go and cure the lepers, I must go and prevent these poor people from being overwhelmed by other social movements and becoming the slaves of intolerable situations." The difficulty, the obstacle becomes attractive. What once aroused fear, was boring, was tiresome, instead then becomes the force which attracts, which makes one committed, which binds, and which makes the apostle – let us say the great word, but said in a general sense, 'Martyr', that is to say, witness.

And this phenomenon is tremendous. Whoever knows how to look at the phenomena of the Church – we have this responsibility and this good fortune – cannot but say, "Thank you God, for giving this vision to me, of seeing so many who are enthusiasts of the Gospel, of the Gospel which is difficult, of the Gospel which is painful, of the Gospel which costs, of the Gospel which does not yield, of the Gospel which collides against all the mentalities and all the vices and obstacles of the world". The Gospel, I repeat, makes those who preach it happy and turns the difficulties into incentives, the dangers into attractions, and the defeats themselves – it seems a paradox – the defeats, that is to say, the failures into merits (...but I did what I could!) and thus into peace which descends serenely into those hearts which have not even had the satisfaction of the success of their labours.

Now we can understand the testimony which our visitors bear today, and which deals with the pivot of Christian life, which is Baptism.

The word 'catechumenate' refers to baptism. It was the period of preparation for baptism. Nowadays, baptism does not have the same development, at least in its didactic preparation. And so our visitors [the Neocatechumens] today say: We will carry out this preparation *after baptism*. The sanctifying grace received was not sufficient; on the contrary, sanctifying grace has done no more than light a fire which needs to spread itself into the whole of the baptised person's life. Saint Augustine says this: "If we cannot have the catechumenate beforehand, we will carry it out afterwards." That is, the instruction, completion and education, the whole of the Church's educative work, after Baptism.

The sacrament of Christian regeneration must once again return to being what it was in the consciousness and custom of the first generations of Christians. The praxis (the practice, isn't it so?) and norms of the Church have introduced the holy rule of conferring baptism on the newly born. What instruction do they receive? It is necessary therefore that the godfather should take the infant's place, speaking on its behalf. But the latter does not benefit from the attestation given by the godfather to the priest. What has happened is that the preparation has been liturgically concentrated in the baptismal rite. The liturgy in fact still bears traces of this preparatory initiation which preceded baptism, and which during the early times when society was profoundly pagan, was called the catechumenate. Later, the Church condensed this period. Why? Because all families were Catholic, all were good, all were Christian; the orientation of society was fundamentally Christian. The children would continue to learn 'along the way'.

But today our society is no longer uniform, homogeneous. It is pluralistic, and indeed in itself is full of contradictions and obstacles to the Gospel. In the social environment of today, this method needs to be completed by instruction, by initiation after baptism, into the proper life style of the Christian. This has to come after baptism.

This is the secret of your formula, which provides religious assistance, a practical training in Christian faithfulness, and effectively integrates the baptised into the community of believers which is the Church. They have already entered it from the supernatural point of view, but it was like a seed that has not yet had the advantage of developing.

Here we see the rebirth of the name 'Catechumenate'. This certainly does not intend to invalidate or to diminish the importance of the baptismal discipline as currently practised, but seeks to apply it according to a gradual and intensive method which recalls and renews in a certain way the Catechumenate of earlier times. The person who has been baptised needs to understand, to think over, to appreciate, to give assent to the inestimable treasure of the Sacrament he has received.

We are happy to see that this need today is understood by the institutional church structures: the parishes, the dioceses in particular, and by all the other religious families. In this area of structures, as I have said, the parish is fundamental.

Here we see a catechesis taking shape, which is subsequent to the one that baptism did not have. 'Pastoral work for adults', as it is referred to today, is taking shape, creating new methods and new programmes, and also new ministries. What a great need there is for people to help. And so we see catechists, nuns, and families too, who are becoming the teachers in this evangelisation that takes place after Baptism. New subsidiary ministries are supporting the ever more demanding roles of the priest and the deacon, in teaching and in participating in the liturgy. New forms of charity, culture and social solidarity are increasing the vitality of the Christian community and, before the world are becoming its defence, its apologia and its attraction.

Many people are attracted to these Neocatechumenal Communities, because they see that there is a sincerity, a truth in them, something alive and authentic, Christ living in the world. May this happen with our Apostolic Blessing.

Visit of Pope John Paul II to the Parish of Our Lady of the Blessed Sacrament and of the Canadian Martyrs

(*Rome, 2nd November 1980* – Cf. the Italian edition of *L'Osservatore Romano*, 3rd-4th November 1980, augmented by material from a tape recording)

1. **Above all, I want to tell you that I love you**, seeing so many of you meeting together, adults, young people, children, with your priests. I love you. I have followed with interest the information given to me by your presbyter. This is not the first time that I have heard him speak of his enthusiasm for the Neocatechumenal movement, which being 'way' is also movement. I have also listened with great interest to the testimony of your first catechist.

What can I tell you? Most importantly, **the word which came up most often was the word faith**. All of you are faithful, I mean you have faith. There is more to say: many have faith, but **you have followed a way to discover your faith**, to discover the divine treasure that you carry within you, in your souls. And you have made such a discovery, **discovering the mystery of baptism**. It is true that in the world there are a great many people who are baptised. Certainly they are still a minority among the people of the world, but they are many. Among these baptised, I don't know how many are aware of their baptism, not simply of the fact of being baptised, but of what it means to be baptised, of what baptism means.

Now **the road or the way to discover faith through baptism is the road that we all find in the teaching of Christ, in the Gospel**.

We find it reflected too in a profound way in the letters of St Paul. He has shown us the immense depths of the mystery of baptism, comparing immersion in the baptismal waters with immersion in the death of Christ, a death which has brought us redemption, and a death which brings us resurrection. Thus the whole paschal mystery is summed up in the sacrament, I mean in the mystery, of baptism.

Look. To discover the dynamic depths of our faith is to discover the full meaning of our baptism. If I understand correctly, **your way consists essentially of this**: **to discover the mystery of baptism, to discover its full content**, and so to discover what it means to be Christian, to be a believer.

This discovery is in the line of tradition, it has roots which are apostolic, Pauline, evangelical. At the same time, this discovery is original. It has always been so, and will always be so. Every time that a Christian discovers the depths of the mystery of his baptism, he is accomplishing an act which is completely original. It is not possible to do this except with the help of the grace of Christ, and the light of the Holy Spirit, because it is a mystery, because it is a divine, supernatural reality, and natural man is not able to understand it, to discover it, to live it. So it must be concluded: all of you who have had the grace to discover the depths, the full reality, of your baptism, ought to be very grateful to the giver of grace, to the Holy Spirit, who has given you such light, who has given you the help of the grace to receive this gift in the first place, and then to continue. Here we conclude the first part of the reflection.

2. Here briefly is the second part: to discover baptism as the beginning of our Christian life, of our immersion in God, in the living God, and in the mystery of redemption, the paschal mystery, to discover our baptism as the beginning of Christian life, must constitute the beginning of the whole of our Christian life, step by step, day by day, week by week, stage by stage of our life, because Christian life is a dynamic process. One begins with, one normally baptises little children soon after birth, but then they grow. Man grows, the Christian must grow too. And so we must project the discovery of baptism on the whole of life, on all aspects of life. We have to see also, on the basis of this sacramental beginning to our life, the whole sacramental dimension of our life, because the whole of life has a multifold sacramental dimension.

There are the sacraments of initiation: Baptism and Confirmation, through which one reaches the fullness, the central point of this initiation in the Eucharist. Moreover we know very well that the Fathers of the Church spoke of the sacrament of Penance as a new baptism, as a second baptism, a third, a tenth, and so on.

We can speak too of the last baptism of human life, the Sacrament of the Sick. There are also the sacraments of community life: the Priesthood, Marriage. Christian life has a totally sacramental structure, and we have to frame the discovery of our own baptism against such a background, which is essentially sanctifying, because the sacraments make way for the Holy Spirit. Christ has given us the Holy Spirit in its absolute fullness. We need only to open our hearts and make way. **The sacraments make way for the Holy Spirit who works in our souls**, in our hearts, in our humanity, in our personality. He builds us anew, he creates a new man.

So **this way, a way of faith, a way of baptism rediscovered,**

has to be the way of the new man. This new man sees what is the true proportion, or rather, the disproportion, of his created being, of his creaturehood, with respect to God the creator, and to the infinite majesty of God the redeemer, God the holy one and sanctifier. In the light of this, he tries to fulfil himself. Thus life takes on a moral aspect. This must be another fruit, indeed I would say the same fruit, of rediscovering the sacramental structure of our Christian life, because sacramental means sanctifying. At the same time, we must discover the ethical structure, because that which is holy is always good, it doesn't have room for evil, for sin. Certainly the Holy One, the most Holy of all, Christ, accepts sinners, he welcomes them, but to make them holy. This, then, is the whole programme. So we have the second point, the second conclusion. Discovering baptism as the beginning of our Christian life in all its depths, we then need to discover the consequences, step by step, in our whole Christian life. So, to do this, we need to follow a way, **we must follow a way**.

3. The third point: That discovery must become leaven in us. **This leaven shows itself, taking flesh and becoming alive, in the fulfilment of our personal Christianity, in the building up, if we can say that, of the new man. But this leaven also realises itself in an** apostolic dimension. **We are sent; the Church is apostolic, not only founded on the apostles, but permeated throughout her body by a spirit and charism that is apostolic**.

Certainly, this apostolic spirit must always be co-ordinated in a social and communal dimension of the whole body, and for this reason, Christ has also constituted the hierarchy. The Church has her hierarchic structure, as the Second Vatican Council's fundamental document, *Lumen Gentium*, reminds us. This is about the leaven and the apostolate.

4. The final point. There could be many other ones, but I want to end with this one. My dearest ones, **we are living in a period** in which we are experiencing a radical confrontation – and I say this, because it is my experience over many years – **a radical confrontation that is everywhere**. There is no one single manifestation of this, but many throughout the world: faith and anti-faith, Gospel and anti-Gospel; Church and anti-Church, God and anti-God, if we can put it like that. An anti-God does not exist, an anti-God cannot exist, but an anti-God can exist in man, the radical denial of God can be created in man. We are living this experience in our history, and more so than in previous times.

In this age of ours, we need to rediscover a radical faith, radically understood, radically lived, and radically fulfilled. We have need of such a faith. I hope that your experience is born within such a perspective, and may lead towards a healthy radicalisation of our Christianity, of our faith, towards an authentic evangelical radicalism. This is why you have need of a great spirit, of great self control, and also, as your first catechist has said, of great obedience to the Church. This has always been the case. This witness was given by the saints: by St Francis, by various charismatic people in different ages of the Church. This radicalism, I would say this radicalisation of faith is needed, yes, but it must always be situated within the life of the Church, and with her guidance, because the Church in her entirety has received the Holy Spirit from Christ in the persons of the apostles after his resurrection.

I see that you meet, I myself have met you, in different groups, in different parishes in Rome, but I think that the biggest group is here. So I am giving a longer talk. One that's not been prepared specifically, but is always present in my mind and heart. So it's not, may we say, a magisterial speech, but a spontaneous pastoral discourse.

This joy that surrounds you, that is in your songs, in your behaviour, may very well be a sign of your southern temperament, but I hope it is a fruit of the Spirit, and I wish that it may be so. Yes, the Church needs joy, because joy, with its different expressions, is a revelation of happiness. So, here man finds himself faced with his fundamental, we can almost say his natural, vocation: man is created to be happy, for happiness. If he sees this happiness, if he meets it in the expression of joy, he can start a way. Here I must say to you: the songs are good, your expressions of joy are good, but the Spirit is the one who initiates this way.

That is, more or less, all that I wanted, all that I have been able, to tell you in these circumstances, and I think that I have said enough, and maybe even too much.

I give you the blessing, together with the cardinals and bishops present here.

Visit of Pope John Paul II to the Parish of the Immaculate Conception at the 'Cervalletta' – Tor Sapienza.

(*Rome, 7th March 1982* – Cf. the Italian edition of *L'Osservatore Romano*, 8-9th March 1982, augmented by material taken from a tape recording.)

I think, first of all, something must be said about your parish priest. I think that the parish priest, like any other priest, **should always be one of us**. And your priest is this; he is not the only one, but I see him so more than others, here too in this environment, one of us. And there is another thing: to say that a parish priest is in love may seem like a contradiction.

But I tell you that **he must be in love** and I see that he is in love, in love with all the groups, but perhaps a bit 'more' with your group. This could have led to favouritism, but it has not. I see this because it is fairly clear, and it seems to me that through your community, he has fallen in love with the whole of his parish. And the parish is larger than your community but that's the way Jesus arranged things. He spoke to us of **leaven**: the dough and the leaven, and the leaven is always a part, something small, and the mass is the mass – but it needs leaven.

I think that the parish priest and his collaborators have found a leaven in your community, which I have also seen in other groups, but perhaps in your group in a special way. He has "walked in this Way" as you say in your language – I already know you a little from meeting you in several parishes in Rome – and not always in parishes, but mostly in parishes. I think that your community in this parish is very well organised. It is growing together with the parish priest and together with the parish. As he said, ten or fifteen years ago he saw the difficulties of this parish, what there was and what was missing and together with you took on the appropriate apostolic commitments.

What is most significant, particularly in your communities in general, and in your community here, could be said in two words. One fundamental word which always comes up when listening to someone in the Neocatechumenal way, is the word **discovery**. Discovery is always something great. If you make some scientific discovery, if you discover a new continent, like Christopher Columbus did, then what a discovery that is. But without any doubt, all discoveries of a physical nature cannot be compared to those of a spiritual nature. For you, 'discovery' is the word which sums up each one of you and your community.

It is the discovery of the reality of baptism, which is a wonderful reality, an amazing reality. Even in theological terms, if we listen to what St Paul says in his letters, it is an amazing reality.

If we then take it existentially, as a way of being, the rediscovery of baptism is even more wonderful, more astonishing than baptism in general. It is a sacrament of the Church, yes, but I mean my baptism, my reality, the gift given by the Heavenly Father through Jesus Christ to me in person, the source of new life, divine life in me. We ought to speak at length about this, and look at the texts of St Paul word by word.

Let us return to 'discovery'. This discovery is all the more profound when it comes, as an affirmation, after a situation of contradiction, of negation. It could be said that the preceding negation makes the affirmation that follows it stronger and deeper. As there are ex-Marxists here, we might be inclined to think of dialectics, of Hegelism in fact, the yes and the no, the no and the yes. But this is now transcended, we pass from no to yes, and this **'yes'** is much more dynamic.

We have a wonderful example, the prime example. It is Paul who discovered Christ, and in so doing, discovered his baptism – because discovering Christ means discovering one's own baptism. Paul discovered it after he had been a persecutor, an anti-

Christ let us say. If not an anti-Christ, an anti-Christian, because Jesus says to Paul, "Why do you persecute me?", not "my brothers and my followers", but "me". So the first thing: the discovery is a gift from God, a grace, and a grace cannot be explained. It is to discover one's own faith, one's own Christianity, one's being as a Christian – from this starting point one begins to see all the other elements. There is a new life, a new vision of life. All the elements, all of life, look different. It is a new world. In today's liturgy, we contemplated the Transfiguration: a new world.

There is also another word which is heard more and more often in contacts with Neocatechumenal groups. It is the word 'itinerant'. *Iter* means way or journey, as we know well, but here it means an apostolic way, and the itinerants are those who set off on a journey, begin a way to take their discovery to others. We find ourselves once again in the footsteps of the Apostles, of Christians, of all Christians, of every generation. Christianity – the Gospel – is not a theoretical method which can be transmitted as something abstract or something that can be deduced. Not at all. It is an existential system: you **must be** a Christian by conviction.

A Christian who has **discovered** the value of his being Christian, of his faith, of his divine sonship, of his likeness to Christ, has finally discovered the reality of Christ in him, he has discovered his Baptism. Then such a man is able to **transmit,** not only is he able, but **he is driven**, **he is driven**; **he cannot remain silent**, but he has to walk, he must walk, it is, we could say, a natural motion. There is a propulsion which is found within, and the movement follows, it is propelled. That is enough, no more. It's enough or we would go on too long.

May you continue in this way in this parish well organised, well organised in the life of this parish. May you remain leaven, because it seems to me that this word – we are speaking of the way you are organised in the parish – is the most important: **be leaven**. The mass of dough is great, twenty thousand parishioners. I think that nearly all of them are baptised – so there are many baptisms to be discovered. Therefore be leaven, continue to be leaven. Enough. A blessing and then you can go home. Sing another song. For you, to sing means to pray. We can sing the Our Father together once, because the Pope knows it too.

Private audience of Pope John Paul II for the Bishops and Parish Priests attending the convention on 'Penance and Reconciliation' promoted by the Neocatechumenal Communities

(*Rome, 10th February 1983* – Cf. the Italian edition of *L'Osservatore Romano*, 11th February 1983, and the English edition, 7th March 1983.)

Dear Brothers!

1. I am happy to have the opportunity today to meet a group of members of the Neocatechumenal Communities gathered in Rome to meditate together on Reconciliation and Penance in the mission of the Church, which is the theme of the next Synod of Bishops.

I greet the bishops, pastors and priests here present, who have come from all the continents for this occasion.

I would like my words to be a reflection on the spiritual and ecclesial experience which you intend to follow through, that they may be for you an incentive towards an ever greater commitment in offering, within the context of the modern world, a clear and genuine example of profound Christian faith, lived constantly in intimate, docile and happy union with the pastors of the Church.

Your witness is meant to be fundamentally one of announcing the Gospel message, which has as its centre the proclamation that Jesus of Nazareth is the Messiah, the Lord, the incarnate Son of God, who died and rose again for our salvation. Evangelization – said Paul VI – will always contain – as the foundation, centre and the same time summit of its dynamism – a clear proclamation that in Jesus Christ, the Son of God made man, who died and rose from the dead, salvation is offered to all men, as a gift of God's grace and mercy (Apostolic Exhortation *Evangelii Nuntiandi*, 37).

One of the typical manifestations of your communities is precisely the evangelization carried out in countries and environments which either have never heard the Christian message or have become almost deaf to this message, because of the prevalence of ideologies, concepts, of refusal or indifference to the problem of God itself. This is why you intend to prepare and train catechists, who will have to strive first of all to study thoroughly and live personally the mystery of Christ, "catechizing" – I wrote in the apostolic exhortation about catechesis in our time – "is, in a certain way, to lead a person to study this mystery in all its dimensions... to reveal in the Person of Christ the whole of God's eternal design which is fulfilled in him... The definitive aim of catechesis is to put people not only in touch but in communion, in intimacy, with Jesus Christ: only he can lead us to the love of the Father in the Spirit and make us share in the life of the Holy Trinity" (Apostolic Exhortation, *Catechesi Tradendae*, 5).

I have made note of the commitment of your communities in the meritorious work of catechises. During these years the Episcopal Conferences have intensified their efforts in this field of exceptional importance for the very life of the People of God. To follow the methods, the indications, the routes, the texts, offered by the Episcopates, as also to exercise the ministry of catechesis in communion and in ecclesial discipline, with regard to the fundamental ministry of the bishop and of the priests associated with him, will be a precious help for your catechesis on all levels and it will certainly produce great spiritual fruits among the faithful.

The specific end of every work and form of catechesis will be that of making the seed of faith, deposited by the Holy Spirit with the first announcement and effectively transmitted through Baptism, germinate, grow, and develop.

2. In your communities you want to investigate, not only on a theoretical level, but in a totally special way in its vital dimension, the significance, the value, the richness, the demands of Baptism, the sacrament which is the necessary condition for salvation; which unites one with the death, burial and resurrection of the Saviour; which makes one live Christ's life itself, which makes the baptized person a temple of the Spirit, an adopted son of the heavenly Father, a brother and heir of Christ, a member of Christ's Body, which is the Church. Such thorough study is directed to the rediscovery and evaluation of the riches proper to Baptism, received usually in infancy, and to which, therefore, it is necessary to refer not as a purely juridical fact, but as the true founding moment of the whole Christian life.

By cultivating what we could call a baptismal spirituality, you intend to animate, direct, enrich your pilgrimage of faith, which is the logical development of the intrinsic demands of the sacrament, so that your witness will be always more authentic, sincere, consistent, active and so that you can always be more available to respond readily to the divine call.

Such readiness must be manifested in the continual meditation on and attention to Sacred Tradition and Sacred Scripture, which form "one sacred deposit of the Word of God, which is entrusted to the Church" (Dogmatic Constitution *Dei Verbum*, 10).

From this follows the need for a constant and serious work of personal and community investigation of the Word of God and of the teaching of the Magisterium of the Church, through participation in serious biblical and theological courses. Such a commitment to study and reflection is shown to be more than ever necessary for those who, having to fulfil the role of catechist, have the duty to feed their brothers and sisters with solid spiritual food. Always keep in mind the solemn and strong statement of the Second Vatican Ecumenical Council: "The Church has always venerated the divine Scriptures just as she venerates the Body of the Lord, since, from the table of both the Word of God and of the Body of Christ she unceasingly receives and offers to the faithful the bread of life, especially in the Sacred Liturgy" (Dogmatic Constitution *Dei Verbum*, 21). From Christ the Word to Christ the Eucharist, because the Eucharistic Sacrifice is the source, the centre, the culmination of the whole Christian life.

Celebrate the Eucharist and, above all, Easter, with true piety, with great dignity, with love for the liturgical rites of the Church, with precise observance of the norms established by competent authority, with the desire for communion with all the brethren.

3. Your willingness to respond to the divine appeal likewise must be manifested in continual, untiring daily prayer, an expression above all of adoration which man, fragile, weak, aware that he is a contingent creature, offers to God, the Transcendent, the Infinite, the Omnipotent, the Creator, but also the loving and merciful Father; prayer that therefore also becomes intimate and affectionate dialogue between Father and Son.

Prayer which becomes the suppliant chorus in the Pater Noster, taught to us by Jesus himself: prayer which becomes the solemn and conscious profession of Christian faith in the Creed or Apostolic Symbol; prayer which finds in the Psalms the various and complex inner nuances with which the one who is praying – the People of the Promise, the new Chosen People that is the Church, the Christian in various spiritual situations – can turn to God, his hope, his rock, his salvation: "If the Psalm prays"; St Augustine suggests to us, "pray; if it laments, lament; if it exults, exult; if it hopes, hope; if it fears, fear. All the things which are written here are our mirror" (*Enarr.* in Ps. XXX,II, s.III, 1: CCL 38, 213).

4. Your willingness to respond to the divine appeal is manifested in fulfilling, day after day, the compelling word of Jesus: "Turn away from sin and believe in the Good News" (Mk 1:15). This conversion, this "change of mentality", is above all the rejection of true evil, sin, which draws us away from God. This conversion is a continuous journey of return to the house of the Father, like the return of the prodigal son (cf. Lk 15:11-32). This conversion finds its salvific sign in the Sacrament of Penance or Reconciliation.

Freedom from sin, I wrote in the Bull of Indiction of the Jubilee for the 1950th Anniversary of the Redemption, "is... a fruit and primary requirement of faith in Christ the Redeemer and faith in his Church... At the service of this freedom, the Lord Jesus instituted in the Church the Sacrament of Penance, so that those who have committed sin after Baptism may be reconciled with God whom they have offended, and with the Church which they have wounded" (Bull *Aperite Portas*, 5).

The ministry of reconciliation – this wonderful gift of the infinite mercy of God – is entrusted to you priests. Be ministers who are always worthy, ready, zealous, available, patient, serene, following with faithful diligence the norms established in this matter by ecclesiastical authority. The faithful will thus be able to find in this sacrament an authentic sign and instrument of spiritual rebirth and of gladdening interior freedom.

And all of you, brothers, celebrate the Sacrament of Reconciliation with great confidence in the mercy of God, in full adherence to the ministry and discipline of the Church, with individual confession, as repeatedly recommended by the new

Code of Canon Law, for the pardon and peace of the disciples of the Lord, and as the efficacious announcement of the Lord's goodness to everyone.

5. Along your spiritual journey try to harmonize the requirements of the catechumenate with the commitment to the necessary dedication to the brethren, to the family, to professional and social duties. Above all, do not yield to the temptation to close yourselves in on yourselves, isolating yourselves from the life of the parochial or diocesan community, since only from an effective insertion in those larger organisms can they draw authenticity and effectiveness from your apostolic commitment.

I do not want to conclude these reflections of mine without reminding you and the communities you represent of what I said recently on the occasion of the official presentation of the New Code of Canon Law: the Christian must dispose his own soul to welcome it and to put it into practice. Laws are a munificent gift of God and their observance is true wisdom. The law of the Church is a means, and aid, and also a protection for keeping in communion with the Lord. Therefore the juridical norms, just as the liturgical ones, have to be observed without negligence and without omission.

I am sure that your Communities, moved by the fervour to distinguish themselves in the celebration of Baptism, the Eucharist and Penance, also want to distinguish themselves, under the Church's guidance, in this commitment of fidelity to common discipline.

Dearest Brothers!

While I offer these thoughts of mine for your reflection, I invoke the abundance of divine grace upon you here present, and on all the communities which you represent. I entrust everyone to Mary Most Holy, incomparable example of ardent faith and docile acceptance of the will of God.

May she who "advanced in her pilgrimage of faith and loyally persevered in her union with her Son unto the cross" (*Lumen Gentium*, 58) comfort you with her maternal smile in the daily pilgrimage of the following of Christ.

With my Apostolic Blessing.

Pope John Paul II's greeting to those participating in the convention on 'Penance and Reconciliation' during the Sunday Angelus

(*St Peter's Square, 13th February 1983* – Cf. the Italian edition of *L'Osservatore Romano*, 14-15th February, 1983.)

I wish to address a warm greeting to the large group here present who have these days participated in the convention in Rome on 'Penance and Reconciliation', sponsored by the Neocatechumenal Communities.

I want to express to you once again, dear brothers and sisters, my satisfaction for this congress of yours which has assembled about sixty bishops and two thousands pastors and priests coming from the five continents to reflect on the theme of the next Synod of Bishops.

In the meeting I had with you last Thursday I was able once more to appreciate the enthusiasm that distinguishes you.

Continue with tireless and ever renewed generosity your commitment to the apostolate and Christian witness, particularly in the field of catechetics, in which you have produced so many good fruits in these years.

May my Apostolic Blessing accompany you and all the members of the Neocatechumenal Communities in the world.

Visit of Pope John Paul II to the parish of St Francesca Cabrini

(*Rome, 4th December, 1983* – Cf. the Italian edition of *L'Osservatore Romano*, 5-6th December 1983, augmented by material taken from a tape recording.)

I am very happy to see you, and your families and your children. We are all children of God, we become children of God through Baptism, a great Sacrament, tremendous, I would say. It does not seem so because it is a very sweet Sacrament which works through water, with oil, with Holy Chrism (this morning I baptised a baby girl).

And this Sacrament, Baptism, which is so sweet and which we usually confer on newborn babies, this Sacrament has tremendous depth, stupendous depth, because it immerses us in the redemptive death of Christ, immerses us, so we can rise with Christ and thus participate in his work. It is the only way to be children of God, the only sacramental way to be sons, to share in the life which Christ has brought us, showing it by his Resurrection.

What I say to you touches what is specific about your movement which is called Neocatechumenal. The Catechumenate was a very ancient institution of the Church. How many catechumens passed through this ancient Rome of the Caesars, this Rome, this pagan Rome, and how many were prepared with the Catechumenate and the Baptism of adults! But today Baptism, the same Sacrament, has become the sacrament of little children, of newborn babies and this catechumenal way is deferred until after Baptism: Catechumenate thus becomes life-long; yes, we are Catechumens all our life long!

There is no institutional Catechumenate as it existed in the days of the early Christians, so the Catechumenate has become the task of our Christian life, of our life of faith. In fact, your movement, and here I welcome the one who inspired it (I know him well), your movement is centred on this process of becoming children of God, of becoming Christians. It is very important!

Many people think, 'But we are Christian'; they say, 'we are Christian' without knowing this, because it is not enough to be Christian, you have to become Christian, to become Christian every day, to discover every day what *cristianus* means, *Cristo adscriptus*. For the first time in the city of Antioch they began to call the disciples of Jesus 'Christians', followers of Christ. This has to be discovered, to be discovered every day, to be discovered more and more, because the mystery of Baptism is so profound, it is a divine and at the same time a human mystery, the human being becomes the adopted child of God... enough!

You reflect a lot concretely, you meditate a lot on this truth. I have to say that here in the parish of St Francesca Cabrini, that your movement here is leaven, leaven which must permeate the dough and the world of Christians in general. Not everyone is aware, not everyone fulfils it; here you are leaven, you must permeate this community, of about 20,000 people, permeate it with a new awareness of human dignity combined with the reality of divine sonship.

You do well, very well! Sing, sing! Because song always demonstrates joy, this discovery of the divine and the human reality. Baptism brings with it great joy which must be expressed in song. I have seen during my visit that the parish sings with great energy, with enthusiasm! **You must sing**. You must sing because this song brings with it a spiritual meaning, an inner meaning of our soul; in fact we almost do not have enough means of expressing this, this meaning, this mystery, this reality which is the fruit of our Baptism.

Dearest ones, thank you for your presence, for your animation of the life of this parish. I bless you with all my heart, your families, the different groups (because I have heard that you belong to different groups, twelve communities, like the twelve apostles). Your presbyters are amongst you; I have met your itinerants. I bless you with all my heart.

Private audience of Pope John Paul II
for 2000 priests of the Neocatechumenal Communities

(*Rome, 9th December 1985* – Cf. the Italian edition of *L'Osservatore Romano*, 11th December 1985.)

Dearly beloved!

1. I have listened with great interest to the words addressed to me by Kiko Argüello in the name of all of you. He has described how all the communities of the Neocatechumenal Way, throughout the various nations of the world, have committed themselves

to continuous prayer and meditation for the Extraordinary Synod which is being celebrated twenty five years after the conclusion of the Second Vatican Council.

Your spiritual participation in the preparation and your presence at the closing ceremony of the Synod have been a significant and solemn manifestation of your fidelity to Christ the Redeemer and to the pilgrim Church which transmits grace to men, especially in the sacramental signs which are a memorial of and make real the efficacy of the Redemption.

In this audience I am glad to recall the many meetings I have had with your communities, particularly during pastoral visits in my diocese of Rome, meetings in which I have encouraged your spiritual experience, which is based on the fundamental experience of the Sacrament of Baptism, on the awareness that to realise the baptismal dimension means above all to live the authentic identity of being Christian. It means uniting oneself intimately to the Eucharistic Christ; it means loving concretely and effectively all men as brothers in Christ; it means making and directing one's moral choices in conformity and harmony with the baptismal promises. "This way, way of faith, way of Baptism rediscovered," I said to your friends in the parish of Canadian Martyrs in Rome, "must be a way of the new man. The latter sees what is the real measure, or better, the nothingness of his created entity, of his creatureliness with respect to the Creator, to his infinite majesty, to God the redeemer, to the holy God who makes holy, and he tries to fulfil himself within that perspective" (*Insegnamenti* III 2 [1980], p. 1044).

2. The majority of you are made up of a large number of pastors and priests who work within the ambit of the Neo-catechumenal Way. In the decree *Presbyterorum Ordinis*, solemnly approved on 7th December 1965, the Second Vatican Council gave its attention and care to the ministry and life of priests. In this important document – which I invite you to meditate on again – the Council, taking the Word of God, together with the teaching of the Fathers, the Magisterium and the living Tradition of the People of God, as its basis, underlined that presbyters, in virtue of the sacred ordination and the mission that they receive from the Bishops, "are promoted to the service of Christ, Teacher, Priest and King, participating in his ministry, by which the Church here on earth is constantly built up into the People of God, Body of Christ and Temple of the Holy Spirit" (*Presbyterorum Ordinis*, 1).

Pastors and priests here, you certainly wish for a word from the Pope to understand even better what the Church of today expects from you. I give it very willingly because I am sure that my exhortation can only have a positive and beneficial influence on your Communities and on individuals,

3. The aims proposed by your Neocatechumenal Communities certainly correspond to one of the most agonising questions

of the pastor of souls today, especially those in the great urban agglomerations. You try to reach the mass of adults who are baptised, but have had little instruction in the faith, in order to lead them, along a spiritual way, to rediscover the baptismal roots of their Christian existence and to make them always more aware of their duties. From this derives the necessity that your position as leaders of the Communities be very clear so that your actions may be in harmony with the real demands of the pastoral situation.

The first demand that is made on you is to know how to keep faith, within the community, with your priestly identity. In virtue of Holy Orders you have been signed with a special character which conforms you to Christ the Priest, so that you can act in his name. (cf. *Presbyterorum Ordinis*, 2). The sacred minister, therefore, must be welcomed, not only as a brother who shares the way in the Community but above all as the one who, acting *in persona Christi* carries in himself the irreplaceable responsibility of Teacher, Sanctifier and Guide of souls, a responsibility which he can in no way renounce. Lay people must be able to recognise this reality from the responsible behaviour which you maintain. It would be an illusion to believe you can serve the Gospel by diluting your charism in a false sense of humility or in a misunderstood manifestation of fraternity. I repeat what I had the opportunity to say to the Ecclesiastical Assistants of the International Catholic Associations: "Do not let yourselves be deceived! The Church wants you to be priests and the lay people you meet want you to be priests and nothing other than priests. The confusion of charisms impoverishes the Church instead of enriching her" (*Discorso* of 13th September, 1979, n. 4: *Insegnamenti* II/2 [1979], p. 1391).

4. Another delicate and irrenounceable responsibility that I hope you undertake is to build up ecclesial communion, not only within your groups, but with all the members of the parochial and diocesan communities. Whatever service has been entrusted to you, you are always the representative of and the *providi cooperatores* with the Bishop, to whose authority you should feel particularly united. In effect, in the Church it is the right and duty of the bishop to give directives for pastoral activity (cf. Can. 381 ff.) and everyone has the obligation to conform to these. Do this in such a way that your communities, while losing nothing of their originality and richness, can be inserted harmoniously and fruitfully into the family of the parish and the diocese. With regard to this I expressed myself last year, on the occasion of the Plenary Assembly of the Congregation for the Clergy: "It is the task of the pastors to make an effort to see that the parishes benefit from the positive values that these communities can bring and as a result be open to the communities. However it must be very clear that the Communities cannot put themselves on the same plane as the parish community itself, as a possible

alternative. On the contrary, they have the duty to serve the parish and the local Church. It is precisely this service, given in conjunction with the parish and the diocese, that the validity of these experiences within the Movements and Associations can be seen." (*Discorso* of 20th. October 1984, n. 7 – the Italian edition of *L'Osservatore Romano*, Spanish edition, p. 841)

5. Here I offer another point for reflection. Exercising your ministry for the guidance of the Neocatechumenal Communities, you do not feel sent only to one particular group but to serve the whole Church. "The spiritual gift which priests have received in ordination – the Second Vatican Council reminds us – does not prepare them merely for a limited and circumscribed mission, but for the fullest, in fact the universal mission of salvation… The reason is that every priestly ministry shares in the fulness of the mission entrusted by Christ to the apostles" (*Presbyterorum Ordinis*, 10).

The consciousness of this mission and the need to conform to it should help to give greater encouragement to your apostolic initiatives, to be open to the problems and needs of the whole Church. Moreover, this same awareness, which makes you feel and live more deeply the bond with the universal Church, with its visible Head and with the bishops, makes easier the most important task of the priests within the communities, that is, the vigilance over correct comportment as regards both ideas and activities. Beloved priests, strengthen always in yourselves this vital link with the whole of Catholicism. It will be of great help to you, especially when you feel tired or disheartened when you see that, because of deafness and the indifference of hearts, all your efforts awaken no response. Then you can be consoled with the thought that you are not alone and that your work, if it meets with failure in one part of the Mystical Body of the Church, is certainly not useless, because God uses it for the good of the whole Church.

6. Dearly beloved priests, I end this meeting which I am pleased to have with you, renewing my confidence in your service to the Church and urging you to put all your trust in him who has loved us as his chosen ones and has called us to participate in his priesthood. It is precisely because of this that St Paul reminds us that in all our tribulations 'we conquer in him who loved us.' (Rm 8:37) I end with the exhortation by the author of the Letter to the Hebrews: 'Be as confident now then, since the reward is so great. You will need endurance to do God's will and gain what he has promised' (Heb 10:35-36).

Under the gaze of Mary Immaculate, Mother of Priests and Queen of Apostles, continue on your way with new enthusiasm. May my Apostolic Blessing accompany you and all the Neocatechumenal Communities entrusted to your guidance.

I want to add again: Happy Christmas to you all.

Among you I have found many priests, but also many lay

people, many married itinerants. I must say to you that the first people who went to Bethlehem, who recognised the Mystery of the Incarnation, were itinerants: they were shepherds. Then Jesus himself became itinerant when he was thirty, beginning with the messianic declaration at Nazareth. As well as that, he made all his Apostles itinerant, sending them all over the world.

The Church, too, is certainly itinerant, on a way, and we can say that the Pope tries more and more to be itinerant, even if with more 'sophisticated' and, perhaps, less authentic methods than yours, for you are poor itinerants, with no aeroplanes. But we hope that all of us, the Pope too, will always be, using all possible means, itinerants of the Gospel, that is, itinerants of the Mystery, of this Mystery that was revealed by the birth of Jesus, by the incarnation of the Son of God and then by his mission, by his death on the cross and by his resurrection. This is how a life was revealed to us, a new life, a divine life, eternal life.

We are itinerants of this life. It would not be possible for us to be itinerants of this life, of eternal life, if the same life had not been given to us first. We already have this life, and this life impels us, this life comes from Jesus Christ. This life comes to us through Jesus Christ in the Holy Spirit. He is the source of the divine life in creatures, the source of divine life in us. It is he who drives us. Jesus Christ the itinerant impels us, the itinerant of the Father, for it is the Father who sent him and made him itinerant among us.

So Jesus Christ the itinerant pushes us; the one who was sent, the missionary, because in the mission the Word of God *missiones divinarum personarum* – as I learned from St Thomas. *Missio* means to be sent and therefore to be itinerant. Christ impels us in the Holy Spirit because the Holy Spirit is sent too, sent in a different way – not like Christ, not in a visible, incarnate, human form – a Holy Spirit, not incarnate, but sent. It could be said that the mission of the Holy Spirit is even more penetrating, for it descends into what is the most intimate of man, of every creature. As St Augustine said, 'Intimior intimo meo'. This then is the mission of the Holy Spirit, of the Spirit that is sent. And you become itinerants with the strength of the incarnate Son who gave us an example of the visible mission. Thanks to the mission of the Son and Holy Spirit, with the life which comes through them from the Father, you become itinerant.

As St Paul says, the mission compels us; woe to me if I do not evangelise!

I wish you the joy of the Christmas feasts. I wish you the joy of the itinerant shepherds who found the way to Bethlehem. I wish you the joy that comes from those who convert. There are many among you who are converted, who have found Christ, who have rediscovered God, coming often from the opposite shore. I wish you again the joy that comes from the conversion of people, of souls. As Christ said, 'There is more joy in heaven for

one sinner who converts than for ninety nine just men.' I wish
you this joy and that in this way your itinerancy and your Neocatechumenal Way will be rewarded.

Once again I wish you 'Happy Christmas'. To make things
more simple I say it in Italian but it should be said in many
languages. I want to extend this wish for a Happy Christmas to
all the communities, to all the peoples from whom you come, to
your parishioners, to your colleagues, to your families.

May Jesus Christ be praised.

Visit of Pope John Paul II to the Parish of St Maria Goretti

(Rome, 31st January 1988 – Cf. the Italian edition of *L'Osservatore Romano*, 1st-2nd February 1988.)

I thank you for this meeting, and for all the testimonies
you have given. Listening to you and meeting you I always think
of the catechumenate, and I think of it not only in historical
categories.

Certainly the catechumenate belongs to the history of the
early and missionary church, but through your 'Way', and through
your experiences one can see what a treasure the catechumenate
has been for the Church as a method of preparation for baptism.

When we study baptism, when we administer this essential
sacrament of our faith, when we read St Paul's words to the
Romans, we see ever more clearly that its practice nowadays has
become increasingly inadequate and superficial. If we consider
the sacramental nature of baptism, and consider the baptismal
promises which, in their content, constitute a completely new
programme of life, the life of Christ, all this of course is practised
and fulfilled in the liturgy of the Church today. But at the same
time we can see how without a prior catechumenate, this practice
becomes insufficient and inadequate for that great mystery of
faith and God's love which is the sacrament of Baptism: this
immersion in the death of Christ and his resurrection; that is
immersion in the very life of God, immersion in the Holy Trinity.

Naturally, there is an explanation for the circumstances which
caused the catechumenate of the early, missionary Church to
disappear with time, as baptism took place more and more in
families where parents, urged on by faith, wished to have their
infants baptised. Certainly these children could not be prepared
for baptism with the methodology of the catechumenate. They
were too young. Yet this methodology has been kept alive in
mission countries. Sometimes it seems to me that the faith of
those neophytes, of those new Christians of Africa, and of the
other countries of the world, who have to undergo a catechumenal
experience quite similar to the experience of the early

catechumenate lasting for more than two years, is more mature. It seems to me that they themselves then become more mature Christians than we are – we who belong to nations, countries who boast of an old-established Christianity where the catechumenate, in its primitive and missionary sense, has disappeared. Of course that catechumenate didn't completely disappear. It has been replaced by a catechesis carried out by the Church, through instruction, teaching and through Christian education in the family. All this is an equivalent of the catechumenate in the early and missionary sense of the word. But this is something done after the sacrament. All of you belong to the category of Christians because all of you have received baptism as it is received today: in the family, in the parish, in the contemporary Church.

However, I have to say that your Way is striking – and indeed the word 'Way' is very appropriate; through your Neocatechumenal Way one can almost reconstruct what was once the true catechumenate, and perhaps it can be made even deeper. For this is how we arrive at all the **fruits of baptism** lived out, just as they were lived by the early communities, by the early Christians, by the first generation of Christians who were ready to face everything, even martyrdom for Christ, and who led lives of great fidelity.

Of course, they were sinners too, because man, even after baptism, remains a potential sinner. However, there was a tremendous strength in this baptism, in this Christian life of the first Christians, which, in times of hostility and opposition, of persecution, of paganism, of a pagan and very worldly culture – we know well what the life of Rome was like in those early years of the Christian era – was able to give life to a Christianisation which spread not only among people, among families, but reached out to entire nations. Of course the more Christianisation increased in quantity, the more it began to decrease in quality.

Certainly today, especially in countries where Christianity is long established, the European countries particularly, we sense the exhaustion of our inner Christianity, of what should be the fruit of our baptism. Baptism is a sacrament that contains the programme of the entire Christian life. Of course, it is not the only sacrament, but it is the first and fundamental sacrament. We know very well that a building grows on its foundations.

It is often said, and often we read too, that baptism, **our baptism, must last our whole life long**, must bear fruit throughout our life. But in our environment, in our countries, in our traditionally Christian society, often we see the opposite; in Rome, too, we see this. We are living in a period of dechristianisation. It seems that the faithful, those baptised years ago, are no longer mature enough to oppose secularisation and the ideologies which are contrary not only to the Church, to the Catholic religion, but also to religion in general; they are atheistic, indeed anti-theist. You, with your Neocatechumenal Way, in different environments, try to rebuild what has been broken down: you seek to rebuild it in a more authentic way, that, I would say, approaches the experience of the early Church.

This is how I see the origins of the Neo-catechumenate, of its way. Someone – I don't know if it was Kiko or someone else – asked himself: "Where did the strength of the early Church come from, and where does the weakness of today's Church – a Church with much greater numbers – come from?" I believe he found the answer in this Way.

I hope you will continue in this Way, to continue to accept all the demands which it makes, because it is not a short Way. If you consider the missionary catechumenate, it sometimes looks hard – four years! You are more demanding; yours lasts seven years or more! So then I hope that you will continue always to be demanding in your Way, and I hope above all that you continue to produce all these fruits, because among your communities it is evident how all the fruits of the Holy Spirit grow from baptism, all the charisms of the Holy Spirit, all vocations, the whole authenticity of the Christian life in marriage, in the priesthood and all the various professions, finally in the world.

You need courage to take your experience, your witness, into the more dechristianised environments of the world. But this is providential, because such environments cannot be approached in any other way; those human communities so destroyed, so disintegrated, so far, not only from faith, but from being human. They can only be approached with a great experience of faith, with a deep conviction, with a life entirely permeated by the Holy Spirit.

I hope that you may receive all these fruits in this parish, which seems to me to be based on the Neocatechumenal experience.

I think there is a way **to rebuild the parish on the basis of the Neocatechumenal experience**. Of course this method cannot be imposed on everybody; but if there are many candidates, then **why not**? **It is authentic and is consistent with the very nature of the parish, because just as each one of us Christians grows from baptism, so does the Christian community grow naturally from baptism**. The Church grows from baptism; she grows in the **Eucharist**, yes; but she grows from Baptism, for there is **no Eucharist without Baptism**. The parish is a basic community in the Church. It can grow authentically in the experience and on the basis of the neocatechumenal experience; it would be like the renewal of the early community that grew out of the catechumenal experience.

May the Lord bless you, my dearest people, may he bless your families, bless your candidates for the priesthood and the seminarians from 'Redemptoris Mater', bless your young people and your children who, thanks be to God, are numerous. They are also a cause for great hope because the world, secularised, dechristianised, agnostic, which no longer has faith in God, is losing faith in itself, is losing faith in man. How else can the falling birth rate be explained? Indeed, how else to explain the anti-birth mentality of communities, of nations, of groups, and of political circles? The explanation is in the lack of faith in man.

But this lack of faith in man derives from a lack of faith in God. Man has his dimension, his origin and this origin of his is God himself because man has been created in God's image and likeness. This explains who man is, how he can live and how he can die. You need courage to live in this world and in this meeting with these families and these itinerants I see a sign of Christian courage.

Homily of Pope John Paul II during the Eucharist celebrated at Porto San Giorgio, and the sending out of the families for the 'New Evangelisation'

(Porto San Giorgio, Ascoli Piceno, Feast of the Holy Family, 30th December 1988 – Cf. the Italian edition of *L'Osservatore Romano*, 31st December 1988.)

May Jesus Christ be praised.

Dearly beloved, we are living the Christmas period. In this period we live in faith the great divine mystery, the mystery of the most Holy Trinity in mission. It was known and confirmed that God was one and only one. We can also accept what Paul said when he spoke at the Areopagus, that God is that spiritual absolute in whom we live, in whom we move, in whom we have our being. But what was not known, and what many today still have difficulty in accepting, was the profound reality of God the Trinity in whom we live, in whom we move. And he, Trinity in mission, is not only an absolute being, above all others, but the Father in his infinite, inscrutable reality who generates his Word from eternity without beginning.

And with this his Word he lives the ineffable mystery of Love, which is a person and not only an interpersonal relationship; it is a person, the generated Son, Spirit, Love breathed out.

Every year the holy time of Christmas reminds us of this mystery of the Trinity in mission, here in the Night of Bethlehem, this mission of the Son, sent by the Father to bring us that Holy Spirit by whom he was conceived in the Virgin. He comes to bring us this Spirit. The night of Christmas is this night in which the reality of God-communion, the unity of the Divinity, absolute unity, unity of communion, comes close to our human mind, to our eyes, to our history and becomes visible. That is, the hidden mystery, the *Mysterium absconditum a saeculus* becomes visible, the mystery hidden from all time is revealed, becomes visible. By means of this poor reality of the birth of the Lord, of the Crib, of the Night of Bethlehem, of Mary and Joseph, the great mystery of the Trinity in mission is revealed. This is our God: this is our God! Ineffable mystery!

This is how we must speak, this is what we must confess, witness to, knowing our inadequacy in front of the inscrutable mystery of God, divine unity, unity of the divinity, and at the same time unity of communion.

During this Christmastide Holy Mother Church has us celebrate today another human mystery: the Holy Family of Nazareth.

We contemplate this reality, this mystery of the Trinity in mission. During the Christmas period we contemplate it with a special depth and intensity and with intense joy because this mission – the Word sent to the world to speak in person of his Father, of the divine reality, he, the Word, comes in this night as a human baby, poor, stripped of everything; in this moment already stripped – he could not be born in any other way. No human richness could provide an adequate context for the human birth of the eternal Son of God. Only that poverty, that abandonment, that Crib, than Night of Bethlehem could do so. It was right that no lodging could be found in that little town.

Dearly beloved, we contemplate this divine reality, **the Most Holy Trinity in mission**, and at the same time we feel how inadequate to talk of this mystery are our human concepts, our poor human words. Nevertheless, he who was sent to us, the Word, comes to speak and comes also to make us speak. More than that, he sought out those people who were most simple to take up this Word, this divine Word; he sought out the most simple.

We have to say that we are contemplating today the family in mission, because the Holy Family is nothing other than this: the human family on the divine mission. And here, this human family like a smaller community, shows itself to be, at the same time, like a big human community which finds itself on the divine mission: this is **the Church**. Particularly in the Second Vatican Council the Church has recognised her family and her missionary character. She is a great family in mission. Inside this great family-Church is every human family, every family community, as family in mission. A lot is talked about the family as a smaller, more basic society and all this is true.

But when we see the principle mystery constituted by the Trinity in mission we cannot see the family outside this: it, too, is in mission. And its mission is really fundamental, fundamental for the divine mission of the Word, for the divine mission of the Holy Spirit; it is fundamental.

The divine mission of the Word is that of speaking of the Father, of giving witness to the Father. It is the family which is the first to speak, the first to reveal this mystery, the first to witness before the new generations to God, to the Father. Its word is more efficacious.

And so every human family, **every Christian family, finds itself on a mission**. It is the mission of Truth. The family cannot live without Truth; more than that, it is the place where there is an extreme sensitivity towards the Truth. If truth is lacking in relationships, in the communion of persons – husband, wife, fathers, mothers, children – if truth is missing, communion is broken, the mission is destroyed. You all know well how subtle, how delicate, how very vulnerable, is this communion in the family. And so in the family is also reflected – together with the mission of the Word, the Son – the mission of the Holy Spirit which is love. The family is in mission, and this mission is fundamental for every people, for the whole of humanity; it is the mission of Love and of Life, it is the witness of Love and of Life.

Dearly beloved, I came here very willingly. I accepted very willingly your invitation on the Feast of the Holy Family to pray with you for the most fundamental and most important thing in the mission of the Church: for the spiritual renewal of the family, of the human and Christian families of all peoples, of every nation, perhaps particularly those of our western world, which is more advanced, more marked by the signs and benefits of progress but also by the failures of this one-sided progress. If one is talking about a renewal, about a regeneration of human society, even in the Church as a society of men, one has to begin with this point, with this mission. Holy Church of God, you cannot carry out your mission, you cannot fulfil your mission in the world, if not through the family and its mission.

This is the main reason why I accepted your invitation to be together and to pray together in this gathering made up above all of families, of couples, of children indeed of itinerant families.

It is a beautiful thing. We see that the Family of Nazareth was also an itinerant family. And it was so straightaway, from the first days of life of the Divine Infant, of the Word Incarnate. It had to become an itinerant family, itinerant and also refugee.

Many painful realities of our time – that of refugees, for example, or of emigrants – are already engraved, are present in **the Holy Family of Nazareth**. But for you this Family is above all an itinerant family because it goes everywhere: it goes to Egypt, it comes back to Nazareth, it goes back to Jerusalem with the twelve year-old Jesus, it goes everywhere, always as itinerant to bring a testimony of the family, of the divine mission of a human family.

I think that you as Neocatechumenal, itinerant families do the same thing: in yourselves you constitute the aim of your itinerancy which is that of bringing everywhere, to different environments, perhaps to the most dechristianised environments, the witness of the mission of the family. It is a great witness, great in human terms, great in Christian terms, divinely great, because such a witness, the mission of the family, is conclusively inscribed in the path of the Most Holy Trinity. In this world there is no other more perfect, more complete image than that which is God; **Unity, Communion**. There is no other human reality which corresponds more, which humanly corresponds more to that divine mystery.

And so, bringing as itinerants the witness which is properly that of the family, the family in mission, you bring everywhere the witness of the Most Holy Trinity in mission. And so you make the Church grow because the Church grows from these two mysteries. As the Second Vatican Council teaches us, all the vitality of the Church comes finally, or principally, from this mystery, from this mystery of the Trinity in mission. Together with this you bring the witness of the family in mission which tries to walk in the footsteps of the Trinity in mission. And in this way also a message is brought, the message of Bethlehem, the message of Christmas, a joyful message.

We know that this message too, according to traditions and customs, is always linked to human families. It is the feast of the family. This feast needs to be given a deep breath of life, a full dimension, full in human terms, full in Christian terms, divinely full because this human mystery, this human reality of the family is rooted in the divine mystery, in the mystery of God communion.

You are communion, communion of persons like the Father, the Son and the Holy Spirit.

You are communion of persons, you are unity. You are unity and **you cannot not be unity**. If you are not unity, you are not communion; if, instead, you are communion, you are unity. There are many families in this world of progress, rich, opulent, who lose their unity, lose communion, lose their roots. Here **you are itinerants** to bring the witness of these roots; this is your catechesis, this is your Neocatechumenal testimony: this is how the fruitfulness of Holy Baptism is spoken of. We know well that the sacrament of Matrimony, the family, all this grows in the sacrament of Baptism, from its richness.

To grow in baptism means to grow in the paschal mystery of Christ. Through the sacrament of water and the Holy Spirit we are immersed in this paschal mystery of Christ which is his death and his resurrection. We are immersed so as to find again fullness in life and of the person but, at the same time, in the dimension of the family – communion of persons – to bring to, to inspire with this newness of life different environments, societies, peoples, cultures, social life, economic life... All this is for the family. You must go throughout the world to say to everyone that it is 'for the family' not 'at the cost of the family'. Yes, your programme must be fully evangelical, full of courage, courage in giving witness, courage in asking, asking before everyone, above all before our brothers, before human beings, before our sisters, all these families and all these couples, all these offspring. But also before others. With this great witness, the family in mission as image of the Trinity in mission, must also carry forward a socio-political, a socio-economic programme, I would say. The family is involved in all this and can be helped, carried along, privileged, or it can be destroyed.

You must, with all your prayers, with your testimony, with your strength, you must help the family, you must protect it against every kind of destruction. If there is no other dimension in which man can express himself as a person, as life, as love; it has also to be said there is no other place or environment in which man can be so destroyed. Today many things are being done to normalise this destruction, to legalise this destruction; a profound destruction, deep wounds in humanity. Much is being done to systematise, to legalise this. In this sense people speak about 'protecting'. But the family cannot really be protected without going to the roots, without entering into its deep reality, into its intimate nature; and this intimate nature is the communion of persons in the image and likeness of the divine community. Family in mission, Trinity in mission.

Dearly beloved, I do not want to go on, I do not want to prolong this. I leave you these reflections which come to me spontaneously. Today is the day on which above all else the Holy Family must speak to us and this is my humble prayer: that this Holy Family of Nazareth, through our assembly, through our songs, through our prayers and also through these my words, may speak to all of us.

Amen.

Bibliography

Argüello F. (Kiko), *Le Comunità Neocatecumenali*, in *Rivista di Vita Spirituale,* 2 (1975) pp. 191ss.

Id., *Il Convegno dei Parroci delle Comunità Neocatecumenali in vista del Sinodo su 'La catechesi del nostro tempo', Roma, 10-13 gennaio 1977* (pro manuscripto), specialmente pp. 103-127: *Catechesi sul Cammino Neocatecumenale.*

Id., *Breve relazione sul Cammino Neocatecumenale* (presentata ai Padri Sinodali durante il Sinodo su 'Penitenza e Riconciliazione', 21 ottobre 1983), in Felici S. (a cura di), *Catechesi Battesimale e Riconciliazione nei Padri del IV secolo*, LAS, Roma, 1984, pp. 153-158.

Id., *La Virgen Maria y el Camino Neocatecumenal*, in *Ephemerides Mariologicae*, 36 (1986) pp. 302-309.

Id., *Il Cammino Neocatecumenale per vivere in pienezza il proprio Battesimo* (sulla missione delle Famiglie nella Nuova Evangelizzazione), in *Avvenire*, 30 dicembre 1988.)

Blazquez Ricardo., *Neo-Catechumenal Communities – a theological discernment*, St Paul Publications, 1988.

Id., *Un Camino de iniciación cristiana*, in *Iniciación cristiana y Neuva Evangelización*, DDB, Bilbao, 1992, pp. 338-380. In the same volume can be seen what the author says about the Neocatechumenal Way in the conclusion (pp. 71ff) of the chapter *Tiempos nuevos de Evangelización*, pp. 21-81.

Id., *Il Cammino Neocatecumenale e la formazione al presbiterato nel Seminario 'Redemptoris Mater' di Roma*, in *Communio*, 112 (luglio-agosto 1990) pp. 82-101. The same work has been published by the author with the title: *Seminarios para la Nueva Evangelización*, in *Iniciación cristiana y Nueva Evangelización*, DDB, Bilbao, 1992, pp. 381-418.

Bugnini A., *La riforma liturgica (1948-1975)*, CLV Edizioni Liturgiche, Roma, 1983.

Catecumenato per la maturazione nella fede, in *Notitiae*, 10 (1974) pp. 228-230.

Comunidades neocatecumenales, a cura di Aa. Vv., in *Comunidades plurales en la Iglesia,*, Ediciones Paulinas, Madrid, 1981.

Cordes P.J., *Dentro il nostro mondo. Le forze di rinnovamento spirituale*, Piemme, Casale Monferrato, 1989.

Id., *El Camino Neocatecumenal: itinerario de formación católica*, in *Ecclesia*, 1508 (22 dicembre 1990).

Della Torre L., *Le Comunità Neocatecumenali*, in *Rivista di Pastorale Liturgica*, 48 (1971) pp. 512-515.

Diez Moreno J.L., *Los 'Kikos' a cara descubierta. 'Lo nuestro, un calco de San Ignacio de Loyola'*, in *Vida Nueva*, 1828 (8 febbraio 1992) pp. 23-30.

Favale A., *Movimenti ecclesiali* (IV: Comunità Neocatecumenali), in De Fiores S. – Meo S. (a cura di), *Nuovo Dizionario di Mariologia*, Edizioni Paoline, Cinisello Balsamo (MI) 1985, pp. 965-968.

Gennarini S., *Una testimonianza di evangelizzazione nei Paesi dell'Est* (Intervento all'assemblea speciale del Sinodo dei vescovi per l'Europa), in *L'Osservatore Romano*, 8 dicembre 1991.

Giudici E., *Il Neocatecumenato: cammino di rievangelizzazione per i lontani (itinerario di riiniziazione cristiana per adulti)*, Roma, 1985–1986. Esercitazione di licenza presso la Facoltà di Missionologia della Pontificia Università Gregoriana.

Goffi T., *La spiritualità contemporanea*, in *Storia della spiritualità*, EDB, 1987, vol. 8, pp. 316-317.

Grasso L., *Le Comunità Neocatecumenali*, in *Rivista di Pastorale Liturgica*, 16 (1978) pp. 20-22.

Higueras J.F., *Comunidades Neocatecumenales en la parroquia de S. Pedro el Real (La Paloma) de Madrid*, in *Evangelización y hombre de hoy. Congreso*, Madrid, 1986, pp. 325-330 (a cura della 'Secretaria General del Congreso').

Id., *La Parroquia y el Camino Neocatecumenal. Una experiencia*, Edibesa, Madrid, 1992.

The Neocatechumenal Way in the Discourses of Paul VI and John Paul II – published by the Neocatechumenal Centre, Rome.

Il Neocatecumenato. Un'esperienza di evangelizzazione e catechesi in atto in questa generazione. Sintesi delle sue linee di fondo. Pubblicato a cura del Centro Neocatecumenale, Piazza San Salvatore in Campo, Roma, 1976 (pro manuscripto). Il testo è stato consegnato a Papa Paolo VI in occasione dell'udienza generale del 12 gennaio 1977. È poi stato anche in parte pubblicato in *Rivista di Vita Spirituale*, (1977) pp. 98ss e in *Communio*, 32 (1977) pp. 58ss.

Lau Engels, *Der Neokatechumenat*, in *Liturgisches Jahrbuch*, 29 (1979) pp. 180-185.

Nuova Evangelizzazione – III Millennio. Neocatecumenato.

Czestochowa 1991, a cura del Centro Neocatecumenale, Piazza San Salvatore in Campo, Roma, 1991 (pro manuscripto).

Pirlo P., *The Neocatechumenate: an experience in the revival of the Catechumenate after the Second Vatican Council.* Thesis presented to the Faculty of Sacred Theology and the Graduate School University of Santo Tomas, Manila, 1992.

Riflessioni sul capitolo IV dell'O.I.C.A. (e commento di G. Pasqualetti), in *Notitiae*, 9 (1973) pp. 274-282.

Teodoro E., *La liturgia nel Cammino Neocatecumenale. Aspetti positivi*, in *Rivista di Pastorale Liturgica*, 177 (marzo-aprile 1993) pp. 62-71.

Voltaggio F., *La Parola di Dio nelle Communità Neocatecumenali*, in Zevini G. (a cura di), *Incontro con la Bibbia. Leggere, pregare, annunziare*, Roma, 1978, pp. 187-191.

Zevini G., *Le Comunità Neocatecumenali. Una pastorale di evangelizzazione permanente*, in Amato A. (a cura di), *Temi teologici-pastorali*, Roma, 1977, pp. 103-125.

Id., *Informazioni su esperienze di iniziazione cristiana degli adulti nelle Comunità Neocatecumenali*, in *Concilium* 2 (1979) pp. 109-122.

Id., *Neocatecumenato*, in De Fiores S.-Goffi T. (a cura di), *Nuovo Dizionario di Spiritualità*, Edizioni Paoline, Cinisello Balsamo (MI), 1979, pp. 1056-1073.

Id., *Il Cammino Neocatecumenale. Itinerario di maturazione nella fede*, in Favale A. (a cura di), *Movimenti ecclesiali contemporanei. Dimensioni storiche, teologico-spirituali ed apostoliche*, Roma, 1982, pp. 231-267.